The Blues Dream of
Billy Boy Arnold

Billy Boy Arnold, 1951
Photo courtesy of Billy Boy Arnold

THE BLUES DREAM OF BILLY BOY ARNOLD

Billy Boy Arnold
with Kim Field

The University of Chicago Press
Chicago and London

CHICAGO VISIONS AND REVISIONS

A series edited by Carlo Rotella, Bill Savage, Carl Smith,
and Robert B. Stepto

The University of Chicago Press, Chicago 60637
The University of Chicago Press, Ltd., London
© 2021 by The University of Chicago
All rights reserved. No part of this book may be used or reproduced in any
manner whatsoever without written permission, except in the case of brief
quotations in critical articles and reviews. For more information, contact the
University of Chicago Press, 1427 E. 60th St., Chicago, IL 60637.
Published 2021
Printed in the United States of America

30 29 28 27 26 25 24 23 22 21   1 2 3 4 5

ISBN-13: 978-0-226-80920-5 (cloth)
ISBN-13: 978-0-226-80934-2 (e-book)
DOI: https://doi.org/10.7208/chicago/9780226809342.001.0001

Library of Congress Cataloging-in-Publication Data

Names: Arnold, Billy Boy, author. | Field, Kim, author.
Title: The blues dream of Billy Boy Arnold / Billy Boy Arnold ; with Kim Field.
Other titles: Chicago visions + revisions.
Description: Chicago : University of Chicago Press, 2021. | Series: Chicago
    visions and revisions | Includes bibliographical references and index.
Identifiers: LCCN 2021010983 | ISBN 9780226809205 (cloth) |
    ISBN 9780226809342 (ebook)
Subjects: LCSH: Arnold, Billy Boy. | Blues musicians—Illinois—Chicago—
    Biography. | Harmonica players—Illinois—Chicago—Biography. |
    Blues (Music)—Illinois—Chicago—History and criticism. | LCGFT:
    Autobiographies.
Classification: LCC ML419.A76 A3 2021 | DDC 788.8/21643092 [B]—dc23
LC record available at https://lccn.loc.gov/2021010983

♾ This paper meets the requirements of ANSI/NISO Z39.48-1992 (Permanence
of Paper).

*Dedicated to the memory and the music of
John Lee "Sonny Boy" Williamson*

Contents

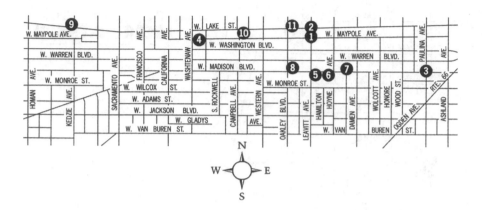

BILLY BOY ARNOLD'S
WEST SIDE
L E G E N D

1. Mr. Upchurch's home
2. Blind John Davis's apartment
3. Homesick James's apartment
4. Radio station WGES
5. Ralph's Club
6. The Purple Cat
7. The Seeley Club
8. The Happy Home Lounge
9. The second Sylvio's
10. Ruby Lee Gatewood's club
11. The first Sylvio's

Research: Scott Dirks

Maps: Fred Ingram

Photograph by Russell Lee,
courtesy of Library of Congress,
Prints and Photographs Division,
FSA/OWI Collection,
LC-DIG-fsa-8a29892

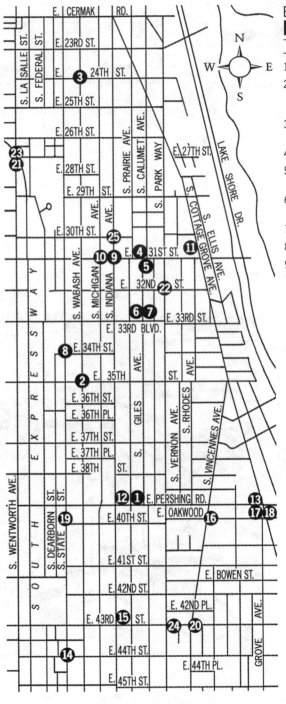

BILLY BOY ARNOLD'S

NEAR SOUTH SIDE

L E G E N D

1. Wendell Phillips High School

2. Spot where "Big Boy" Crudup used to play under the elevated train tracks

3. Moseley Grammar School

4. The Plantation Club

5. Butcher shop owned by Billy Boy's uncles

6. Sonny Boy Williamson's apartment

7. Douglas Elementary School

8. Tampa Red's apartment

9. Pawn shop where Billy Boy met Junior Wells and the Aces

10. Bob Myers's apartment

11. Sam and Gussie's Lounge

12. Hollywood Rendezvous

13. Forest City Joe Pugh's apartment

14. Clifton James's apartment

15. Indiana Theatre

16. Oakwood Boulevard jazz scene

17. The DuSable Hotel

18. The Macomba Lounge

19. Musicians Local 208

20. Pepper's

21. Club Alibi

22. Earl Hooker's mother's apartment

23. Club Alabam

24. Checkerboard Lounge

25. The Harmonia Hotel where Billy Boy played with Otis Rush

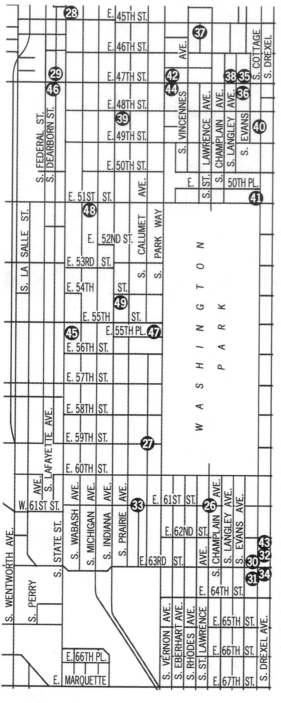

BILLY BOY ARNOLD'S
FAR SOUTH SIDE
L E G E N D

26. Early apartment of the Arnold family
27. The Arnolds' first apartment of their own
28. Club Georgia
29. Billy Boy's father's stable
30. Where Billy Boy sold the *Chicago Defender*
31. The Pershing Hotel and the Circle Inn jazz club
32. Cotton Club
33. Billy Boy meets Big Joe Williams getting off the elevated train
34. Restaurant where Billy Boy met Ellas McDaniel, Jody Williams, and Roosevelt Jackson
35. The 708 Club
36. Corner on 47th where Billy Boy first played with Ellas McDaniel
37. 45th Street Baptist Church where Ellas McDaniel and Roosevelt used to hang out
38. Ellas McDaniel's apartment
39. Theresa's Lounge
40. Chess Records office
41. United Records office
42. Vee-Jay Records office
43. Trianon Ballroom
44. The Regal Theater
45. Club DeLisa
46. Cadillac Baby's club
47. The Rhumboogie
48. Kid Rivera's Barrelhouse
49. Little Walter's girlfriend's apartment, where he died

Preface

: : BILLY BOY ARNOLD

You have to really love music to do it professionally. I just wanted to be able to perform, like the musicians I idolized. It wasn't about the money.

What I've said in this book is authentic and exactly the way it went down. If I say I did somethin', I did it. If I didn't do it, it's not in here.

I don't like people who come up and say, "Hey, I did this and I did that," or who make things up to be accommodating. I call those kind of people "recognition freaks." They're tryin' to get recognized. I talk about what I know. I won't embellish it. I didn't put nothin' in this story to make me look better or anyone else look worse. I'm not that kind of person. I don't believe in that. That ain't what I'm about. I like the real deal.

I remember everything 'cause this is very important stuff to me.

Introduction

: : KIM FIELD

Commentators often glibly divide the human race between the dreamers and the doers, but history may actually belong to those who embody both dispositions. William "Billy Boy" Arnold is a self-confessed romantic, but he was born a man of action.

By the time he was five, he had found his life's passion—the blues.

At twelve, he knew that music would be his vocation.

Six years later, he was a recording star.

Single-minded self-propulsion has been the story of Billy Boy's life, and so it is the theme of this memoir. *The Blues Dream of Billy Boy Arnold* is a revelatory account of a remarkable and unique journey—by someone who was both a keen observer and an important participant—through no fewer than five landmark events in the history of American music: the creation of the Chicago blues style, the birth of rock and roll, the arrival of white musicians on the Chicago blues scene, the appropriation of the Chicago blues sound by white rock groups in the 1960s, and the transition of black blues to a predominantly white audience.

Billy Boy Arnold is the only musician alive today who has lived the entire history of the Chicago blues scene. Its zenith was the mid-1950s, when the new, raw, amplified approach of Muddy Waters and Howlin' Wolf reigned supreme, but the city had established itself as a major blues center two decades prior to that, thanks to the extensive and impressive output—much of it captured by producer Lester Melrose and released on RCA Victor's Bluebird label—of Windy City legends like Tampa Red, Big Bill Broonzy, Big Maceo Merriweather, and Jazz Gillum. Thrilled by these recordings as a schoolboy, the young Billy Boy made a commitment to seek out what he calls "the blues world."

Had he not become a musician, Billy Boy might have made an excellent police detective. Henry Morton Stanley's legendary search for David Livingstone has nothing on the twelve-year-old Arnold's dogged pursuit of his idol, blues legend John Lee "Sonny Boy" Williamson, across the South Side of Chicago.[1] Billy Boy's method was to accost anyone carrying a guitar and ask that person two questions: Do you know Sonny Boy Williamson? How do you get to make records? Those weren't idle questions. They were focused queries that demonstrated the interrogator's desire to make contact with the blues world and his determination to find a place for himself in it.

Billy Boy's youthful single-mindedness earned him two momentous meetings with his hero, but the promise of a deeper, mentoring relationship was abruptly shattered when Williamson was murdered two weeks after their second meeting. Although the profound shock of Sonny Boy's premature death still reverberates for Billy Boy, at the time it made him determined to expand his blues circle by seeking out popular artists like Blind John Davis, Big Bill Broonzy, and Memphis Minnie. More importantly, Billy Boy launched his own career by singing and playing on the streets. The ambitious teenager had already spent five years in the blues world

---

1. All references to "Sonny Boy Williamson" in this book are to the blues harmonica player and singer John Lee Williamson, who died in 1948. The blues artist Aleck "Rice" Miller (ca. 1912–1965) also performed and recorded as "Sonny Boy Williamson." Miller is referred to in this book as "Rice Miller."

when Muddy Waters assumed the throne as the Windy City's blues king in the early 1950s, and before Billy Boy reached voting age he had joined the slim ranks of Chicago blues artists who had a bona fide hit record on their résumé.

In 1955, six months after Elvis Presley's recording debut blew open the door to rhythm and blues for white teenagers, Billy Boy contributed to two of the earliest and biggest rock-and-roll hits ("I'm a Man" and "Bo Diddley"), both produced by the legendary Leonard Chess.

In the early 1960s, when young white musicians like Paul Butterfield and Charlie Musselwhite began jamming in the black blues clubs, Billy Boy was one of the first established Chicago blues stars to work with them and accept them as equals.

By the middle of the decade, when blues-based British bands like the Yardbirds and the Animals made their assault on the American pop charts, they came armed with cover versions of American blues records, including Billy Boy's Vee-Jay sides.

By the 1970s, Billy Boy and the other black blues artists were navigating a profound cultural shift as the blues audience became mostly white, a simultaneously challenging and liberating sea change that rejuvenated the careers of those who were able to make the transition.

I first became a fan of Billy Boy's music in the 1970s, when I bought the LP *Blow the Back Off It*, a collection of his recordings for Chess and Vee-Jay on the British Red Lightnin' label. When Billy Boy resurfaced in the 1990s with two comeback CDs on Alligator Records, I was impressed all over again with the vitality of his sound.

The first time I saw Billy Boy perform on stage was in 2015, when he came to Dimitriou's Jazz Alley in Seattle as part of the Harmonica Blowout series hosted by Mark Hummel. This was an ideal showcase for Billy Boy, since the program was designed as a tribute to Sonny Boy Williamson, and Billy Boy gave compelling and faithful performances of several of his hero's tunes.

Mark made an evening full of great music even more memorable by inviting me to join him, Billy Boy, Steve Guyger, Rick Estrin, Rich Yescalis, and an all-star backing band on stage for the finale. Afterward, I made my way upstairs to the dressing room to thank Mark, but when I popped my head in the door, the only person in the room was Billy Boy. He looked up and complimented me on my harmonica playing. I planted myself in a seat across from him, and it wasn't long before he was telling me about the meetings between his twelve-year-old self and Sonny Boy. I left our brief encounter very much taken by Billy Boy's friendly but dignified personal manner, his passion for the music, and his detailed recall of events that had occurred sixty years before.

All of that rattled around in the back of my head for the next couple of years as I learned more about Billy Boy's significant and enduring career. I kept coming back to his remarkable personal story and how it needed to be documented—in his own voice. I talked with several friends who knew Billy Boy, and they all praised his talent, his warmth, his integrity, his uncanny memory, and his willingness to share his story.

In 2018 Mark Hummel brought Billy Boy to the Alberta Rose Theatre in Portland, Oregon, for another Harmonica Blowout. I called Mark about a week before the show, told him that I had been thinking about approaching Billy Boy about a memoir, and asked if he would reintroduce me to Billy Boy at the Portland show. A few days later Mark did just that during intermission at the Alberta Rose. I told Billy Boy about my background as a musician and a writer, did my best to explain why I thought his memoir would be not only a great read but a historically important and culturally valuable document, and asked him whether he would be willing to let me pay him a visit in Chicago to explain more about how I might help him with such a project. Billy Boy was amenable.

A couple of months later, I enlisted the help of Dick Shurman, the Grammy Award–winning blues producer and a close friend of

Billy Boy's, in arranging a lunch with the three of us in Chicago at the Valois diner in Hyde Park, a favorite eatery of both Billy Boy's and Barack Obama's. I had barely launched into my sales pitch when Billy Boy interrupted me and got right down to business: "If Dick says you're all right, that's good enough for me. When do we get started? Do you have a tape recorder with you?"

Over the next year and a half, I taped more than sixty hours of interviews with Billy Boy, transcribed them, and, with minimal editing, created a narrative from those transcriptions. I want to make it crystal clear that I am Billy Boy's partner in this effort, not his ghostwriter. My goal was to faithfully capture Billy Boy's story in his own voice, and Billy Boy insisted that every word in the published version of his story be his, true and free of embellishment.

I think that Billy Boy and I both succeeded. The interviews naturally encompassed Billy Boy's career and the blues legends he knew and worked with. (And what a list that is: Sonny Boy Williamson, Big Bill Broonzy, Tampa Red, Memphis Minnie, Blind John Davis, Muddy Waters, Little Walter, Howlin' Wolf, Elmore James, Junior Wells, Rice Miller, Otis Spann, Jimmy Rogers, Earl Hooker, Johnny Shines, and James Cotton, among many others.) Billy Boy also reflected on his childhood, the early days of the Chicago blues scene, the history of the black neighborhoods in Chicago, what it was like to spend a night in a South Side blues club in 1955, the workings of the music business, his brush with Jim Crow while touring the South, the experience of performing in foreign countries, his lifelong effort to improve himself, his struggles to collect the royalties to which he was entitled, and the future of the blues. *The Blues Dream of Billy Boy Arnold* has a chronological structure, not just because that is a traditional and logical approach, but because it's the best way to convey the swiftness of Billy Boy's early rise and the cumulative impact of the cultural shifts that influenced him and the blues.

Billy Boy Arnold is a vigorous eighty-five-year-old who is in his eighth decade as a performing musician. He remains a committed disciple of Sonny Boy Williamson and the deep blues, but his best-known recordings show the influence of the rock and roll that he also loves and helped create. Billy Boy's musical influence has been extensive and international—his recordings and songs have been covered by Eric Clapton, Jimmy Page, Jeff Beck, David Bowie, the Blues Brothers, Canned Heat, Hot Tuna, John Hammond, Tom Jones, Aerosmith, Gary Moore, and the Red Devils. Billy Boy may be self-effacing by nature, but he also has a solid sense of what he has accomplished in life.

Billy Boy's memory is nothing short of phenomenal. He possesses an encyclopedic recall of the details behind countless blues recordings—the labels that issued them, the studios where the sessions took place, the years they were released, which tunes were on the B sides, the backing musicians involved, and so on. You can show him an old photograph and he will inform you that it was taken on Mother's Day in 1957. Navigating the urban grid is the first thing that city boys like Billy Boy learn to do, and his recollections almost always snap to a precise location. His ability to instantly recall the specific addresses and street corners in Chicago where his contemporaries lived and where the long-gone music clubs, record stores, and theaters were located makes his remembrances all the more fascinating and unassailable. Billy Boy's geographic recollections were the inspiration for the maps of the circa-1955 South and West Sides of Chicago that appear in this book.

When he wasn't recording or performing himself, Billy Boy was on the scene as a devoted fan of the music, so his story is much more expansive than a recounting of his own exploits. Billy Boy is an intelligent and thoughtful man with a wry sense of humor (there is a lot of laughter on those interview tapes that was unfortunately lost in translation), but he could not be more serious about the importance of black music in America and its history. Bill Greensmith and Mike Vernon are two of the earliest British blues researchers (they began documenting the genre in the 1960s), and Bill told me recently that back in the day he and Mike considered Billy Boy to be one of the first serious blues historians.

The most majestic music about the human condition ever created deserves an honest and eloquent spokesperson from within the ranks of its creators. *The Blues Dream of Billy Boy Arnold* is that inside story.

Easter morning on the South Side of Chicago, 1941
Photograph by Russell Lee, courtesy of Library of Congress, Prints and Photographs
Division, FSA/OWI Collection, LC-DIG-ppmsc-00256

1

Born in Chicago

When Ray Charles was eight or nine years old, back in the late 1930s, most black people didn't have record players in their houses 'cause they lived on a very meager level economically. Ray would go into a café right there in his home—Greenville, Florida—and he would listen to all kinds of music on the jukebox. He would listen to country music and black jazz.

In his book *Brother Ray*, Ray Charles says that his favorites was the blues records by the black artists. He called 'em "those black-bottom goodies." And the artists he named were Sonny Boy Williamson, Arthur "Big Boy" Crudup, and Tampa Red. Those were his guys.

They're mine, too.

Ray Charles was about five years older than I was. I'm a big fan of his. What I like about him is that he can play all kinds of stuff, but he can really get down and play them "black-bottom goodies." Today the white people call them "the Delta blues," 'cause a lot of great artists—like Muddy Waters, John Lee Hooker, Pinetop Perkins, and Pops Staples—came out of the Mississippi Delta.

My grandfather and his brothers and sisters—there was about fourteen or fifteen of them—came from the Delta. They lived about fifty miles south of Clarksdale, Mississippi, in a town called Mound

African American family arrives in Chicago from the rural South, ca. 1920
Shutterstock

Bayou.[1] This was my mother's father. Now, I wasn't on the scene then, but I've heard that it was an all-black town. My mother's mother was born in Paris, Tennessee. Her family migrated to Toledo, Ohio, where my mother and her brothers and sisters was born. My mother was born around 1916, so her family must have moved to Toledo in the late teens or early twenties. Later they moved from Toledo to Chicago.

My father's mother and father were from Georgia—I think from Athens or somewhere around in there. My grandfather and his brothers and sisters, they all came to Chicago when my father was about six or seven years old.

My people, like most black people, left the South for economic

1. Founded in 1887 by former slaves, Mound Bayou, Mississippi, was the nation's largest and most self-sufficient African American town in the United States during the first half of the twentieth century.

reasons and to get away from the pressures of Jim Crow. The black people in the South was under siege, just like the people in Europe was under siege during the war. Just imagine. When you're under siege—*goddamn*, you want to get *away* from that.

Here's an example. In Bo Diddley's hometown—McComb, Mississippi—the business district was only three blocks long, and the train stopped there. Down South, you couldn't just walk away from all that Jim Crow pressure. You had to slip away or run away. So don't come up to the station there with no suitcase to get on the train. One of the whites would say, "Ain't you old man Smith's boy? Where you goin'?" Then they'd hold you and whup your ass. It sounds funny, but it was tragic. If you wanted to leave, you had to slip out of town, mostly.

All the blacks had to go to the business districts in these little Jim Crow towns to do their business, and they wasn't friendly places for black people. If you wanted to do any shoppin', you had to run into the Jim Crow whites. You might have to get off the sidewalk to let them by. Some of them was hostile and wanted to pick a fight or start somethin' with you. And some of the blacks couldn't be pushed around. It was chaos. And the blacks always lost, 'cause the law was on the other side. I'm not tryin' to get into a racial thing. That's the way it *was*.

Down South, there wasn't no work in the small towns. Black people worked in the fields or drove a tractor. You would pick cotton from sunup to sundown for a dollar *a day*. You wasn't makin' no money *at all* drivin' that tractor down South. Elmore James drove a tractor. B. B. King did, too. Rice Miller was drivin' a tractor when he made his first record for Chess Records, "Don't Start Me Talkin'."

But if you came to Chicago in 1939 or '40, you could probably get a job makin' fifty cents an hour. When I was a kid, during the war, around 1941, I remember my auntie sayin', "Well, this job pays fifty cents an hour." So if you're makin' fifty cents an hour for eight hours, that's a hell of a lot better than a dollar a day from sunup to sundown. In Chicago, a black man could make a hundred dollars a week workin' construction. And in Chicago you wasn't exactly under the pressure you was down South. 'Cause, like I said, they was under siege, you know?

So that's why black people jokingly called Chicago the "Promised Land." Economically, times was better. There was lots of jobs. You could make a livin', and that alone made Chicago a great place to come to. During the war, there was defense jobs, and women were workin' and the men were workin'. There was always construction jobs for the black men. They was makin' money workin' on the tunnels and stuff like that. You could drive a cab. Muddy Waters drove a venetian blinds truck. When my father and his brothers and sisters came here from Georgia, they worked at the stockyards.

And you wasn't under siege like down South. Bo Diddley's mother sent him from Mississippi to Chicago to stay with her sister when he was five years old, so he wouldn't have to live down there under the stress. His auntie raised him. He didn't know nothin' about the South. There was no restrictions in downtown Chicago. There was no color line at restaurants and movie theaters, nothin' like that. If a black person wanted to go to a movie theater in downtown Chicago, you just went in and paid like anybody else.

Chicago was the railroad center of the Midwest. This was before the airplane got to be a popular form of travel. There was all kinds of big train stations in Chicago with trains comin' in from everywhere. You'd come into Chicago at seven or eight o'clock in the mornin', and maybe your connectin' train wouldn't leave until three or four o'clock, and so there was plenty of restaurants and shops with no color line.

My parents met in Chicago. I was born there on September 16, 1935. My parents had eleven children. I'm the second to the oldest. My father and his brothers was in business together. They had a sort of partnership. His two younger brothers ran a butcher shop, and my father had a couple of trucks and a horse and wagon. He sold vegetables. My father was a rough-type guy who drove his horses and trucks fast.

The first home I can remember was an apartment at 61st and St. Lawrence. It was a big flat, and we lived there with my mother's two younger sisters and their children. There was four of us cousins born in 1935. My cousin Archie was born in June of 1935. My other cousin—my mother's sister's child, Marva—was born in March of 1935. My father's sister's son, Leon, is nine days older than me, and he was born in 1935, too.

Chicago is a big place, but black people only had a small part of it. They had the South Side and the West Side. The city used redlining to keep the blacks limited. The biggest black neighborhood was on the South Side. The South Side extended north to south from 22nd Street to 67th Street, and west to east between Wentworth and Cottage Grove. South of 67th Street, it was all white out to the 70s and 80s and 90s, where I live now. West of Wentworth was white. Blacks didn't start movin' south of 68th Street 'til around the early 1970s. When you went east of Cottage Grove, the whites had that. When you crossed Cottage Grove Avenue, you steered into the white part of the city, with better buildings and everything.

The South Side was the old part of Chicago. Of course, blacks always got what the whites didn't want anymore. When the whites would move out, the blacks would get the area, and they would take over the neighborhood. The black neighborhood was only two or three blocks from Lake Michigan and the beach at 31st Street, and it expanded south of there. It was almost on the lakefront, so that made it in a way a kind of choice area. And the South Side had a lot of old buildings that was still in good condition.

The South Side was a viable neighborhood, and it was all black. You had your own culture, so to speak. All the businesses on 31st Street, where my uncles had their butcher shop, was black-owned businesses. They had black drug stores. They had black taverns and nightclubs. Black restaurants. There was a black theater—I think it was called the Terrace—at 31st and Indiana. So you was in your *own* environment.

The more sophisticated blacks lived south of 47th Street. You'd hear jazz on the radio and on the jukeboxes. North of 47th Street on down to 29th, 26th, and 22nd was where the blues people lived.

A lot of people don't realize that the South Side in those days was like a hundred or a thousand small towns like they had down South. It was so diversified. You had people from each state. When people would come to Chicago from different places, they would always seek out people from the same hometown, from the area they had come from. You'd find 'em all sort of huddled together. There was people from all over, and they brought these country things with 'em—"I put a spell on you," and all that hoodoo and black magic. Sonny Boy made that record, "I'm goin' down to Louisiana and get me another mojo hand. 'Cause I got to break up my woman from lovin' that other man." And Memphis Minnie—I think she was from down there in Louisiana—sung about that hoodoo stuff.

If you walked across the South Side from 31st and Cottage Grove to 31st and Wentworth, man, it was like going through three or four or five little towns. And then, if you went south to 35th Street, there was another black business district. There was three or four movie theaters from 31st to 34th on State. Balaban and Katz was a white company that built all these great big theaters in Chicago in the 1920s, including the Chicago Theatre in the Loop.[2] On the South Side, in the black neighborhood, they owned the Regal and the Tivoli. All the jazz bands in the '20s and '30s played those theaters—Ma Rainey and all of 'em. Oh, man, those were some beautiful theaters. They was like castles. I don't see why they ever tore those theaters down, but they're all gone now.

The Pershing Hotel, at 64th and Cottage Grove, was the big black hotel on the South Side. It was near the Tivoli Theatre and a couple of other big theaters. The Pershing was a big, first-class, full-service hotel. It had a lounge, it had a barber shop, it had a beauty shop, it had a restaurant. Downstairs in the basement they would hold jam sessions with a jazz band. All the black entertainers and celebrities of note would stay at the Pershing when they was

2. The Balaban and Katz Theater Corporation was founded in Chicago in 1916. Within ten years, the company owned more than one hundred theaters across the Midwest, including fifty in Chicago.

in Chicago. The downtown hotels was expensive and there was the racism.

The South Side was rough. *All* the black neighborhoods was rough. The white cops could be brutal. They policed the black neighborhood kind of harshly, you know. But when I was a kid, I didn't run into any direct confrontations with the police.

They had some black cops on the South Side. They had one black cop named Two-Gun Pete that made his reputation by shootin' and killin' his own people.[3] His real name was Sylvester Washington. When I was a kid, I would hear all the adults talk about Two-Gun Pete. Fifty-Eighth Street was a famous street on the South Side. There was a lot of businesses there. My grandfather lived around the corner. And Two-Gun Pete, he cleaned up 58th Street. If Two-Gun Pete caught young black guys hangin' out, he would pistol whip them and beat them up. He shot several of them and he killed several more. He did all kinds of terrible things. And he had a reputation, so I guess they let him get away with it.

Some of the black people admired him for cleanin' up the neighborhood. They talked about him like he was Hopalong Cassidy or somethin'. When I was a kid, I used to sell two magazines meant for blacks, *Our World* and *Ebony*, and one time one of 'em had an article written up about Two-Gun Pete. And in it he said, "One time, I almost had to shoot a white guy." And I looked at that word "almost." I knew goddamn well that Two-Gun Pete knew better than to shoot a white person. Ain't no way in hell he would have done that, 'cause

---

3. Sylvester "Two-Gun Pete" Washington (1905–1971), whose nickname came from his penchant for wearing a brace of pearl-handled revolvers, was a member of the Chicago police force from 1934 until 1951. Washington claimed to have made more than twenty thousand arrests and to have killed a dozen men during his time policing Chicago's Fifth District. Music industry legend Quincy Jones grew up in the Fifth District and wrote about Two-Gun Pete in his autobiography, Q (Doubleday, 2001): "Every weekend we watched a legendary black cop named Two-Gun Pete who carried two pearl-handled revolvers shoot black kids in the back in broad daylight, right in front of a Walgreens drugstore—the kids dropped like potato sacks. We fantasized about making Two-Gun Pete pay" (13).

Ready for action, police officer Sylvester ("Two-Gun Pete") Washington awaits instructions from Chicago ward boss Joseph T. Plunkett, 1948
Joseph Scherschel/Getty Images

he knew that would have been the end of his life. But Two-Gun Pete could kill all the black people he wanted. He brutalized a lot of his own people.

Two-Gun Pete was a guy that I had no respect for. And I'm surprised some of them guys didn't give him what he gave some of them other people. They should've killed *him*, the way he brutalized people. They should have annihilated *his* ass. Wiped him out. Two-Gun Pete was mentally ill and an Uncle Tom and an asshole and everything else you want to call him.

I met Two-Gun Pete once in 1957. He owned his own hotel on 39th, near the outer drive. A couple of musicians—Abb Locke, who was my saxophone player, and George Coleman, who became a famous saxophone player—lived upstairs above the club. There was a bar downstairs. I went in there one day and Two-Gun Pete and his daughter was workin' behind the bar.

I went up to the bar and said, "I'm lookin' for George Coleman. What floor does he live on?"

Two-Gun Pete kind of tore into me. He said, "Man, I don't know what them motherfuckers is doin', if they're knockin' dick heads and bumpin' dick heads or what." That's the way he talked. Crazy bastard.

I never really had any trouble in white neighborhoods when I was a kid. You might have your little gangs and stuff like that. When I was a kid in 1947, '48, and '49, we would walk about eight blocks over the color line on Wentworth to go to see the movies on Halsted—there was about five or six movie theaters within two or three blocks on Halsted—or go to the Sears and Roebuck department store and dime stores over there. You would walk through the white neighborhood to go to the movies.

We would walk over to Halsted and go to the show, and if we stayed late, like until seven o'clock, on the way home we would pass four or five clubs that had country and western bands playin' fiddles and violins and all that. There was the Wagon Wheel and the Sawdust Trail and Club Columbia. The country and western bands would be playin' in the windows with their cowboy hats on. They had hillbilly bands all up and down the North Side in those days, too.

: : :

When you'd leave the downtown area and head west, you would cross the Chicago River and run into the Skid Row area around

Madison Street. It was like New York City's Bowery. You'd go over there and that's where all the alcoholics and wineheads and bums would be. When we would go through there when we was kids, we'd see very few black down-and-outers. I don't know whether that was 'cause of discrimination or what. They was almost all white, and you'd see hundreds of 'em lyin' on benches or sittin' there, drinkin' wine. There was a lot of flophouses on both sides of the street where you could get a room for fifty cents or a quarter a night, and there was restaurants or bars where you could get pints of cheap wine.

If you kept headin' west, past Des Plaines Street, you'd get to South Paulina Street, and that's where the black neighborhood on the West Side started. That neighborhood went as far north as Lake Street and as far south as Van Buren. The eastern boundary was around South Paulina and the western boundary was around South Homan. After that, you're gettin' out in the suburbs.

The West Side was one of the oldest parts of Chicago. The white people lived there for 100 or 150 years, and when the West Side started goin' downhill, the white people started sellin' out to the blacks. The place was already run-down when the blacks got in there. There wasn't many Hispanics on the West Side when I was a kid. It was mostly black. There were a lot of older frame houses and stuff like that. The West Side seemed more rural and less sophisticated than the South Side. It was more unkempt. Some liked the West Side and some liked the South Side. It depended a lot on where your people lived when you came to Chicago. The people was the same.

:::

My first musical memory is from when I was about four or five years old. They used to have sound trucks that would go through the black neighborhoods. On each side of the truck was an advertisement for some kind of product, and they would come through there playin' music to get people's attention. They would only move about three to five miles an hour, so you could follow 'em. And they would play a song like "Summit Ridge Drive" by Artie Shaw or Tommy Dorsey's

"T.D.'s Boogie Woogie" or Glenn Miller's "Tuxedo Junction." Those were my favorites.

When I would hear those songs, I would just run and follow that truck as far as it would go just to hear 'em. Now I learned later that "T.D.'s Boogie Woogie" was based on a record by a black piano player named Pinetop Smith, but at that time I wasn't thinkin' about blues or about bein' no musician. I just *loooooved* that music.

My father used to take me into speakeasies—after-hours places where he and his buddies would be drinkin' and all that—and he would point to me and say, "He likes music." They would have juke-boxes in these places. Around that time Nat King Cole was singin' blues. My mother's younger sister went to school with Nat King Cole at Wendell Phillips High School down on 39th. And he had this record out, "That Ain't Right," and they would play it on those tavern jukeboxes. I still remember some of the lyrics:

Baby, baby, what is the matter with you?
Baby, baby, what is the matter with you?
You got the world in a jug
And you don't have a thing to do

I took you to a nightclub
And bought you pink champagne
You rolled home in a taxi
And I caught the subway train

That ain't right
Baby, that ain't right at all
Takin' all my money
Goin' out, havin' yourself a ball

Yeah, I loved that song. I was just a kid and I didn't know who the artists were, but even then I loved them "black-bottom goodies" that Ray Charles talked about. The blues players had that expression in their music and that inflection in their voice and everything.

My mother's sister had a phonograph, and she and my mother would play all the latest blues records. Jazz Gillum's[4] "Key to the Highway," Big Maceo Merriweather's[5] "Worried Life Blues," Arthur "Big Boy" Crudup's "Gonna Follow My Baby," "After Hours" by Erskine Hawkins with Avery Parrish on piano—stuff like that. I heard Lil Green's records—"In the Dark" and "Why Don't You Do Right."

They had one record by Sonny Boy Williamson, "Mattie Mae Blues."[6] My mother's cousin was named Mattie, so I think she was the one who bought that record. The flip side was "Coal and Iceman Blues," and Sonny Boy played harmonica on there. I didn't know it was a harmonica. I just knew that it was some kind of interestin' sound. It sounded weird to me.

This was about 1940 or '41, so I'm hearin' these records when I'm about four or five. I used to babysit my brother Jerome and my sister Margot when my mother would take my oldest sister to school, and I would sing 'em those blues songs that my mother and aunties would play on the phonograph. I would sing the words— I knew the lyrics—and I would make the music—the guitar or the piano—with my mouth. I knew how it sounded.

4. Harmonica player and singer William McKinley "Jazz" Gillum (1902 or 1904– 1966) began his performing career in Chicago in 1923 as Big Bill Broonzy's partner. Gillum recorded for the Bluebird label, both under his own name and as a sideman, from 1934 until the late 1940s. His best-known tune, "Key to the Highway," became a blues standard. Gillum began recording again in the 1960s, but his comeback ended in 1966, when he was shot and killed during street brawl.

5. The pianist and singer Major "Big Maceo" Merriweather (1905–1953) was active in Chicago during the 1940s. Merriweather's first recording for the Bluebird label, "Worried Life Blues," was a major blues hit in 1941. Merriweather's playing was a huge influence on Muddy Waters's pianist Otis Spann. Merriweather was inducted into the Blues Hall of Fame in 2002.

6. John Lee Curtis "Sonny Boy" Williamson (1914–1948) was an early blues star who set the model for using the harmonica as a solo instrument in a group setting. During his ten-year career as a recording artist, Williamson was remarkably prolific, making hundreds of recordings as a bandleader and an accompanist. One of the earliest of these, "Good Morning, School Girl," is still a staple of the blues repertoire. Williamson achieved national popularity and exerted a profound influence on younger Chicago bluesmen like Muddy Waters, Little Walter, and Jimmy Rogers before his murder in 1948.

This was before television, so there were movie theaters galore and people played records. Black people played jazz, gospel, and blues records. My grandmother used to sing spirituals and church hymns while she was cookin', but she didn't play spiritual records. I never went to church myself. I wasn't brought up religious. A lot of musicians came out of the black churches. That's where they learned that rhythm and different techniques.

My father was like a lot of black people who would put the blues down. He didn't like blues. He called it "cabbage blues." But his sister would play that "Key to the Highway" record.

My auntie had all the latest blues hits, and I remember when I was seven years old she was playin' Arthur "Big Boy" Crudup's record with "Greyhound Bus" and "Gonna Follow My Baby" on it. I remember a friend of mine's mother tellin' me, "Arthur 'Big Boy' Crudup used to play there on 35th, between State and Wabash, up under the elevated train." I heard his records all the time. Everywhere you'd go, they'd have Arthur "Big Boy" Crudup's records. So I got the sense as a kid that Arthur "Big Boy" Crudup was one of the major, dominant blues guys at that time.

In 1942 we lived at 43rd and Evans, and our landlady had a stack of records. That's when Lonnie Johnson's "Jelly Roll Baker" record came out, and the landlady would play that a lot. I really liked that record.

After a couple of years, the families moved apart, and my parents got their own apartment on 59th and Calumet. My mother didn't have a record player, and so for a time I didn't hear any blues at home. When I was nine years old, my cousin Leon and I would go to this restaurant called the Big Apple down the street from where we lived, and I would put nickels in the jukebox to hear Eddie "Cleanhead" Vinson's "Cherry Red Blues." I *loved* that record. I loved his singin' and I loved those horns and stuff, you know.

In 1947 my mother's father and mother went back to Toledo, Ohio, and opened up a restaurant and a hotel. My grandfather bought my mother a record player, and he would pick out records from his jukebox and send them to my mother.

"G. M. & O. Blues," Sonny Boy Williamson's 1945 paean to the Gulf, Mobile and Ohio Railroad
Kim Field

I had started to play records for myself. Some of them was jazz, some was blues. One of 'em was Sonny Boy Williamson's "Mellow Chick Swing" and "G. M. & O. Blues." Sonny Boy was playin' the high register on the harmonica on "G. M. & O. Blues," and that just fascinated me.

I asked my mother, "How does a guy learn to play harmonica like that?"

And she said, "Oh, that's a gift."

So I'm thinking, *damn, why didn't I have that gift?*

One day I was playin' "G. M. & O. Blues" when my father and my mother was sittin' in the kitchen, and my mother said, "Oh, that's that man that made 'Mattie Mae.'" 'Cause if you heard Sonny Boy Williamson sing and you'd hear him again two years later, you'd know that voice. It was that distinctive.

My father said, "That guy came into Club Georgia the other day." My father's first cousin Ed White—we called him "Big White"— owned a club on 45th and State. It was called "Club Georgia" 'cause the whole family was from Georgia. My father told us that Sonny Boy came in there and was singin' and playin', and that everybody started callin' out, "Hey, Sonny Boy! Hey, Sonny Boy!" and throwin' money to him.

So that's how I found out that Sonny Boy lived in Chicago. I said, "Wowee." I thought blues singers was like movie stars—that they lived way off somewhere, like in Hollywood. I decided that I would try to find him. After that, every time I saw a guy on the street with a guitar, I'd give him the third degree and ask him if he knew Sonny Boy.

Me and my brother Jerome both went to Moseley Grammar School, an all-black elementary school at 24th and Wabash. At eight o'clock in the morning when you went to school, they'd have a drum and bugle corps playin'. I loved music, so the first morning we went to Moseley and I heard that music, I got elated. I got *excited*. I suggested to a friend named Victor Belcher that we join the drum and bugle corps. So we showed up one morning and lined up to talk to Mr. King, the band director. Mr. King was one of them big-time musicians—he played at the Regal Theater in Chicago—and he was tough. If you made the wrong note, he'd slap you. *Wham!* So there was three or four of us kids waitin' for our turn, and after he slapped a couple of kids, we took off runnin'. "Hey, where you all goin'?" he shouted at us.

Even when I was young, I was a romantic. When I first went to school at the age of five, I was in love with two girls in the first grade: Dosie Lee Marshall and Josephine Baker. She wasn't Josephine Baker the famous dancer, just a girl in my class. And I would come back home, and I would tell my older sister and my brother Jerome about my girlfriends. Every class I was in I fell in love with some girl. When I was eleven or twelve, I fell in love with one of my schoolteachers, Miss Wills. She was black and she was as pretty as she could be.

Around the same time, I became infatuated with the actress Yvonne DeCarlo. There was a movie that came out in 1945 called "Salome, Where She Danced," and she was the star. There's some beautiful music in it, and it felt bluesy to me. I must have seen that movie a hundred times when I was a kid—it played all over Chicago. I didn't know what instruments they used for the soundtrack—I know there was an organ in there—but I *loved* that music. And I fell in love with Yvonne DeCarlo 'cause she was so beautiful and the sexy way she danced and everything. Like I said, I'm a romantic.

In the summertime, we would go over to Maxwell Street. It was a real colorful place. There was a lot of gypsy storefronts over there. You could find them all up and down Maxwell Street—these gypsy storefronts with women readin' fortunes. And there was a huge market there where you could buy anything you wanted. There was blues players there, but I didn't pay any attention to that. My cousin and them went to the Montefiore school over there, and in the summertime we would go over there 'cause we could go over to the lunchroom and eat a free lunch. They didn't know who was who. They didn't know one kid from another.

I started workin' little jobs when I was a kid. I would work on my dad's horse-drawn watermelon wagon in the summertime. There was still horses all over the South Side and West Side of Chicago in those days. The *Sun Times* newspaper, the milk dairies, and the coal and ice men—before refrigeration, people used to have ice delivered—all used horse-drawn wagons. There was a place called Blue Front Stables at 41st and Emerald where they would rent a lot of horses. My father owned several horses of his own that he kept in a converted garage at 47th and Dearborn.

In the summertime, there'd be watermelon wagons crawlin' all over the South Side and the West Side. My father and his brothers would take a couple of wagons and go out to the watermelon track out on Archer Avenue where they had freight trains loaded with watermelons. People would show up with trucks and horses and wagons and everything, bid for a load of watermelons, and then sell 'em in the neighborhood.

Us kids thought the watermelon trucks and the horses was exciting, and we liked to eat the watermelons. My dad and the other

Watermelon wagon on the South Side of Chicago, ca. 1950
Photograph by Joanne Marten; The Art Institute of Chicago/Art Resource, NY

guys on the watermelon trucks would be hollerin' the "watermelon call" all up and down the street. It sounded somethin' like Howlin' Wolf. The soul singer Sam Cooke and his brother L. C. worked on the watermelon wagons in Chicago, too.

I also worked at my uncles' butcher shop on the weekends, and on top of that I was makin' five, six, seven dollars a week sellin' copies of the *Chicago Defender*, the black newspaper, at the corner of 63rd and Cottage Grove. The area around 63rd and Cottage Grove was popular with a lot of sophisticated blacks. The Pershing Hotel was right down the street.

One day I saw Joe Louis, the heavyweight champ, standing out front of the Pershing. I said, "Hello, Joe Louis!" He looked at me like I was crazy. I ran into Amos Milburn the same way. It was 1950, and he had just made this big record, "Bad Whiskey." I said, "Hey, Amos Milburn!" And he looked at me and snubbed me. You would see Sarah Vaughan at the Pershing—she would be gettin' her hair or her nails done.

Newsboy selling copies of the *Chicago Defender*, 1941
Photograph by Russell Lee, courtesy of Library of Congress, Prints and Photographs
Division, FSA/OWI Collection, LC-USW3-000698-D

There was a great big nightclub near the Pershing called the Circle Inn where they had jazz, so a lot of jazz musicians hung out there. It was a great big club and I used to walk through there sellin' the *Chicago Defender* to people.

I bought my first harmonica around this time. I bought an

American Ace model and a double-reed harmonica. They wasn't good for blues, but I didn't know what kind to buy. I was walkin' through the Circle Inn one day, tootin' on a harmonica, and this little dark guy came over and said, "Hey, boy, come here. Let me see that harp."[7] And he took that harp and he choked it—today they call that "bending" a note—and played some pretty blues runs on it.

I said, "What's your name?"

And he said, "Rhythm Willie."

I asked him, "Do you know Sonny Boy?"

And he said, "Yeah, I know Sonny Boy." He knew of Sonny Boy 'cause Sonny Boy was a big-time recording artist.

I found out later that Rhythm Willie played with all the jazz bands in Chicago at the more upscale places like the Cotton Club. He wasn't a blues guy. He could play standards and jazz tunes—any kind of popular song—on the harmonica. I don't know whether he did any singin' or not. That was the only time I saw him. I never did hear him play. He wasn't associated with the blues guys. He could play standards on the harp, and he was well respected in that jazz circuit around 63rd Street.[8]

:::

So, thanks to these little jobs, I began to have a little spendin' money, and I spent that money on blues records. I'm talkin' about the 78-rpm shellac records they had back then. Those 78s really had a sound.

They had record shops galore, all over in the black neighborhood. There was a big record shop called Rose downtown at Adams and

7. Blues musicians commonly refer to the harmonica as a "harp."

8. Willie Hood, a.k.a. Rhythm Willie (1910–1954), was a highly skilled and distinctive harmonica player who first recorded as an accompanist for blues artists Peetie Wheatstraw and Lee Brown. The Chicago-based Hood seems to have performed in the city's jazz and supper clubs and not in the blues bars on the South and West Sides. Hood cut four instrumental sides under his own name for OKeh in 1940 and recorded with Earl Bostic's band seven years later. His last recordings, two instrumental numbers with an orchestra, were made in 1950.

Wabash when I was a kid. They carried all the major labels like Capitol, Decca, and RCA. Most of the blues records was on RCA Victor, and they had bins of them at Rose. A lady who worked there told me that they got a lot of their records from jukebox distributors all over the country. Some of 'em was well worn, 'cause they'd been on the jukeboxes, but you could find most all the records there. And Rose had seven or eight listenin' booths where you could listen to records before you bought them. I used to go to Rose on Saturdays sometimes and stay there almost all day, listenin' to different records. It was an experience, you know.

After my father told me about Sonny Boy and Club Georgia, I went to Rose and I said, "What you got by Sonny Boy Williamson?" And they had seven or eight titles by him. Sonny Boy had recorded for Bluebird, and those records sold for forty cents. RCA Victor deleted their Bluebird label in 1945 and put the best-sellin' blues artists like Sonny Boy on the RCA Victor label. Those records sold for seventy-nine cents.

RCA Victor records printed the whole lineup on the record label. It would say, "Sonny Boy Williamson, Blues Singer with Harmonica, Tampa Red on Guitar, Big Maceo on Piano, Judge Riley on Drums, Ransom Knowling on Bass." So I began to study those labels and learn more about the musicians who played on these records.

That was my thing—buyin' blues records. Like some kids collected stamps, I collected blues records. I liked different types of music, but I didn't buy any jazz records. I was always interested in the blues. I liked the way the blues artists sang, I liked the way they played their instruments, and the musical parts of it.

All my friends knew that I liked blues, and their people had blues records. Most of 'em had one or two Sonny Boy records at home, and my friends would take those records from home and give 'em to me. A boy named Johnnycake said, "Hey, Billy, we got that Sonny Boy record 'Good Morning, School Girl' at home, and I'll get it for you." He looked for it, but it must have got broke. He said, "I got another record by him," and he gave me "My Little Machine."

The flip side was "Jivin' the Blues." A girl I knew named Muriel gave me "Collector Man Blues."

I would take those records home and hole up in the bedroom where we had the phonograph and play them for hours and hours. I wouldn't let any of my brothers and sisters touch those records. To me, they were sacred. I didn't like every blues artist, but there were some that I really liked. Tampa Red. Big Bill Broonzy. Walter Davis.

But I *really* loved Sonny Boy. I really liked his singin'. He had a voice that was more unique than all the other blues singers. He had the blues appeal in his voice—he could make a song sound real bluesy. He was the originator of that. He didn't sing in anybody else's style. And he was creative and personable on those records. The little innuendos and things he would do with his voice was really intriguing to me. You know, like in one song he said, "Come back tomorrow, 'cause Sonny Boy ain't got a doggone thing." Little things like that. One of my favorite songs of his was "Black Gal Blues." I think he did a beautiful job on that and on so much other stuff.

When I was about twelve, Muddy Waters had made a record on Aristocrat Records and I saw a picture of him with his guitar in a record shop. I went in there and I said, "Let me hear that guy's record." And they put it on and it had that slide guitar. I had never heard slide guitar before. To me it sounded like Hawaiian music, and I wondered where did that kind of music come from? 'Cause I was used to listenin' to Big Bill and Roosevelt Sykes, Memphis Slim, Memphis Minnie—people like that.

One afternoon a couple of years later, I was sellin' papers in front of the Pershing when I saw this guy gettin' out of a 1940 black convertible Buick. Now, I didn't know who he was, but he pulled a guitar out of the trunk. Like I said, every time I saw a guy with a guitar, I would give him the third degree, so of course I had to speak to him.

I asked him, "Do you make records?" He said, "Yeah."

I asked, "What's your name?" And he said, "I'm Muddy Waters."

I said, "Did you know Sonny Boy?" And he said, "Yeah, that was my partner."

And I said, "Well, how do you get on records?" And he said, "Well, you have to get in with a record company. And if they like you, they record you."

I said, "Where you goin' now?" And Muddy said, "I'm going to the Pershing Hotel to play for my manager." I walked with him over to the Pershing. Muddy had that big record out—"Rollin' Stone." And it was a big one, man. They was blastin' that all over Chicago. That was a hell of a hit for Muddy. And that's how I first met Muddy Waters.

All of my contemporaries—my cousins and the kids in the neighborhood—was listenin' to Billie Holiday, Sonny Stitt, the Orioles, James Moody, and people like that. None of the other kids liked blues. They would say, "Oh, man, I don't like that." Everybody laughed at me 'cause I liked blues. My mother's brother, my uncle, said, "Billy, he's like a *farmer*. He likes the blues."

When I was a kid and I would talk to my friends about the blues, they would ask me, "How come all the blues singers live in run-down, raggedy houses?" I couldn't answer that. I was just in love with the music.

Not too long ago, my youngest sister said to me, "Well, you had a calling." I had never thought of it that way, but I think she was right. It had to be a calling. 'Cause I felt the lure of the blues when I was four or five years old, when I first started hearin' it. So it must have been a calling, 'cause I really *loved* that music. And it wasn't about money or fame and all that. It was somethin' that was born *in* me.

Some black people frowned on anything that black people came up with on their own, unless they was tryin' to sing like Al Jolson or Bing Crosby or Perry Como. But that's some *other* person's talent or creation.

I saw this in my own family. My mother liked music. My father didn't. He was one of those people who tried to put the blues down. See, my mother's family was black Africans, and my father's people was not as black. When I say "not as black," I mean not only in skin color, but in soul, too. The blues wasn't what they really liked. They were the type of people that frowned on the blues. When I went over to my father's family's house, they wasn't as expressive as my mother's family. My mother's family was the black soul of Africa, and that's where the warmth was. When I would be around 'em, I felt warm and close to 'em.

I didn't express it that way then, but now I can look back on it and see it. That's where I heard the blues, and that's who played the blues—my mother's family. And the rest of the kids in the family, you know, they didn't listen to the blues. Blues didn't move them. But I was always conscious of the adults in the family, and I really liked my mother's father and her sisters and brothers 'cause they was really soulful. All I can say is that they had that black African soul in 'em. It was there. And that's where the blues came from. When you heard John Lee Hooker and Muddy Waters and Big Bill, they had that same soul. And so that's how I really got into the blues.

I didn't know the story of my people in America. I didn't know the prejudices and what they was goin' through. I was just a kid, but this was music that I really, really loved to my heart. I could feel it—the soul of the musicians and the songs. And as I got older, I realized that it was somethin' about the black people in America that was different from other people. And that includes how we got to America and everything else.

Like I said, I've always been a romantic, and the blues was about singin' about women and love and all that. Well, most music is. What would music be if it wasn't about singin' about some beautiful girl or somethin'? And the blues is about relationships, you know. The main theme of the blues is relationships between men and women. And love. So I liked that about the blues, too.

The Europeans had their twelve-tone music system, and their black slaves in America would learn their hymns and their music, but they did somethin' different with it. What they did was flatten the third and the seventh tones in the scale. This amazed the Europeans, but that sound was part of black people's African heritage. And that's the blues sound. Louis Armstrong and all them guys who came out of New Orleans and everything took the blues scale and the African soul and feelin' and the rhythm—blacks had brought that rhythm from Africa, that's how they expressed themselves—and they called it "jazz."

The boogie-woogie piano bass line, like the one Pinetop Smith recorded on "Pinetop's Boogie Woogie"—that's the black blues sound. That's the basis of blues, jazz, and rock and roll. And the white people didn't want to accept it or popularize it, 'cause it was black music and you wasn't supposed to recognize blacks as bein' great at anything or havin' anything to offer. Well, they have to recognize it now, 'cause black music was the original music of America and now it dominates worldwide. That's just the way it is.

I was always proud of myself as a person, even as a child. I never wanted to be anybody else. I loved the music that black people created, even though a lot of black people didn't. I think deep down they kinda liked it, but they was taught from slavery to not like anything created by other blacks. The white people didn't want you to feel proud of bein' black. They made you feel that everything you did was less than anybody else. I wasn't like that. I never felt that way. I *liked* the black culture and the music and everything, 'cause that's how I am as a *person*. It wasn't how I was raised. Yeah, there was racial prejudice among the blacks, too. I used to hear other adults, like on my father's side, who thought that they had been dealt a better hand 'cause they had a little lighter skin. But I didn't think that way. And when they'd say things like that, I'd speak out and speak up.

I loved my mother's family's culture 'cause they was African—not only in person, but within their soul. And that's what I liked. That's the way I felt. It was just *in* me. It was in me to love that music, 'cause it was comin' from the soul of the black people. And I wasn't thinkin' about that then, but now I can look back and see where the blues came from. The blues came from hardships and such like that, but black people made music out of it. That's how they survived. And I was proud of 'em and I was proud of myself.

And so it was in my nature to love the blues. That's why I had that calling.

Over time, the blues became somethin' that I also wanted to *do*. Sonny Boy Williamson's harmonica just fascinated me. Every time I'd buy one of his records, I'd get deeper into that fascination. *Wow! How does a guy make the harmonica play like that?* So I went to Sears and bought a harmonica and started to try to play with the record. Tryin' to get that *gift*. Some of my friends and family was shocked when I told 'em I wanted to learn how to play the harmonica. "What is *this*?" 'Cause a lot of people was tryin' to put blues down.

I wanted to be around the musicians who played the blues. I was livin' right in the middle of the Chicago blues world on the South Side, and so I decided to seek it out.

Blues luminaries gathered at Club Georgia in the late 1940s. *Seated, left to right*:
Muddy Waters, Sonny Boy Williamson, Lacey Belle Williamson (wife of Sonny Boy),
and Andrew ("Bo") Bolden. *Standing, left to right*: son of club owner Ed White, Eddie
Boyd, and Zadie Belle White (sister of Ed White)
Bill Greensmith/Blues Unlimited

2

Sonny Boy Williamson

By the time I was twelve, I had a burnin' desire to meet my idol, Sonny Boy Williamson, and to be a singer and a harmonica player. I could have tried to be somethin' else and went to school for somethin', but it was that blues music that took a grip on me, and I wanted to *make* that music.

I found out that Sonny Boy played at the Plantation Club at 31st and Giles on Wednesday and Thursday nights. I remember passin' by the Plantation Club and seein' a sign outside that said, "Sonny Boy Williams." The people that ran the Plantation Club was from Jackson, Tennessee, Sonny Boy's hometown.

My father had told me that Sonny Boy was workin' on the weekends at his cousin Big White's Club Georgia on 45th and South State Street. I have a *Chicago Defender* clipping from that time that says, "Big White invites you to enjoy the music of Sonny Boy Williamson, Friday, Saturday, and Sunday at Club Georgia."

Big White had a jazz band in Club Georgia at first. I think it was led by a saxophone player named Dick Davis. Sonny Boy was immensely popular in Chicago 'cause his records was all over the jukeboxes. Sonny Boy was so popular and dynamic that he could go and get a job anywhere. Get hired just by showin' up by himself with a harmonica. Sonny Boy came into Club Georgia one night and the band knew him, even though they was jazz players. Sonny Boy

Chicago Defender advertisement for "A Battle of the Blues" between Sonny Boy Williamson and Lonnie Johnson at Club Georgia, 1947
Scott Dirks

went up on the bandstand and played and the people loved him. Big White fired the jazz band and told Sonny Boy to bring his trio in the next week. Sonny Boy played there Friday, Saturday, and Sunday for about two years. Eddie Boyd was his piano player, and for the last six months he had Lonnie Johnson playin' with him there, too.

My father told me that when Sonny Boy would leave Club Georgia at intermission time, all the people would follow him down the street. And my father would say, "Hey, y'all get Sonny Boy and bring him back. He took all the people with him!" Memphis Slim said Sonny Boy always had an entourage with him. Every time you'd see him, he'd have four or five guys followin' him. There was a party everywhere he went.

But I was only twelve—too young to party or to even get into the Plantation Club or Club Georgia. How was I supposed to make contact with my idol?

I had a cousin named Archie who was three months older than I was. We was real close. We used to run together all the time. He had a younger brother named Herbie who was eight at the time. I would call Herbie up and play him Sonny Boy's records. I would say, "Listen to this, Herbie," and play the "Sonny Boy's Cold Chills" record for him over the phone.

One day I was at Archie's house and I decided to call Club Georgia—I knew the phone number—to see if I could talk to Sonny Boy.

I rang the club and told the bartender or whoever it was that answered, "I want to speak with Sonny Boy." He said, "Well, he's on the stage right now."

I could hear Sonny Boy playin' in the background. It was a big wall of sound. I mean, it was *full*. It was a roar. And Sonny Boy was singin' and playin' harp through the same amp. Sonny Boy never got the chance to play amplified harp on his records, but I definitely heard him play amplified harmonica at Club Georgia that night over the phone. That's where Little Walter got that idea to play harp through an amplifier, 'cause Sonny Boy was the first guy that was doin' that. I know that Muddy Waters also told people that Sonny Boy played amplified harmonica in the clubs.

I gave the bartender my auntie's phone number—I can't remember my own phone number today, but I can still remember hers from back in the day: WAterfall 8-1669—and asked him to have Sonny Boy call me back.

In about twenty minutes Sonny Boy called back. I guess he must have taken a break.

"This is Sonny Boy," he said. He had a real rough-sounding voice.

I was intimidated, and my mind went blank. All I could think of to say was, "What's your latest record?"

Sonny Boy said, "'Sugar Gal' and 'Willow Tree.'"

He must have detected that I might have been a kid, 'cause then he said, "Well, I got to get back right now."

I said, "Okay," and hung up.

I had actually talked to my idol, and I had heard that wall of sound and that amplified harmonica, and, oh *man*, it was like nothin' I had ever heard before.

:::

One day in April 1948, around Easter time, I was working at my uncles' butcher shop on 31st and Giles. I had just made twelve years old that September.

A guy walked past the shop with a guitar, so naturally I ran out to talk to him. Just as I did that, somebody across the street hollered at him, "Hey, Bill!"

I found out later that the guy with the guitar was a blues musician named Lazy Bill Lucas. If you ever met Lazy Bill, you never forgot him, 'cause he had an affliction that made his head go 'round and 'round. Lazy Bill played guitar and piano.

The guy who hollered approached Lazy Bill at the same time I did. They started talkin', but I jumped in and asked Bill if he knew Sonny Boy Williamson.

Bill said, "Yeah, I know Sonny Boy. Sonny Boy lives at 3226 Giles."

Children queued up for a movie matinee at the Regal Theater, 1941
Photograph by Edwin Rosskam, courtesy of Library of Congress, Prints and Photographs Division, FSA/OWI Collection, LC-LC-DIG-fsa-8a15699

That was just a block and a half away! I ran inside the butcher shop, found a pencil, and wrote that address down on a piece of paper.

Not too long after that I ran past the building at 3226 Giles. I was by myself, and I was shy, so I just yelled out, "Hey, Sonny Boy!" and kept on runnin'.

On Saturdays us kids would usually go to the movies. Television had just come out, but most people couldn't afford one. But there was movie theaters everywhere. I'd usually go with my cousin Archie and his friend Pat Shay Jones, who lived right around the corner from Archie. We was all twelve-year-old kids.

Archie and Pat Shay Jones wasn't into the blues, but they knew I liked it. I had told 'em about findin' out where Sonny Boy lived, so one Saturday I said, "Hey, come on, let's go over to Sonny Boy's house before the show."

And they said, "No, let's go to the show first, and *then* we'll go over to Sonny Boy's house."

We was out on 94th and Prairie, so we took the streetcar to 63rd and Halsted, where there was about five or six big movie theaters. We went to the early matinee and we got out about two o'clock.

I said, "Come on, let's go over to Sonny Boy's."

We rode the elevated train down to 33rd Street. We walked over to 32nd and Giles, found number 3226, and rang the bell. A very attractive lady came to the door.

I said, "We want to see Sonny Boy."

She said, "Sonny Boy is up on 31st Street somewhere," so we left.

A couple of weeks later, me and Archie and Pat Shay Jones went to the movies again and stopped by Sonny Boy's house a second time. We rung the bell and a well-dressed man came to the door and said, "Can I help you?"

I'd never seen Sonny Boy and didn't know what he looked like.

I said, "We want to see Sonny Boy."

He said, "This is Sonny Boy."

Sonny Boy had on a shirt and tie. He didn't have a suitcoat on. But he was well dressed, like he was goin' somewhere. He was just sharp lookin', you know. He had a head full of long hair—real long, black hair piled high on his head. His complexion was jet black. He doesn't look as black in his photographs as he did in person.

I said, "We want to hear you play your harmonica."

He said, "Come on up. I'm proud to have you all."

Thirty-two twenty-six Giles was a small, three-flat building. Sonny Boy lived in the front apartment on the second floor, so me, Archie, and Pat Shay Jones followed him upstairs, past the kitchenette and the bathroom that the people who lived there shared.

When we got into the apartment, there was a man and a lady sittin' there. They was immaculately dressed, too. The man was Johnny Jones, the piano player. I remember that he had a scar right by his eye with a piece of tape on it. I assumed that the woman was his wife. Sonny Boy's wife, Lacey Belle, was there, too. She was the nice-lookin' lady who had answered the door the first time we went by Sonny Boy's house. They was all dressed like they was goin' somewhere special. They said they was goin' to Gary that evenin' to play a gig.

Sonny Boy introduced us to his wife, Johnny Jones, and the other lady like we was his guests. He said, "They came to see Sonny Boy."

I asked him, "Sonny Boy, how did you learn to play harmonica like that?"

He said the same thing my mother said: "That's a gift."

So my thing was, *How do you get a gift? Why don't I have that gift?* I hadn't yet learned that you get the gift by keepin' on tryin' and doin' it over and over.

I had my American Ace and my double-reed harmonica with me, so I showed 'em to Sonny Boy. I asked Sonny Boy, "Let me see your harmonicas."

Sonny Boy asked his wife, "Where's my harps?" and then he found a couple in the inside pocket of his suit jacket and pulled them out. They was Marine Band harmonicas.

I said, "Sonny Boy, how do you make the harmonica say 'wah wah wah'?"

He said, "You have to choke it." White harp players call it "bendin' a note," but all the black harp players from Sonny Boy on up called it "chokin'" a harp.

Sonny Boy said, "I play with my tongue." He looked over at Johnny Jones.

"He plays with his lips. He can play just as good as I can," Sonny Boy said, and he asked Johnny Jones to blow some harp, but Johnny wouldn't play.

Sonny Boy had two record players in his apartment, so I said, "Play your record and I'll sing and play the harmonica along with it. I can sing and play the harmonica just like you."

Sonny Boy put on his current record, "Sugar Gal," and I stood there, singin' his song and tryin' to play the harmonica along with the record. I knew every word, and I was tryin' to sing just like him.

I didn't know how to choke a harp, but I thought I could play one just like him. And Sonny Boy got a real big kick out of that.

I said, "Sonny Boy, how do you choke it?"

Sonny Boy started to show me somethin', and then he said, "Oh, it's hard to show somebody."

Lacey Belle told him, "Oh, don't discourage him, Sonny." She asked me how old I was, and I told her I was twelve.

She said, "Well, Sonny started playin' the harp when he was nine."

Sonny Boy had an amplifier there with a bullet mic—a small, round microphone that fit in your hand. He told us that the amp was brand new. "I paid two hundred dollars cash for that," he said. He plugged the microphone in to it and turned on the amplifier. Archie took the mic and started sayin', "Calling all cars, calling all cars" into it. Imitating the police, you know.

Sonny Boy had somethin' like a stutter. When he would sing, he didn't hardly have it. But when he talked, he had a stutter.

Sonny Boy told me, "I bet you got some pretty sisters." He figured I must have some older sisters, but my sister was only a year older than I was.

So I made a kind of a face and I said, "Well, my sister is only a year older than I am. She's thirteen."

Someone came to the door, and Lacey Belle said, "Somebody let that man with a guitar in." This guy had come up there with a guitar, and Sonny Boy told him, "Let's work on this new song." And they started singin' and playin' it, and us kids just listened. It really sounded great. I remember it was called "You Sure Make a Man Feel Good." I don't know who that guitar player was. He was a young guy. I saw him once after that, but I never got his name.

We were at Sonny Boy's apartment for an hour or an hour and a half. He didn't rush us. Finally, being kids, we decided that we wanted to go and do somethin' else, so I shook his hand and I said, "See you, Mr. John Lee Williamson." I had seen his full name on the record labels, you know. And he got a big kick out of that.

When we left, Sonny Boy told me, "Come on by, and I'll show you everything I know."

When we got back to Archie's house, he told his mother, "Billy got a lotta nerve. He went right up to Sonny Boy's house and rang the doorbell and told him that he wanted to see Sonny Boy and hear him play the harmonica." But I didn't think of it that way. I loved Sonny Boy's harmonica playin' and I had heard so much about his personality. That made me determined to meet my idol and to learn to play the harp. Fortunately for me, Sonny Boy turned out to be a warm, friendly guy.

After visitin' Sonny Boy, I wanted to play the same harmonica that he had. I had noticed that Sonny Boy had two Marine Band harmonicas, so me and Archie went to a music store downtown one Saturday and I bought a Hohner Marine Band. It cost me two dollars and fifty cents. I remember that exactly.

: : :

Two weeks later, I came back to see Sonny Boy a second time. This time it was just me and Archie that went.

Sonny Boy answered the door and said, "Sorry, I don't have any new comics."

Sonny Boy lived right across the street from Douglas Elementary School. The Scott brothers—Walter, Kenneth, Scott, and Butch—went to Douglas. Their mother and their uncles played the guitar, and they all grew up to become musicians. They used to go across the street to Sonny Boy's for lunch. Sonny Boy liked comic books, so he traded comic books with the Scott brothers and other kids who went to Douglas. But I didn't know nothin' about that then.

I said, "Sonny Boy, don't you remember showin' me how to play the harp?"

And he looked at me and said, "Oh, yeah, this is my little buddy. The one who wants to be like Sonny Boy."

Sonny Boy took us upstairs. He had friends visitin'. I remember that they was drinkin' a half a pint of Gordon's gin and smokin' Camel cigarettes.

Sonny Boy was talkin' about a jealous husband who lived in his building. "He keeps his eyes on his wife," he was sayin'. "I heard he's watchin' for her."

One of the guys Sonny Boy was drinkin' with was his neighbor, and Sonny Boy told him, "Go and get your bam bam."

The guy went down the hall and came back with a gun. He said, "Man, I got this for them jitterbugs." In those days they called gang members "jitterbugs."

Sonny Boy said, "Well, I hope they don't try and mess with me."

Sonny Boy noticed that I had a Marine Band harmonica with me. It was a brand-new C harp. That was Sonny Boy's main harp, 'cause on most of his songs he played in the key of G on a C harmonica.

He asked me, "How much did you pay for that harp?" I told him I paid two dollars and fifty cents.

Sonny Boy said, "Where did you get the money for that harp?" I told him, "I sell papers on Friday and I work at my uncle's store."

Sonny Boy told me and Archie, "Don't steal. If you need show fare, come by, and if I ain't got it, my friend next door got it and I'll get it from him. But don't steal."

Sonny Boy told his friends, "You see, he sells papers and he buys harmonicas and records."

Sonny Boy asked me, "Let me take this harmonica to work tonight and you can come by tomorrow about two o'clock and pick it up."

Sonny Boy didn't know that I lived up on 94th Street. The blacks had moved into the neighborhood out there. Sonny Boy lived on 31st, in the area where most of the blacks lived. It was a rough neighborhood, but all the black neighborhoods in Chicago was tough. Sonny Boy lived near my uncles' butcher shop, so I figured I could come back the next week when I'd be down there workin'.

So I said, "Okay."

Sonny Boy had stacks of 78 records in his apartment. When we showed up, he was playin' a jazz saxophone record—I don't know who the artist was—and Sonny Boy was sayin', "Man, that cat can blow."

I said, "Sonny Boy, I thought you just liked blues."

He said, "Oh, yeah, I like blues, too." He showed me one of his records—"War Time Blues." It was on the Bluebird label. Then he pointed to an RCA Victor record and said, "The difference between these two records is night and day."

Now I didn't ask him to explain that. All I knew was that RCA Victor records was sellin' for seventy-nine cents and you could buy all the Bluebird records for forty cents. RCA Victor was a big label, so I took him to mean that he thought that RCA Victor was a step up.

I asked him, "Sonny Boy, who got you on records?" Sonny Boy told me it was a guy named Eli Oberstein. I found out years later that he was head of artists and repertoire for RCA Victor at that time.

I said, "How did you make that harmonica sound on 'G. M. & O. Blues'?"

He told me, "Put your tongue on the lower register, below the note you want. You put your tongue there and you suck in and blow out and you can get chords and single notes. Get that hard sound, that chokin' sound." That's how Sonny Boy got that ringin' sound, with his tongue.

Sonny Boy had a lot of hats, and Archie was standin' in front of the mirror and he's puttin' Sonny Boy's hats on. He had Sonny Boy laughin'. Sonny Boy said, "I would like for y'all to hear my band, but y'all is too young to let y'all in." I should have told him that Club Georgia was my father's cousin's place, but I didn't think of it.

Finally, Sonny Boy said, "Let me call a cab, 'cause I got to work in a few minutes." He called a cab, and when it drove up we went down with him to the street. We said good-bye to him, and he climbed into the cab with my Marine Band harmonica.

: : :

About a week or so later, me and my cousin went to see Sonny Boy a third time. We went by his house and rung the bell. The lady who lived on the first floor answered the door.

She asked, "Oh, who you lookin' for?"

We told her that we wanted to see Sonny Boy.

"Oh, haven't you heard?" she told us. "They killed him. He got killed. You didn't know?"

I said, "No, I didn't know that." 'Cause I didn't live in that neighborhood.

Then the landlady said, "They crushed his brain. His wife took his body back down South to Jackson, Tennessee, to bury him. She'll be back in a couple of weeks."

I couldn't quite believe it. When I got home, I decided that I needed to get verification from someone else about Sonny Boy bein' killed, so I called up Club Georgia. Some guy answered the phone, and I asked him, "What time does Sonny Boy go on?"

"He got killed," the guy on the phone told me. "He got cut up down on 31st Street."

I hung up the phone. I was devastated. I had just met my idol, who had turned out to be a nice, warm person, and I wanted to get to know him more.

I went back to Sonny Boy's after his wife, Lacey Belle, returned from Jackson, Tennessee, and the funeral. She had some guests there, and she told 'em, "This little boy, he was takin' lessons from Sonny Boy."

Then she looked at me. "Oh," she said. "We've been lookin' for you to come by. He had your harmonica. Let me pay you for it."

I told her, "No. I don't want you to pay me. He was my friend. I don't want you to pay me for it."

I told her that I was surprised that someone would want to kill Sonny Boy 'cause he was such a nice guy.

Lacey Belle told me, "Well, evidently somebody didn't think so."

She said that it would have had to have been more than one per-

Sunnyland Slim (*left*) and Sonny Boy Williamson
Billy Boy Arnold

son who killed him. She said that he was good in a fight and could whip the average two guys. Lacey Belle told me that when they carried his body out of the house the morning after he died, all the schoolkids from Douglas was cryin', 'cause they liked Sonny Boy and traded comic books with him.

I got to see Lacey Belle on several occasions after that. She was a very nice woman.

:::

Sonny Boy wasn't stabbed, like the guy at Club Georgia told me. Most people think that Sonny Boy was attacked on his way home from his gig. That's not true, either. I have a copy of the police report about his death, and years later I heard the real story about what happened that night by someone who knew a person who was there when Sonny Boy was killed.

Sonny Boy was a big gambler. He liked to shoot dice. When he came to Aurora, Illinois, for his first recording session for Bluebird, he got in a craps game and won fourteen hundred dollars. And people who knew him said that he used to win a lot of money gamblin' when he played in Cairo, Illinois. It was drinkin' and gamblin' that turned out to be Sonny Boy's downfall.

Sonny Boy was a bad actor. When he'd been drinkin', he would get into fights. In 1938 he had a fight with Memphis Slim when they was playin' at the Triangle Inn over on the West Side. Sonny Boy thought that Memphis Slim had shortchanged him on the money, and Sonny Boy hit him and knocked him out. Sonny Boy wasn't big, but he was powerful built and he was quick as a cat.

Lacey Belle told me, "I tried to tell Sonny Boy, 'Don't drink,' but the public really liked him." She was talkin' about how people would always buy him drinks.

Sunnyland Slim, the piano player, had a place at 29th and Prairie, just a few blocks from Sonny Boy's house. It was a big flat—six or seven rooms—and he ran an after-hours joint out of there. The musicians would go over there to hang out when they would come off their gigs and the clubs was closed. There would be four or five card games and crap games goin' on. You could come in there and buy liquor and soul food—red beans and rice, whatever. And you could buy sex, too. It was a house of ill repute and a gambling joint.

Sonny Boy was killed on June 1, 1948. He played a gig that night at the Plantation Club, but instead of goin' home he went to Sunnyland's place. There was a lot of people in there that night. Sonny Boy ended up in a back room playin' craps. He told his wife later that night that he had won more money than he had ever won. Well, everyone is against you when you win that kind of money.

A big commotion—some kind of fight—broke out during that

| John Lee Williamson | | 3226 Giles Ave. | | 4 |

| ATE OF ACCIDENT | DATE OF DEATH | DATE OF INQUEST |
| 6-1-48 | 6-1-48 | 7-Y-48 |

CRONER'S VERDICT: (CAUSE OF DEATH)

FRACTURED SKULL

Intracranial hemorrhage

MURDER

Below give names of persons arrested or wanted in connection with this death and Coroner's recommendation

Unknown   Robert Marty
                                DEPUTY CORONER

CORONER'S VERDICT CARD

RWARD ONE OF THESE CARDS TO THE RECORDS DIVISION WITH ALL INFORMATION REQUESTED HEREIN ON EVERY DEATH IN WHI.
A CORONER'S INQUEST HAS BEEN HELD

Form U F 51 10M 53   13

Coroner's verdict on the cause of the death of Sonny Boy Williamson
Billy Boy Arnold

craps game. The house man went and got two or three guys. They hit Sonny Boy in the head with a hammer or somethin' and fractured his skull. Crushed his brain. When they brought Sonny Boy out of the back room, they had him under both arms and his feet was draggin' on the floor.

They had to get him out of there, so they put him in a car and drove him the three blocks to his house. Sonny Boy's landlady said that she heard a commotion outside and several people talkin'. They leaned him up against the door, rung the bell, and drove away.

Lacey Belle told the police that when she got downstairs, Sonny Boy was layin' against the door and that he said, "They got me. They got me." He had a cut over his right eye, but Lacey Belle didn't see no blood, so she helped him upstairs. She thought he'd just been drinkin'. And when she took his clothes off, he said, "Lawd, I'm dyin'." She called the police station and they rushed Sonny Boy to Michael Reese Hospital on South Ellis, but he was dead on arrival.

The people involved had to put that rumor out there that Sonny

Boy died on his way home, but all the Chicago musicians knew the real story behind it. A lot of 'em was probably glad to see him go. Everybody's tryin' to get ahead, you know. Sonny Boy was the tops in Chicago, the front runner. He would have five or six records on the jukeboxes at a time. He was lively on the bandstand and very popular with the black audience. One time, he was on a gig and not feelin' too good, 'cause he had a problem with his heart. So the club owner said, "Sonny Boy, you just sit on the stage and let the band play. Don't play a lick. As long as the people see you on stage, they'll be happy."

Sonny Boy wrote all of his own songs, and he was a one-take artist in the studio. One time, Tampa Red had to make fifty-two takes on one song. Sonny Boy would get in the studio and make eight sides in one session. Willie Lacey, his guitar player, said "Aww, man, he was somethin' else." RCA Victor would bring in Sonny Boy to do two or three recording sessions a year. They always cut at least six sides. He recorded so much material that they was still releasin' his records two years after he died.

Sonny Boy did a dynamite session in May of 1940 for Bluebird with Josh Altheimer on piano and Fred Williams on drums. They sound like a full band, and Sonny Boy was at his best. They made about eight sides at that session, including the famous version of "Decoration Day Blues" and "My Little Machine"—the flip side of that was "Jivin' the Blues." Sonny Boy played a hell of a solo on "I Been Dealin' with the Devil." Sonny Boy's wife told me that that was her favorite record.

Josh Altheimer was Big Bill Broonzy's regular piano player. If you listen to those 1940 records with Sonny Boy, you can tell that Altheimer was a motherfucker on the piano. Memphis Slim and all of 'em would say, "Man, Josh was the best." Altheimer died right after that session. Big Bill started usin' Memphis Slim and Roosevelt Sykes on piano. Sonny Boy and Big Bill and Memphis Slim all played together for quite a while, and then Sonny Boy decided to hire Blind John Davis. Blind John fit right in with Sonny Boy, and Sonny Boy liked him.

In 1945 Sonny Boy cut "You're an Old Lady" and "Early in the Morning." RCA Victor deleted the Bluebird label in 1945, so that was the first Sonny Boy record to come out on RCA Victor. Sonny Boy made two sessions in 1945. "Sonny Boy's Jump," "Elevator Woman," and "G. M. & O. Blues" was recorded then. He did one session in 1946. That's the session where he made "Shake the Boogie" and "Mean Old Highway." In 1947 he made three sessions. He made "Lacey Belle" and "Polly Put Your Kettle On" with Blind John Davis and Big Bill. Then he recorded "Sugar Gal," "Willow Tree Blues," and "Wonderful Time" ("I sho' had a wonderful time last night, at least they tell me I did," you know) with Eddie Boyd and Willie Lacey. His last session was in November of '47, and he got killed in June of '48. Sonny Boy was only thirty-four when he died. He was a year younger than Muddy Waters.

Sonny Boy Williamson was the man who made the harmonica a lead instrument in the blues. His brother said that Sonny Boy used to practice to Leroy Carr's records 'cause there wasn't no harmonica players around then except for DeFord Bailey, who played by himself.[1] Most of the time, Sonny Boy played a C harp in second position, in the key of G.[2] On some of his early sides, he played an F

1. DeFord Bailey (1899–1982) was the first star of Nashville's legendary Grand Ole Opry broadcasts over WSM radio in Nashville and the first African American performer on the program. Bailey sang and played the guitar, bones, and banjo, but he is best known for his complex, unique, and brilliant harmonica playing, which earned him the nickname "Harmonica Wizard." Bailey grew up in a musical family. Confined to his bed at the age of three after contracting polio, he began mastering the harmonica. Bailey first appeared on the Opry in 1926, and during the next two years he recorded for Brunswick and Bluebird. After WSM fired him in 1941, Bailey opened a shoeshine stand in Nashville. He was inducted into the Country Music Hall of Fame in 2005.

2. When players of a diatonic harmonica—such as the Hohner Marine Band harp used by Sonny Boy and Billy Boy—refer to straight harp, or first position, they mean playing a harmonica tuned to the same key as the song (e.g., playing a song in the key of G on a G harmonica). Cross harp, or second position, refers to playing a harmonica tuned a fifth above the key of the song (e.g., playing a song in the key of G on a C harmonica). Sonny Boy Williamson popularized the use of second position, which gives the player the opportunity to "bend" the draw notes (e.g., to lower the pitch of the standard note). Third position refers to playing a harmonica tuned fifths

harp. On "Good Morning, School Girl" and "Sugar Mama," he played an A harp. But a lot of his later records was all played in G. He could take a C harp and play in the high register in C—in first position. Sonny Boy didn't play in third position. Never recorded it, anyway.

Sonny Boy Williamson played guitar, too. He played country and western stuff on it. Jimmie Lee Robinson told me he used to see Sonny Boy playin' the guitar down on Maxwell Street.

Sonny Boy was real aggressive, and if he had lived he would have continued with that amplified harp. He probably would have had the Aces and some of the other younger, more creative musicians like that playin' around him. He might have left RCA Victor and got with Chess. Either way, he would have recorded the way he wanted to record.

Willie Anderson was a Chicago harp player who spent a lot of time around Sonny Boy and Little Walter. One time he told me, "If Sonny Boy had lived, Little Walter wouldn't have become the king of the harp players." I was surprised to hear Willie say that, 'cause he was a real disciple of Little Walter.

If it wasn't for Sonny Boy's records, I would never have tried to play the harmonica. Once I heard him, I wasn't goin' to stop, even if it had turned out that he lived in New York or some other place and I never got the chance to meet him like I did. I still sing a lot of Sonny Boy's songs. It was Sonny Boy's records that made me seek out the blues world, and when I met him, that was my first contact with it.

One time Sonny Boy's wife said, "You're not in the blues world until you make a record."

"You're in the blues world if you are singin' in clubs," I told her. But when I think about it, she was right. 'Cause a record goes everywhere. You can be singin' in a club in Detroit and be the greatest singer or the greatest piano player or the greatest harp player or the greatest guitar player, but if you don't get out of Detroit or put out

---

above the key of the song (e.g., playing a song in the key of G on an F harmonica). Third position is often used by harmonica players to play in minor keys.

a record, you'll just be great right there where you're at, and nobody will ever know who you are. But once you put out a record, then you're in the music world. It was Sonny Boy's wife who put that in my mind, and as I got older, I began to think about that more and more.

Billy Boy Arnold, age fourteen
Billy Boy Arnold

3

Billy Boy

When I was around fourteen or fifteen years old, I would fantasize about what I would do if I was a millionaire.

This was my blues dream: I would hire Big Bill Broonzy, Muddy Waters, Tampa Red, and those guys to play at my club for twenty-five thousand dollars a week, and I would buy each of 'em a house so they would have a nice home. Their music meant that much to me. I loved their music, and I thought they deserved that. That's what I would think to myself.

It would be like what they did with classical music. Classical musicians didn't have to depend on the people. The governor or the king would pay for everything, and the artist would get his own villa. Beethoven and all those people, all they had to do was write music. They was taken care of by the king or the queen, or whoever was the head of the country.

I would also say to myself, "If anybody else anywhere in the world would hear this music, they would like it, too." This was before whites was gettin' involved with the blues. All my friends thought I was crazy.

A couple of months after Sonny Boy got killed, I met Big Joe Williams.[1] He was gettin' off the elevated train at 61st Street with his guitar. He was with a guy with a washtub bass. And, like I said, every time I saw a guy with a guitar, I'd give him the third degree. So I went up to him and said, "Do you make records?" And he said, "Yeah."

I asked him who he was and if he knew Sonny Boy, and that's when I found out that he was the Big Joe Williams who had recorded with Sonny Boy. In fact, he had made his last record with Sonny Boy, "Stack of Dollars," just a few months before I met him.

Big Joe had on some beautiful clothes—a real expensive sport jacket, nice pants and shirt—but it looked like he had had them on for a couple of weeks. He reached in his suit pocket and pulled out a brochure with a picture of him standin' in front of a CBS microphone.

I walked with Big Joe for three or four blocks, and then he set up to play on a street corner. I talked with him about Sonny Boy, and he told me, "Sonny Boy got killed on a zoom."

That was an expression black people used in those days. A "zoom" meant you was just at the wrong place at the wrong time. In other words, wasn't nobody out to get you, you just happened to walk in on a thing and a fight started and you got the worst end of it. Maybe you wasn't even the party that started the fight. Another way to say it would be, "Oh, yeah, he got wiped out on a humbug." A "humbug" was the same thing as a zoom.

That's what Big Joe told me about Sonny Boy. He said, "He

---

1. Guitarist and singer Joseph Lee "Big Joe" Williams (1903–1982) enjoyed a recording career that spanned four decades and many labels, including Bluebird, Vocalion, OKeh, Prestige, and Delmark. His distinctive sound was partly a product of his unique nine-string guitar. Williams recorded several duets with Bob Dylan in 1962 for Spivey Records. The guitarist Michael Bloomfield gives a vivid portrayal of Williams in his book, *Me and Big Joe* (V/Search, 2000).

mighta been comin' out of a hotel with somebody's old lady or wife or somethin'. He got killed on a zoom."

::::

When I would help out my father on his vegetable wagon on trips to the West Side, I got to know an old guy we called Mr. Upchurch, who lived over on Maypole Avenue. Mr. Upchurch was the grandfather of Phil Upchurch, the famous guitar player who was raised up on the West Side and played on a lot of blues and jazz records. I would stop by on Saturday, and Mr. Upchurch would be sittin' out on the porch. He had the gift of gab, you know, and I enjoyed talkin' with him.

One day I was talkin' to Mr. Upchurch and I just threw out Blind John Davis's name. All I knew about Blind John Davis was that he played piano on lots of the Bluebird blues records.[2] He was on my mind 'cause he had just made some records for MGM Records.

I asked Mr. Upchurch, "Do you know Blind John Davis?"

Mr. Upchurch said, "Sure, I know John. I been knowin' John since he was about twelve years old. John's uncle got that coal shed over there on Lexington and Leavitt. And John lives right across the street from there."

I said, "Wow." That was another new piece of information about the blues world. I had no idea Blind John Davis lived on the West Side. I had passed a house once on Lexington and had seen a blind guy there, but I didn't know who he was.

So one day, when I was on the West Side, I found the building across from the coal shed, and I went up and knocked on the door. This blind guy answered.

I said, "Does Blind John live here?"

---

2. Before he was thirty, Blind John Davis (1913–1985) had established himself as the house pianist for Bluebird Records, accompanying Merline Johnson, Sonny Boy Williamson, Red Nelson, Tampa Red, Memphis Minnie, Doctor Clayton, and Big Bill Broonzy, among others. After World War II, Davis formed his own trio and recorded for MGM Records. In 1955 Davis's house burned down and his wife died in the fire. Following that tragedy, Davis mostly focused on touring Europe.

Blind John Davis
Alligator Records

And he said, "Yeah."

"The one who used to make records with Sonny Boy?"

And he said, "Yeah, I made a lot of records with Sonny Boy, Tampa Red, and all of 'em."

And I said, "Well, I play harmonica just like Sonny Boy."

And he said, "Well, come on in. Let me hear you."

Blind John let me in. His wife was there. He had a piano in there, so we started jammin'. I was tryin' to sing and play like Sonny Boy. I could play pretty good by then.

That's how I got to know Blind John. When Blind John was a kid, his daddy ran a speakeasy, and there was a piano player who worked there. See, in those days you'd have a speakeasy or a house-rent party and you'd hire a piano player. When Blind John was fourteen years old, he watched his daddy payin' the piano player, and he told his dad, "Pop, if I learned to play a piano, would you pay me, too?" His daddy said, "Yeah." So Blind John sat down there at the piano and went to work! Blind John was an aggressive kid. He'd whup the shit out of you if he got his hands on you, even later when he was a man. He was talented, too. His mother would take him to the theater, and Blind John would hear the music in the movies and come home and play it.

Pretty soon I was spendin' a lot of time over at Blind John's house. Blind John liked his whiskey and moonshine and all of that 'cause he'd been drinkin' since he was fourteen years old. When I first went to Blind John's house, there was three or four fifths of sherry in there. Some of 'em was half full or almost full. Some of his buddies was raised up with him and did things for him when he needed anything done, and they would hang around his house and drink sherry wine.

At that time Blind John wasn't workin'. His wife, Hazel, worked. Hazel's mother was white. I met her once at Blind John's house. Blind John was black as midnight, but he would say, "I never did like no black women." He was one of those guys from that school. He believed in that cliché. I didn't feel that way. I will tell you that the blacker the berry, the sweeter the juice, you know?

I got to meet a lot of musicians at Blind John's house. I met Judge Riley there one day. He was a drummer-turned-bass-player who played with Tampa Red and on some of Sonny Boy's last sessions. He said, "Yeah, my wife loved Sonny Boy's music. He got cut up down on 31st Street." I didn't know at the time that that wasn't the real story.

Blind John was RCA Victor's main piano player. The way he got with 'em was he called 'em up and said, "I'm a blind piano player, and I'd like to do some recording for RCA." They said, "Well, you have to talk with Lester Melrose," and they gave him Lester Melrose's phone number.[3] Lester Melrose was the head man for artists and repertoire for RCA Victor.

When Blind John called Melrose, Melrose said, "Well, I'll tell you what. You call Tampa Red up and see if he can use you."

Blind John called Tampa and went up to Tampa's house. Tampa Red was tryin' to record a song of his called "You're More Than a Palace to Me." The Duke of Windsor had abdicated the crown, and Tampa wrote this song about it. And it wasn't blues changes. You had to know a lot about music to play it. Melrose sent tons of piano players up there, and they'd come up there and they couldn't cut it.

So Blind John called Tampa and went up to Tampa's house. Tampa's wife was in the bedroom across the hall, feelin' kind of sick that day. When Tampa started singin' that song, "You're More Than a Palace to Me," and Blind John joined in, she hollered, "Tampa! That's the one! That's the one!" Meanin' that's the piano player who could play that song. 'Cause all the other guys that had come up there couldn't cut it.

That opened the door for Blind John to get in there with RCA

3. Lester Franklin Melrose (1891–1968) was the first great blues record producer. As a Chicago-based freelance talent scout and session manager, primarily for the Bluebird and OKeh labels, during the 1930s and 1940s, Melrose established Chicago as a blues recording mecca. He launched the careers of many blues and jazz stars, including Leroy Carr, Joe "King" Oliver, Victoria Spivey, Lonnie Johnson, Champion Jack Dupree, Big Bill Broonzy, Big Joe Williams, Bukka White, Roosevelt Sykes, Sonny Boy Williamson, Arthur "Big Boy" Crudup, and Jazz Gillum. Melrose typically paid artists only for their recording sessions and assigned composer credits and performance rights to his own publishing company, a practice that enabled him to eventually own the copyright to more than three thousand songs.

Victor. Melrose started usin' him on sessions. When Sonny Boy come up there to record, Blind John complemented his style. He could play with Sonny Boy real good, and Sonny Boy started reques-tin' him for his sessions. Blind John complemented Lonnie John-son, too. He played on Lonnie Johnson's big hit, "He's a Jelly Roll Baker." He played on Memphis Minnie's hits, and on Big Bill's rec-ords. And Blind John is on all the great stuff Doctor Clayton did.[4]

Some of the guys, like Jazz Gillum, didn't like Blind John's playin'. Gillum wanted Black Bob to play piano for him.[5] Gillum was livin' on the West Side, and Melrose sent him to Blind John's to rehearse with him. Gillum came back and said, "Man, I went over there, and it was just a bunch of wineheads sittin' around there." And he wasn't lyin' about that, 'cause at that time Blind John was drinkin' sherry.

Gillum was a consistent songwriter and made a lot of records. He had somethin' going, 'cause if he wasn't sellin', Melrose wouldn't have kept recording him. Jazz Gillum's records was very slow and real bluesy. I never heard nobody say nothin' about Jazz Gillum playin' in the clubs. I never did meet him. I liked his record "Key to the Highway" recording

Blind John also told me a lot about Lester Melrose, the producer of those Bluebird blues records that I had been buyin'.

See, Melrose was a middleman. He was in with RCA Victor. He

4. The singer and songwriter Peter Joe "Doctor" Clayton (1898–1947) made his first records for the Bluebird label in 1935 in St. Louis. After his entire family died in a house fire two years later, Clayton moved to Chicago with the guitarist Robert Jr. Lockwood and began appearing regularly in blues clubs and on sessions for Decca Records. He returned to the Bluebird label in 1941, recording with Lockwood, Ransom Knowling, and Blind John Davis. B. B. King recorded covers of several of Clayton's tunes in the 1960s.

5. The dates of pianist Black Bob's birth and death and his real name are unknown, but the Chicago-based musician recorded extensively as an accompanist in the 1930s for the Bluebird and Vocalion labels. Black Bob lent his talents to re-cordings by many blues luminaries, including Tampa Red, Casey Bill Weldon, Big Bill Broonzy, Joe McCoy, Memphis Minnie, and Jazz Gillum. Memphis Minnie claimed that Black Bob performed and recorded with her as late as 1954.

found the blues talent and he recorded 'em, and then I guess he gave RCA acetates for manufacturing. Melrose's artists didn't have no personal contact with RCA Victor. They worked for Melrose. He had the deal with Victor to put out all those blues records. I don't know what Melrose's cut was. Now, he owned the publishing, and he was probably on salary, too, 'cause he was head of artists and repertoire. And I'm sure he had an expense account, you know, for when he'd go out and get people. Hotels and all that cost money. And he could pocket that money, 'cause he could send 'em to Tampa's house. I'm sure that he told RCA Victor somethin' along the lines of "Well, it should have cost a thousand dollars to get this guy and I only spent a hundred."

Here's what Melrose did with Tampa Red, according to Blind John. It was the old cliché: find one of the blacks that looked halfway white and treat him right. Give him more recognition. Melrose needed to have a guy like Tampa in his pocket to control the other guys. If the artist was from out of town, Melrose would send 'em train fare to come up to Chicago for a session and put 'em up at Tampa's house for a couple of days. Tampa had a big place with several rooms. They would record at Tampa's house, too. When the session was over, they'd go back down South.

Melrose didn't pick Tampa 'cause he was smarter than everybody else, 'cause Big Bill was a very smart guy. Maybe it was 'cause Tampa had been with Victor for a long time. I think Tampa got signed by Eli Oberstein just like Sonny Boy did. Oberstein was with Bluebird before Melrose.

Tampa's house was like Melrose's headquarters. Tampa didn't do all this just 'cause he was glad to do it, of course. Tampa got extra money for all that stuff he was doin' for Melrose, and he probably got a better royalty deal, too. Melrose paid Tampa to let the guys stay there and rehearse and record. Blind John said that Melrose kept money in the bank for Tampa, and that every week Tampa's wife would go to the bank and get some money. Tampa would spend the money, and then he'd send Mrs. Tampa down the street to the bank for more.

Even though Blind John lived on the West Side, he would go stay at Tampa's for two weeks before each session to rehearse and record. He would have a room there, and Melrose had a room there, too. Tampa might have had a couple of other spare rooms for the guys when they would come into town. And that's how they did it.

Walter Davis was another key guy for Melrose. Walter Davis recorded for Bluebird, and he was real popular with black audiences. All his records sold real consistent. He would do a session every three months and record eight to ten songs. He recorded for RCA Victor from 1930 or thereabouts until 1955. I met him one time. Walter Davis was smarter than the other guys that recorded for Bluebird. He left Bluebird in 1951 and sued Melrose. Then Melrose offered him a better contract, and Davis went back to RCA Victor. That was a smart move by Davis. Melrose would probably deal with you straight if you knew how to deal with him, you know.

Those guys who recorded for Lester Melrose, they didn't hardly get no money at all. Sonny Boy's wife told me that after Sonny Boy died, Melrose sent her a check for sixty dollars every now and then. Big Bill didn't get no royalties, and he recorded for Victor for years. I saw a documentary on television about Arthur "Big Boy" Crudup not long ago, and he said he didn't get *any* royalties off of his songs. He said that even before Elvis covered him, when he was recording for Bluebird, Melrose didn't give him no money. When Crudup first came to Chicago, he'd be singin' and playin' his guitar under the elevated train at 35th Street between State and Wabash. He was doin' that so Melrose or somebody would hear him and get him on record.

Crudup was singin' Big Bill's songs at that time. People always make the mistake of tryin' to sing somethin' that's already out, that they know was successful. When Melrose finally heard him, he told Crudup, "Well, you sound like Big Bill. Write your own material and let me hear it."

So Crudup came up with a couple of doozies—"Gonna Follow My Baby" and "Mean Old 'Frisco Blues"—for one of his first Bluebird sessions. I think that was in 1943. Those were two great

Arthur "Big Boy" Crudup
Bill Greensmith/Blues Unlimited

records. That session was a big success, but Crudup didn't get any money. Melrose would give him a few dollars once in a while—money to put in his pocket, you know—but no royalties.

Crudup claimed that when Elvis made that record of his tune "That's All Right," he wrote to Melrose's wife—Melrose had passed by then—and asked her about royalties, but she never answered him. "That's All Right" was Elvis Presley's first hit. If it wasn't for Crudup, the song would have never came to existence, and he didn't get *anything*. He said that when his mother died, he didn't have any money to bury her.[6]

Big Boy Crudup was a great singer, he had his own sound on the guitar, and he was a prolific songwriter. His records came out consistently, and they was very popular with the black audiences. Everybody was buyin' 'em. He came up with several big sellers. He was givin' Tampa Red and them a run for their money, and he recorded for RCA Victor from 1942 until 1954 or '55. You would think that he was makin' *some* money, right?

Crudup recorded in Chicago, but he didn't live here. He was farmin' down South, and he would come to Chicago every three months or so when Melrose would send for him to do a session. He'd record seven or eight sides, whatever, and then he'd go back down South. His records was on the jukeboxes and everything, but he still had to farm. Drive a tractor. He wasn't makin' no money.

I never met Lester Melrose, but I did meet his brother, Walter Melrose. Walter Melrose had an office down on Dearborn and Randolph, and I went down there with Blind John. Walter Melrose had put Blind John and a guy named Peachtree Logan, who was a drinkin' buddy of Blind John's, on MGM Records. Blind John's sessions for MGM wasn't blues, 'cause Blind John was not really a blues man. He could play all the standards. That was the type of stuff that he could do.

I think that Melrose's artists were like me and all the rest of the musicians of my era. We felt that to make a record was to achieve a certain amount of success. But there wasn't a lot of money in it, if Bluebird records was sellin' for forty cents. I wonder what guys like Tommy Dorsey got? He was on Bluebird, but he was definitely reachin' a lot bigger audience. The blues records just went to cer-

6. Dick Waterman states in his book *Between Midnight and Day: The Last Unpublished Blues Archive* (Thunder's Mouth Press, 2003), that while Arthur Crudup received negligible royalties for "That's All Right" during his lifetime, his estate has received "around three million dollars" in royalties from Hill and Range, Presley's music publishing company, since his death.

tain regions where the black audiences was. And the jukebox people would buy those records. Now, one advantage that RCA Victor had was that they had their own distributors. Anything that came out on the jukebox, whether it was music from overseas or blues music or whatever, got distributed by the jukebox people. So that was an advantage. RCA Victor also had their own manufacturin' and pressin' plant in Camden, New Jersey. Camden was a boomin' town in those days, thanks to RCA Victor. And RCA had exclusive franchises. If you owned a record store and wanted to sell Victor records, you had to have a franchise with Victor and you had to take everything they sent you.

Melrose made money collectively on all those records. You didn't need but one artist like Elvis Presley to get rich. But Melrose was handlin' all of 'em, and they may not have been huge sellers, but he made his money. There wasn't LPs at the time, but those 78s sold consistent. He wasn't in it for nothin'. *Somebody* was makin' money, but it wasn't the artists.

I guess there wasn't no big money in blues records. At that time, they was sellin' only to black people. Some artists like Walter Davis had a large followin'—people who bought everything they did. I heard a guy at Vee-Jay say that a Jimmy Reed record was good for fifty thousand records, and those records was considered hits. The jukebox distributors would buy large amounts of records. See, the black people didn't have record players a lot of times, so they'd go to the café, and that's where they'd hear a lot of music. You'd go to the café, and you might hear "You Don't Have to Go" by Jimmy Reed, and you'd say, "Oh, I like that." And if you had a record player, you'd go and buy it and take it home. I have no idea how many jukeboxes there would have been for a black blues record, 'cause they only covered most of the southern states and part of the northern states.

Million sellers were rare in the blues field. They say that Leroy Carr sold a million copies of "How Long, How Long Blues." Sellin' ten thousand or forty thousand records would be good for the record companies, but the artist couldn't count on anything reasonable. He'd have to earn his money in the clubs or otherwise, not

Billy Boy Arnold (*right*) and his friend Ivory Crowley, 1951
Billy Boy Arnold

from royalties. Things changed when white people started buyin' those records. Chuck Berry had million sellers on Chess, and he became a wealthy man off his royalties.

:::

As I became a teenager, the blues was goin' through some changes. The stuff that Sonny Boy, Big Bill, Memphis Minnie, and Tampa Red and them played was sort of becoming dated, compared with the updated sound of new blues stars comin' on the scene.

There was a supermarket in my neighborhood that would play blues records, and that's where I first heard a T-Bone Walker record. T-Bone was really popular back then with black people. He was bluesy and he used horns. He was more acceptable with black people in Chicago than, say, Tampa Red, Big Boy Crudup, or Sonny Boy. By the time I was fourteen, I was a big T-Bone fan. I thought he was the greatest guitar player, and he was one of my favorite singers, too. I started buyin' T-Bone's records. I remember buyin' his record "Hard Pain Blues" and "It's a Low Down Dirty Deal." T-Bone was on a record label called Black and White. To this day, I still really love T-Bone Walker and that beautiful guitar playin' of his. All the guitar players owe a debt to T-Bone 'cause he was the first guy that could play that single-note blues on the electric guitar.

I got the chance to meet T-Bone once when he was playin' at the Tivoli Theatre in Chicago. He was stayin' at the Pershing Hotel right across the street, and I ran into him there. And he had this guy with him, his cousin or nephew or somethin'. Anyway, we ended up goin' up to T-Bone's hotel room, and several people was up there. So I got a chance to meet him and talk with him and shake his hand.

And then B. B. King came out, singin' blues and playin' the guitar in a style derived from T-Bone, and he also had these horns and things. The black people, they were always tryin' to get away from the stuff like Lightnin' Hopkins. So the blues was always catchin' hell tryin' to get up off its knees! Well, I liked other kinds of music, but I still preferred those black-bottom goodies and Sonny Boy's records.

Muddy Waters started makin' his mark. He recorded "Screaming and Crying" and "Where's My Woman Been" for Aristocrat Records in 1950. Aristocrat was Leonard Chess's first record label, before he had Chess Records. To me, that was great music. Muddy had Johnny Jones on piano and Baby Face Leroy on second guitar, and those are really good records. He was still playin' with the slide, and he hadn't used Little Walter on harmonica yet.

Then Muddy came out with "Rollin' Stone" on Chess, and that's when he came to the forefront. "Rollin' Stone" was just him on guitar and Big Crawford on the bass. And Muddy played electric guitar on there. He had done that before, but the electric guitar was really pronounced on "Rollin' Stone." It was real heavy. That record was a smash. It was all over Chicago. It was burnin' up, you know. You'd hear "Rollin' Stone" on all the jukeboxes everywhere, even in parts of the black neighborhood where blues wasn't real popular. So that brought Muddy a lot of recognition. "Rollin' Stone" made Muddy the top man in Chicago. That's when I started buyin' every record Muddy came out with.

Leonard Chess wanted Muddy to keep on with the "Rollin' Stone" sound. He was gonna try to do Muddy like John Lee Hooker and Lightnin' Hopkins. But Muddy didn't have that kind of talent. He was limited in his guitar expression. He was already playin' in the clubs with Jimmy Rogers on guitar and Little Walter on harmonica, so he told Leonard, "Let me bring my band in." But Leonard didn't want to do that. See, before "Rollin' Stone," Muddy had made a couple of sessions with Sunnyland Slim on piano and a regular blues band, and they didn't make no big hits. "Rollin' Stone" made the big hit, so Leonard wanted Muddy to stick with just the guitar and bass.

Leonard finally gave in and put out two records at the same time with Muddy, Little Walter, and Jimmy Rogers on his new label, Chess Records. Chess put out "Ludella" and "That's All Right" on Jimmy Rogers and "Your Gonna Need My Help" and "Sad Letter Blues" on Muddy. Both records had Little Walter's dynamic harmonica playin', and he stole the show.

Muddy was now makin' records with Otis Spann on piano, too. The first time I saw Spann was in 1951, before he joined Muddy. He was playin' down at the Tik Tok Lounge on 36th and State. I think he was playin' with Morris Pejoe. Spann was a new musician who had come into town and he was playin' with different people. And when I heard him, I said, "*Goddamn*, that's the greatest blues piano player that I *ever* heard." And the next thing I knew he was with Muddy. With Jimmy Rogers, Little Walter, and Otis Spann, Muddy had a solid foundation.

I was down on Maxwell Street one day in 1951 or '52 and I went into a record shop down the street from Ora Nelle.[7] Forest City Joe had made a record called "Memory of Sonny Boy" for Aristocrat, which was Leonard Chess's first label, and I wanted to hear it.[8] The young lady in the store played Forest City Joe's record, and she said, "You know, when he made this record for us—well, he sounds better in person. He don't sound really good on record." I wonder if Leonard Chess owned that record shop and whether that woman was his wife or his business partner, 'cause she said, "When *we* recorded him." I didn't know anything about Leonard Chess or Aristocrat at the time.

I never played down on Maxwell Street. When I was a kid, I knew that they had music down there, but when that stuff was goin' in the 1940s, I was too young to appreciate it. That scene went on for quite a while. It lasted up through the '50s. Most of the guys who

7. Dubbed by some Chicago residents as "the Mayor of Maxwell Street," Bernard Abrams established a radio repair business in that neighborhood in 1945. Abrams converted his back room into a primitive studio, and many future blues stars, including Muddy Waters, Johnny Young, Jimmy Rogers, and Little Walter, made some of their earliest records for Abrams's small Ora Nelle label.

8. Joe Bennie "Forest City Joe" Pugh (1926–1960) began his musical career playing the harmonica with Big Joe Williams in St. Louis before moving to Chicago in 1947. Pugh played in a band with Muddy Waters and recorded for Leonard Chess's Aristocrat Records in 1948. He worked in a band with pianist Otis Spann between 1949 and 1954. The following year Pugh moved back to his home state of Arkansas. He resumed recording—this time for Atlantic Records—in 1959 but was killed in a truck accident the following year.

People shopping for shoes on Maxwell Street, 1941
Photograph by Russell Lee, courtesy of Library of Congress, Prints and Photographs Division, FSA/OWI Collection, LC-DIG-ppmsca-01596

started out down there became professionals, and then they didn't play down there anymore. I never did play down there, even before I became a professional. I started out in the clubs. I saw the guys down there a couple of times, but I thought they was just unprofessional guys playin'.

:::

One day in 1951 I was passin' a restaurant on 63rd and Cottage Grove and I saw these guys in there with two guitars and a washtub. They was buyin' some hamburgers. Of course, the guitars attracted me to them, and I came over and introduced myself.

The two guys with guitars turned out to be Ellas McDaniel and Jody Williams, and the guy with the washtub was Roosevelt Jackson. Ellas and Roosevelt were the same age—they were twenty-three. Jody was the same age as me—fifteen.

I told 'em that I played the harmonica, and Ellas said, "Well, we're goin' to the Midway Theatre right down the street to do an amateur show. Come on down to the show." Not to participate, but just to see 'em. So I went down there and caught that show.

Ellas gave me his address. He lived on 47th and Langley. He told me, "Come down there early on Saturday morning. We play on the street corner, and you can play with us." I said, "Okay." And that's how that started.

I got to Ellas's house early on the next Saturday morning, about nine o'clock, and Jody was comin' down the street with a guitar. Jody was a little short guy and he had a great big guitar case.

Ellas's auntie told us, "Ellas is asleep. He ain't up yet." It was summertime, so we sat on the porch there. In about a half hour Ellas came down, and then Roosevelt showed up.

We went up on 47th by the 708 Club and started playin'. We'd play in one spot for about a half an hour or an hour, and then we'd move on down to another corner. Just playin' spots. We wasn't usin' any amplifiers 'cause we didn't have access to electricity out there on the street. We was just playin' acoustic. Ellas would play guitar and sing and dance and draw a crowd.

Ellas, Roosevelt, Jody, and I played intermittently on the streets on Saturdays. Jody and I was too young to play in the clubs. Ellas knew a guy named Joe Brown who ran the Indiana Theatre, and at night Ellas would go in there and count up all the money we'd made on the streets that day and split it with us. I assume it was an even split across all of us, 'cause Ellas was that type of guy.

At first Ellas did all the singin'. He was a good showman. He'd dance and play the guitar. He sung blues and he sung "Mule Train" and "Ghost Riders in the Sky" and stuff like that—whatever was popular. A variety of stuff. Most of the stuff he was doin' on his own. He didn't feature harp particularly. Later he'd let me sing two or three songs, usually the latest Sonny Boy Williamson song. And

Jody would sing a couple. He used to sing Muddy Waters's hit "Appealing Blues."

Roosevelt was Ellas's buddy. They was raised up together around Chicago. They used to hang out at the 45th Street Baptist Church until they got into a little trouble. They went back a long ways with each other. Ellas went to school with Earl Hooker on the West Side at a school over there on Maxwell Street. I don't remember the name of it.

I was just a kid, and Roosevelt said, "We don't need that little old boy following us around." But Ellas said, "That's all right. He's all right." And that was the end of that.

Jody Williams started out playin' classical harmonica. He was playin' the chromatic harmonica like the Harmonicats and stuff like that. Then he met Ellas and decided that he wanted to play the guitar, so Ellas told him, "Come on over and I'll show you." Ellas had Jody tune the guitar like he tuned it. Ellas called it "Spanish tuning."[9] He taught Jody a few things and Jody started playin' rhythm behind him, in the background.

Ellas did a lot of doo-wop-type tunes in those days, and he'd sing a lot of stuff like calypso and music with South American or Mexican rhythms. Ellas didn't use no drums on the street, so he had these maracas and he'd have some of the kids shake them. Jerome Green was one of them. He and his family lived in the same building as Ellas. Jerome was about my age. The maracas fit Ellas's material and gave him some rhythm.

I knew from the very first time I heard Ellas that he was gonna be accepted worldwide, 'cause he had somethin' different. Most of the black musicians thought that he wasn't playin' the right chords like Wes Montgomery and all that. "Ellas ain't playin' shit," they'd say. Most of the guys around Chicago laughed at him, but I knew

---

9. Spanish tuning refers to a practice of tuning the open strings on a guitar to the notes in the G-major chord. For example, a popular open-G tuning is D-G-D-G-B-D (low string to high string). Ellas McDaniel actually used variations of open-E tuning.

he was gonna be a hit even before he made a record, 'cause he had a lot of good ideas, his own personality, his own sound, and his own voice. That's what it takes.

Very few guys come out ready to be a star. I felt that Ellas was really gonna make it, 'cause he was different from anybody else in Chicago. He was *unique*. He was *different*. An original. Ellas was young and he could play a variety of stuff. He was very creative. The other guys was playin' like Muddy Waters, Howlin' Wolf, and all of the regular blues stuff. Ellas could play a little like Muddy Waters, but even if he did another person's song, he did it his own way. He didn't follow anybody. I don't think Ellas had an idol, like the guys who patterned themselves after B. B. King or after Little Walter, or like how I idolized Sonny Boy. Ellas didn't sing all that stuff that Muddy Waters and Little Walter did. He was playin' those little boogies like John Lee Hooker. Ellas is the only guy I know who *always* did his own thing.

Ellas had talent, but he wasn't really pursuin' a career in music. He was just doin' music for fun. The attraction for me was to be playin' with a band. I was just glad to be playin' with somebody. My dream wasn't to be Ellas McDaniel's harp player. My goal was to make records.

Jody had a similar idea. He decided to get away from Ellas eventually, 'cause Ellas wasn't playin' enough music for him. So Jody left and started playin' with people like Jimmy Rogers and Howlin' Wolf, 'cause he wanted to play blues. Jody wasn't playin' nothin' but rhythm and chords when he played with Ellas. After he quit playin' with Ellas, I didn't see Jody for a couple of years. Then in 1953 I went to hear him play with Hubert Sumlin in Howlin' Wolf's band at the Zanzibar.[10] I heard all this guitar, and I thought it was

10. Best known for the recordings he made as a member of Howlin' Wolf's band, Hubert Sumlin (1931–2011) developed a stinging and highly original guitar style that had a huge influence on the blues and rock guitarists who followed him. Sumlin met the bluesman Howlin' Wolf as a child in Mississippi, and when he was twenty-three the Wolf invited him to move to Chicago and join his band. With a few brief

Hubert. But when I got closer, I could see that it was Jody, and he was *swingin'*. I told him, "Man, was that you playin' all that guitar?" Jody was the kind of guy, if he put his mind to learnin' somethin', he wouldn't lose no time on it.

Ellas had just gotten married when I first met him. His wife, Tootsie, was only fifteen years old. She was pregnant when I first met her. Ellas had been married before to another girl for a couple of years or so, but that didn't work, so he married Tootsie. Ellas had a day job, so he wasn't uptight for money. Tootsie's father worked construction, and Ellas worked with his father-in-law. Ellas, Tootsie, and Tootsie's parents all lived in the same building.

Ellas was just a real nice, friendly guy. He didn't drink and he didn't smoke. Ellas was built like Charles Atlas, very muscular, but he was mild mannered. He wasn't threatenin'. Everybody liked Ellas. He had all kinds of friends. If he walked down the street, everybody would be sayin', "Hey, Ellas! Hey, Ellas!"

And if Ellas found somebody with their hood up, havin' trouble with their car, it could be nine below zero and he'd stop and say, "What's going on?" The guy would say, "I don't know, I think it's my clutch," or whatever. Ellas would get up under that hood and get the guy started and say, "No, I don't want no money." Ellas just liked to do things like that.

If you went by Ellas's house on a Saturday when the weather was good and he was back on his construction job, he'd be in the back yard, where he had taken his car apart. The whole motor and every little screw would be layin' out there on a rug. And Ellas would work on it and he'd put that car back together. He was a mechanic. He could fix radios, too. Ellas would see an old radio or a TV in the alley that wasn't workin', and he'd take it home and have it workin'.

Every Sunday Ellas would go check out the Maxwell Street

<hr />

interruptions, their musical association lasted until Wolf's death in 1976. Sumlin continued recording and playing with other members of Wolf's band, earning four Grammy Award nominations. He was inducted into the Blues Hall of Fame in 2008.

market. The market would start about four o'clock in the morning. People would go over there with all their goods. Used tires, an old toilet, an old stove—I mean *everything*. People would take their truck and get there around four o'clock to get a good spot. Then they would park and sell their goods. People would buy whatever you had.

Ellas would go over there about five in the morning to buy stuff. Different trinkets. Ellas was the type of guy who didn't care about clothes. On Maxwell Street you could buy clothes cheap, and it would be new stuff, too. One time Ellas bought a suit for ten dollars. And he said, "Look at my suit." He was braggin' about his suit 'cause it was brand new. I kinda laughed at the idea of a ten-dollar suit, but that's the kind of guy he was.

When the weather got real cold, Ellas didn't do much construction work and we couldn't play on the street corners. So then Ellas would try to get a club gig. He and Roosevelt had played the 708 Club in 1951, but that was before I met him. I've seen pictures of Ellas and Roosevelt playin' there. The people at the club told him and Roosevelt to join the union, but they didn't play there for long. Muddy Waters, Robert Nighthawk, and Elmore James played at the 708 Club, and so they all knew who Ellas was.

Ellas would also get construction work down South sometimes durin' the winters. When springtime would come, we'd start playin' on the streets again. I might not see him for six months or a year.

::::

After I played with Ellas on the street corners, I wasn't with a regular band. I was a kid, so I wasn't able to be in the clubs in the first place. I was doin' all the regular things that kids do.

The same year I met Ellas—1951—I passed a pawn shop on 31st Street and I saw two guys in there with guitars and another guy who was buyin' harmonicas. When I saw these guys with the guitars, I went in there and introduced myself, 'cause I figured they was blues musicians. The guys with the guitars turned out to be Dave Myers and Louis Myers—they was brothers—and the guy

The Aces in 1974. *Left to right*: Fred Below, Louis Myers, and Dave Myers
Bill Greensmith

buyin' harmonicas was Junior Wells.[11] And so I was talkin' to Junior and Dave, and I said that I played the harmonica, and they said, "Well, come on, we're goin' around to the house to practice."

Louis and Dave had an older brother named Bob who was in the service then, and Louis and his wife was livin' in Bob's apartment at 31st and Michigan. So I went there with Junior Wells, Dave Myers,

11. Amos Wells Blakemore Jr., a.k.a. Junior Wells (1934–1998), was raised in West Memphis, Arkansas. Influenced by his cousin Junior Parker, Wells started playing the harmonica and singing at the age of seven. Not long after moving to Chicago in 1948 with his mother, Wells had formed a popular band called the Aces with guitarists Louis and Dave Myers and drummer Fred Below. Wells replaced Little Walter Jacobs as the harmonica player in Muddy Waters's band in 1952 and made his first recordings the following year for States Records. In the late 1950s and early 1960s he recorded for Chief, hitting the R&B charts with "Messin' with the Kid" and "Little by Little." Inspired by artists like James Brown, Wells began to inject a funkier, more soulful approach into his recordings and live shows. Wells and guitarist Buddy Guy teamed up in the 1960s and became hugely popular with white audiences, recording the classic album *Hoodoo Man Blues* for Delmark in 1965 and touring Europe as the opening act for the Rolling Stones.

and Louis Myers. Then the drummer Fred Below showed up for practice. Junior, Dave, Louis, and Fred had a group called the Aces.

Junior was one of the top harp players around town. He didn't really have a style of his own at that point. He told me once that his mother used to go around and listen to Sonny Boy Williamson and come home and tell him about it. He sang all of Muddy's stuff, and the Aces could play those tunes as good as Muddy. Junior wasn't singin' the Sonny Boy stuff he recorded later for States Records in the clubs. He wasn't singin' no "Hoodoo Man" or "You Better Cut That Out" on the bandstand. He was singin' all of Muddy's hits then. Everything Muddy ever did, Junior was doin'. That's what made the Aces go, 'cause Muddy was hot and had all them good records out. Louis and Dave Myers didn't sing at all. Junior was the star of the group and did a great job frontin' the band. When I met 'em, the Aces was playin' at the Zanzibar on 14th and Ashland, and they was really hot.

I hung around the Aces a lot. I used to go over to Louis's house all the time when they would be rehearsin' there. And they took me over to Sunnyland Slim's place, too—the place where Sonny Boy got done in three years before. Sunnyland was still livin' there.

:::

When I was fifteen, I went with Blind John to a Sunday cocktail party at Sylvio's, the big blues club on the West Side. "Cocktail parties" was jam sessions that would happen before the regular gig. They would start about two in the afternoon. Sylvio would put two or three tables together and put out a couple of fifths of whiskey. The party would start at two o'clock in the afternoon, and all the musicians would go up and jam with the band and drink with their girlfriends.

Elmore James and his band was playin' there that Sunday. Elmore had made this hit record, "Dust My Broom," and he had a great band. He had Homesick James on rhythm guitar, Johnny Jones on piano, J. T. Brown on saxophone, and Odie Payne was the drummer.

I don't think he had a bass player. I remember that Snooky Pryor was at Sylvio's that day, too.

Rice Miller walked in.[12] He had played harp on the flip side of "Dust My Broom," and he was callin' himself Sonny Boy Williamson. I knew that he had made a record called "Eyesight to the Blind" that said "by Sonny Boy Williamson" on it.

Rice Miller knew John Lee Williamson. They was friends in Helena, Arkansas, 'cause John Lee Williamson lived there for a while. And Sonny Boy Williamson said that Rice Miller used to come to his house in Jackson, Tennessee, too. They was drinkin' buddies. Rice Miller called himself "Boy Blue" then. He was singin' all of Sonny Boy's songs, 'cause he didn't have no songs of his own 'cause he'd never made no records. He started goin' down through Mississippi and all them places, claimin' that he was Sonny Boy Williamson. And the people at the juke joints went along with the program. They'd say, "Sonny Boy Williamson is gonna be here." Sonny Boy's records was real popular down South, and the people would tell Rice Miller, "You don't quite sound like your records." But he'd say, "Oh, yeah, I'm Sonny Boy Williamson." Then he started doin' that radio show, the *King Biscuit* show, out of Helena, and he was usin' the name Sonny Boy Williamson. Rice Miller didn't live in Chicago. He would just come in and out of town when he started recordin' with

12. Alex (or Aleck) "Rice" Miller (ca. 1912–1965) spent years as an itinerant musician in the Mississippi Delta before being hired as the featured artist on *King Biscuit Time*, a program broadcast across the Delta every afternoon by the Helena, Arkansas, radio station KFFA. Miller played with local musicians like Robert Johnson, Elmore James, Big Joe Williams, and Robert Jr. Lockwood and perfected a sinuous harmonica style that melded seamlessly with his wry singing. KFFA began billing Miller as "Sonny Boy Williamson," clearly to capitalize on the fame of the Chicago-based John Lee "Sonny Boy" Williamson, who was by that time a popular recording artist. This subterfuge has confused blues fans ever since. Miller made his first records (as "Sonny Boy Williamson") in 1951 for the small Trumpet label based in Jackson, Mississippi. Trumpet sold Miller's contract to Chess Records in 1955. Miller recorded about seventy songs for Chess and its Checker subsidiary from 1955 to 1964. Miller toured Europe several times in the 1960s and recorded with the British rock groups the Animals and the Yardbirds.

Chess. In Chicago he wasn't called "Sonny Boy Williamson." He was called "Rice Miller."

I knew the real Sonny Boy Williamson, so I went up to him that day at Sylvio's and challenged him. I told him, "Your name ain't Sonny Boy Williamson, 'cause I knew Sonny Boy Williamson." Johnny Jones was sittin' right there while I was talkin', and Rice Miller said, "He wants my job! He wants my job!" I challenged him on it.

I met Big Maceo Merriweather at Sylvio's, too, in 1957. That was after Maceo had had a stroke. Maceo came into the club for a cocktail party with him and his wife, Big Bill and his wife, and several more people. I got to meet him and talk with him. Big Maceo had a real heavy left hand and he really had a *feelin'* on that piano. Maceo made a lot of great records with Big Bill and Tampa Red, and he had that huge hit of his own, "Worried Life Blues."

I started goin' to Elmore's cocktail parties at Sylvio's on a regular basis and got to know him pretty good. I was just an amateur, but Elmore would always let me come up and sing a couple of numbers with him and the band.

: : :

I started playin' in the clubs with different people around 1953. The club owners didn't know I was underage. I was tall, and I would be with the band. And I didn't go to the bar and drink or nothin' like that.

I did a gig with Johnny Temple. He lived next door to Blind John's mother on the West Side. I had met him over at Blind John's house and he knew I was tryin' to play harp. He got this gig over on the West Side, and he called me up. I think we played somewhere on Roosevelt Road. That was the first time I ever played in a club.

I did a gig with Johnny Shines and a drummer named Scotty on the West Side in 1954. I wanted to play amplified, 'cause everybody was playin' electric guitar and the harp player had to have an amplifier. So I went by Ellas's house—he was an electronics freak—and I told him I needed an amplifier. He had an amplifier that he had made out of orange crates, so he let me use it on that gig with Johnny Shines. I went by his house and got the amp and got on the bus and rode over to the gig.

It was a Sunday afternoon gig and I got there early. Then Scotty came in and said, "How come you ain't playin'?" And I said, "Well, I'm waitin'. Ain't nobody here but me." Scotty said, "Well, when you get to the gig, you're supposed to just start playin'." He knew I was young and inexperienced, and he was just messin' with me.

Johnny Shines was a nice guy. He could play and sing real good. And I was on there, makin' noise on my harp. Later I went over to Maxwell Street and bought an amp. I paid about twenty-five or thirty dollars for that amp. I used a bullet mic. All the harp players in Chicago had them bullet mics.

Then Johnny Young hired me to play harp with him on 43rd and Berkeley every Monday—just guitar and harp. Later we played at a club over on 14th and Ashland. Johnny Young *loved* Sonny Boy. Johnny Young told me that he used to party with Sonny Boy. Johnny worked at the stockyards, and he said that on paydays he would stop at the liquor store and then go over to Sonny Boy's house. They would call a cab. The cab driver would have stopped workin', and he'd drive them all around for free and they'd drink in the cab.

Johnny Young was a great guy. He was real outgoin' and powerful built. He used to be a boxer. He was a nice guy, but when he'd get high, he could be mean. Johnny was from Rolling Fork, Mississippi. He played the mandolin and the guitar. When they had no money for a hotel, Johnny and Good Rockin' Charles—Charles Edwards—used to ride the elevated train from coast to coast. From one end of the line to the other, all night long.

Johnny Young was a character. You'd be on stage with Johnny Young, and his old lady would be there, sittin' in the audience. Johnny would start singin' a song, and she'd say, "Johnny! Johnny!" And he'd say, "What? Hold it. Hold it, band. My wife. What's wrong, baby?" She'd say, "I don't like the drummer." Then they'd start playin' again. And she'd call out, "But Johnny! I don't like the harp

Johnny Young
Bill Greensmith/Blues Unlimited

player. The harp player's not playin' anything." And he'd say, "Hold it, hold it. My wife say she don't like the harp player. Wait a minute, baby." His wife would say, "Johnny! Johnny! It's too goddamn loud!" And he'd say, "Oh, yeah, hold it. Turn it down. My wife says it too loud. You got to turn it down." This would go on for maybe ten or fifteen minutes, before a whole song would even get played.

Johnny Young and Baby Face Leroy and Forest City Joe Pugh was all Sonny Boy disciples. Forest City Joe sang all of Sonny Boy's songs in his style, and Baby Face Leroy could sing just like him, too. Baby Face Leroy used to live over on Lake Street. He once took me over to Homesick James's house at Madison and Paulina. I had seen Homesick James play with Elmore James at the cocktail parties at Sylvio's every Sunday. Baby Face Leroy was a real nice, friendly guy. He was real slim. He had a real pretty girlfriend who took care of him, which he needed 'cause he was kind of a heavy drinker and not in the best of health. Baby Face Leroy could sing a lot of Sonny Boy Williamson's stuff. He could play drums and guitar, but I never saw him play drums in person.

Otis Rush was startin' to play in the clubs, too, around 1953. At that time they was callin' him "Little Otis." He used to play harmonica, too. He played the harmonica and broadcast over the radio. Otis was singin' all of Muddy Waters's hits. He would sing "Still a Fool." And he was singin' Ray Charles's records. "It Should've Been Me"— songs like that. He sung all the latest hits off the jukebox.

One night Harmonica Slim—his name was Charles Willis— and I went to see Otis at the Harmonia Hotel. Otis had Poor Bob Woodfork on rhythm guitar and Good Rockin' Charles on harmonica that night. Charles was good for the first set, but then he got drunk on wine and passed out in a booth. He was plastered.

Otis knew I was tryin' to play harmonica. He said, "Man, you got your harps with you?" I said, "Yeah." He said, "Come up and play. This cat, he's out of it."

So I finished out the night with Otis. When he was payin' me off, he said, "Man, your music just ain't right." I heard later that Good Rockin' Charles came into the club the next afternoon and left with Otis's amplifier. The lady at the bar didn't know who he was. He just said, "I'm with the band," and he took the amplifier and pawned it. Otis got down there for the gig that night and he didn't have no amp!

Otis Rush always was a real nice guy. Real friendly. Otis was cool, he was suave, he had a lot of class, and he always carried himself like a real professional. Otis was really good, but never went over on record like he did live. His Cobra Records stuff was good, but as great as he was, most of his records didn't do him justice. When I heard that he had started drinkin' and kinda actin' out, I said, "No, that can't be the Otis I know." Otis was real *together*. I guess everybody has their breakin' point. He had a lot of talent and power, man. Otis could play that guitar, and he had that heavy voice.

I first saw Jimmy Reed when I was about sixteen. This boy I went to school with, his name was Curtis, he knew that I liked blues. He had some of Sonny Boy's records, too. Anyway, he called me one day and said, "Hey, come over to the house. There's a guy over here with a guitar and a harmonica on a stick with a wire on it." And I went over there, and it was Jimmy Reed. Jimmy worked with Curtis's father at the steel mill in Gary. Then I saw Jimmy Reed again over at Blind John's house. He hadn't made no records then.

When Jimmy Reed's first record, "High and Lonesome," came out in 1953, I knew that he was a special artist. He was different than anybody that I'd heard around. He was original. He wasn't one of them run-of-the-mill guys. I knew he was somethin' mighty special. Jimmy Reed had a unique voice. He had that strained-blues type of voice. He was just born with a voice like that. I knew he was gonna be a great artist. He and his guitar player, Eddie Taylor, had grown up playin' together in Leland, Mississippi. Jimmy Reed specialized in playin' on the high end of the harp. Sonny Boy had played up on the high end on "Springtime Blues" and "G. M. & O. Blues," but that high-end harp playin' was Jimmy Reed's *thing*.

After Jimmy Reed made "You Don't Have to Go," Blind John was his piano player. Jimmy and his wife used to come by on the West Side and pick Blind John up and take him out to Gary. They was playin' out there at the Black and Tan.

: : :

My goal was to make a record. In 1952 or '53 I went to take a look at a recording studio downtown. It wasn't a real professional studio. It

Billy Boy Arnold, age seventeen
Billy Boy Arnold

was a place where people could go and make dubs—demo records. When I dropped by, the Red Devil Trio was in there makin' a dub. I didn't know Little Hudson, the leader, but I knew Lee Eggleston, the piano player. He was a friend of Blind John's, and he had seen me over at Blind John's playin' and practicin' with him. I forget who the drummer was.

Since they was already there, I asked those guys if they would play with me if I did two sides. And they said, "Yeah, we'll play behind you." So I paid fifteen dollars, I think it was, to cut a tune of mine, "Sweet on You Baby," and "Southern Dream," which was a tune of Sonny Boy's. The band didn't charge me nothin' for playin' behind me. Little Hudson was a Sonny Boy disciple. He used to socialize and run around with Sonny Boy. In fact, he was with him the night he got killed. Little Hudson knew that I was tryin' to imitate Sonny Boy on that dub.

I thought the dub turned out real nice, so I went by Chess Records to try to sell it to them. I met with Phil Chess, Leonard's brother. I told him, "I got some songs and I want to make a record."

Phil took me into the stock room in back. He said, "Let me hear you. Play me somethin'. Let's see what you got. Take your harp out and blow."

So he had me stand there and play the harmonica by myself. I was only sixteen and I wasn't polished enough, but I had a lot of nerve and a burnin' desire to make records. So I'm blowin' and playin' and singin' my four or five little songs.

Phil told me, "I tell you what, man. Go home and work on some more material and come back and see me. Maybe we can do some business."

Well, that was a good way of sayin' you ain't got what we want— that I didn't have anything they could use. I was singin' that older style and I wasn't a great harp player or singer at that age.

But I was determined, and I kept at my goal of makin' a real record. I went to United Records, a black-owned company. Memphis Slim recorded for 'em. Those records Memphis Slim and Matt Murphy, his guitar player, made for United are some great blues records.

I had met Memphis Slim once when I was twelve sellin' papers in front of the Pershing Hotel, and I met him again two years later, when I saw a big black Lincoln parked at 94th and Wentworth with "Memphis Slim and the House Rockers" painted on it. Slim was visitin' some people over there. And by me bein' familiar with blues and the names of the artists, I saw him comin' out of this house and I started talkin' to him. I called out, "Memphis Slim!" and ran him down and gave him the third degree. Asked him about Sonny Boy and everybody. And he talked to me. He was real nice.

So here I am two years later at United, and Memphis Slim was there. He saw me and told Leonard Allen, the owner of United, "This guy plays harmonica like Sonny Boy. Yeah, he's good." United was interested in me, but nothin' happened with them.

Finally, in 1953, when I was seventeen, I got to make my first record. I was still livin' with my parents at that time.

I talked to Blind John about my dream of makin' records, and he told me that he would help me get a session. He had a drinkin' buddy named Logan Bennett. They used to chase women together and all that. Logan Bennett recorded for MGM under the name of Peachtree Logan. Blind John played piano behind him, and Walter Melrose, Lester Melrose's brother, produced those records. Peachtree Logan's sister-in-law, Collenane Cosey, had a dowel factory over on 14th and Halsted, and she had wrote a song that Louis Jordan recorded called the "Ration Blues." It was a pretty popular blues song. Her husband was Antonio Cosey, who played saxophone for Red Saunders. The Coseys was tryin' to get into the record business with Peachtree Logan. They had a label called Cool Records that was distributed by RCA.

So Blind John told Peachtree Logan, "I know a boy who plays harmonica. He's good." Peachtree Logan said, "Well, bring him over."

I started practicin' with Blind John. I was singin' a lot of Sonny Boy stuff, but I knew I had to write my own songs to get a record. I couldn't just go in a studio and sing another guy's song. Those guys that made records for RCA Victor and Bluebird, they had to write their own material. You couldn't go there and tell 'em, "I want to make a record," and, when they ask what you got, sing 'em one of Muddy's songs. So I came up with two songs—"Hello Stranger" and "I Ain't Got No Money." Blind John and I went over and met with Peachtree Logan at the Coseys' house and I played 'em these two songs. I sang and played the harmonica and Blind John played the piano.

The Coseys had a son named Peter who was nine years old.[13] He was a little roly-poly kid who was runnin' through the house with his friends while we was rehearsin'. He'd run through the room and say, "Hi, Blind John! Hi, Billy!" Pete Cosey started out playin' the piano. Then he switched to the guitar, and he tuned the guitar down like a piano. He became a great guitar player. He wasn't a blues player. Pete Cosey played some of everything. He played on those psychedelic Chess albums in the 1960s and played with Miles Davis and Sun Ra. He died two or three years ago.

Anyway, after Blind John and I played my tunes, the Coseys and Peachtree Logan said that they wanted to record me, and I said, "Okay." I guess they thought I had potential, and I know they had a lot of faith in John.

The way that Blind John and I planned it, the session was going to be with the same guys that recorded with Sonny Boy. It was gonna be Blind John on piano, Big Bill Broonzy on guitar, Judge Riley on bass, and Charles "Chick" Sanders on drums. That would have been a great deal for me. Blind John told Big Bill that we wanted him on the session, and he said, "I'll do it." Blind John told me that Big Bill said he was lookin' forward to it. Then he and Big Bill went to Paris to play over there for a while.

Before he left for Paris, Blind John told me, "Ask the man for

13. The guitarist Peter Cosey (1943–2012) first made his mark as a session guitarist for Chess Records in the late 1960s and early 1970s, supporting artists like Etta James, Fontella Bass, Howlin' Wolf, and Muddy Waters. Cosey joined Miles Davis's band in 1973 and recorded four albums with him. Cosey developed an influential and unique guitar technique involving alternate tunings and effects. After 1975 Cosey concentrated on live performances and rarely recorded.

some advance royalties." I'm just a seventeen-year-old kid, so I asked Cool Records, "Hey, what about some advance royalties?"

And they said, "Who told you to say that?" I said, "Well, Blind John." And so they knocked him and Big Bill and all the rest of 'em out of the session. They went and got another band, different session musicians around Chicago, while Big Bill and Blind John was in Paris, and that's who I ended up recording with. They wasn't no group, but the record label called 'em "Bob Carter's Orchestra." Bob Carter was the bass player on the session. I had really wanted Big Bill and Blind John and them on there. If they had done it, it would have had the Sonny Boy sound, but with me.

I wasn't happy with the switch. The day before the session I called up and I said, "Let me speak to Peachtree Logan." That was a funny name, you know. Peachtree Logan got mad and said, "Listen, you stay in your place. You're a kid. Stay in your goddamn place."

We made the record at the RCA Victor studio on Lake Shore Drive. There was two buildings there with "RCA Victor" on them. The engineer told me, he said, "Yeah, I recorded Sonny Boy, Big Bill, and Memphis Minnie—all of 'em." So we used the same studio that Sonny Boy and them did their stuff in, and the same engineer.

I sang with that orchestra live in the studio. One of the musicians had a half a pint, and he said, "You want a little taste of this?" I didn't drink, but I took a swig. I wanted to do it. I was glad to be down there. I was ahead of my time—I wasn't ready—but I had a burnin' desire to make records, like Sonny Boy.

It was a split session between me and another guy named Herbert Beard. They only recorded four sides. We each recorded two numbers. I did my tunes "Hello Stranger" and "I Ain't Got No Money." Herbert Beard did "Gal, You Need a Whippin'"—Louis Jordan recorded that song, too—and another tune that I can't remember. "Gal, You Need a Whippin'" started out like this: "Gal you need a whippin' tonight, gal you need a whippin', yes you need a whippin' tonight." That was some record!

Cool Records put out "Hello Stranger" and "I Ain't Got No Money" as a 78 and as a 45—45s had just come out. The record

Cool recording artist Billy Boy Arnold, 1953
Billy Boy Arnold

ended up being pressed by RCA Victor on that real thick vinyl they used in those days. I thought they was goin' to call me "Billy Arnold" on the record label, but when I went over to pick up my copy, they said, "Oh, we gave you a new name—'Billy Boy Arnold.'" I didn't pick that out. I had no inklin' or no idea of callin' myself Billy Boy 'cause of how much I idolized Sonny Boy. The record company gave me that name. I didn't want to be called Billy Boy, 'cause I wanted to be represented as a man. I was only seventeen, but you know what it's like when you're young like that.

That Cool record didn't sell, but it got a lot of airplay. I heard that record on the radio all the time. That was a thrill. I was young, and I had a record out, and it felt great. But all of the kids I associated with—my cousins and them—they still thought I was weird.

The Cool Records people asked me to take a copy of "Hello Stranger" to Leonard Chess to see if he would distribute it. That was the first time I met Leonard. He played it and said, "This has already got too much airplay. I can't use that." And Blind John and Peachtree Logan ended up having a fallin' out.

When I think back about that first record, I kind of laugh about it. I sounded like a little kid on that record, and everybody knew I was tryin' to imitate Sonny Boy. I didn't really know what I was doin', and it didn't go down the way I wanted it to go down. But I was so focused on tryin' to make a record, you know. I just wanted to do it so bad, and I didn't have time to wait, so I did it the opposite way.

::::

When Big Bill and Blind John came back from Paris in the spring of 1951, they did a gig at Sylvio's. I remember that they had a big sign outside of the club that said, "Big Bill and Blind John Davis—Direct from Paris, France—Friday, Saturday, and Sunday."

I knew of Big Bill's music since I was a little kid, 'cause my aunt had his records. And he played on a lot of Sonny Boy's stuff, too. Sonny Boy would say, "Take it away, Big Bill! You got it, Big Bill!" I loved Big Bill's guitar playin' and I loved his singin', but I had never seen him.

Blind John said, "Come on over to Sylvio's on Sunday and I'll introduce you to Big Bill." And, man, I really wanted to meet Big Bill, you know, so I went down there. Blind John was playin' the piano and Lazy Bill Lucas was playin' the guitar. Lazy Bill Lucas was how I found Sonny Boy, 'cause he's the one who gave me Sonny Boy's address in 1948.

So me and Blind John was there, but Big Bill was late in comin'. I was kinda mad, 'cause I really wanted to see Big Bill. And then, about two in the afternoon, a giant of a man came in through the door with a guitar in his hand. Sylvio's was a big club. Real long. And before Big Bill could walk two steps, people was stoppin' him and talkin' to him. It took him a long time to get to the back of the club where we was.

Big Bill Hill, a disc jockey on the radio station WOPA, was drivin' a Yellow Cab at the time. He'd parked his cab in front of Sylvio's and brought in a little transmitter, and he was broadcastin' live from the club. Big Bill and Blind John started playin', and I really enjoyed Big Bill's music.

When Big Bill and Blind John came down on intermission, we walked over to the side of the bar. Sylvio was behind the bar. Big Bill pulled out a bunch of hundred-dollar bills and told Sylvio, "Give me a half a pint." So Sylvio gave him a half a pint and a glass. There was no need for a second glass, 'cause I was a kid and I didn't drink.

Blind John and Big Bill was drinkin' and cussin' each other out. Blind John said, "Goddamn, man, you was late comin' in!" And Big Bill said, "Listen, you son of a bitch, have a drink and shut up!" And then Blind John said, "Don't call me no son of a bitch." And then I said, "Yeah, Big Bill, you shouldn't have called him a son of a bitch." I'm a little kid, you know. Big Bill said, "Come on and have another drink, you son of a bitch." And they drank some more and they downed that half a pint and then Big Bill said, "Let's go down and listen to Memphis Minnie." She was playin' a block from Sylvio's, near Blind John's house.

So we left out of the club—it was intermission time—and now I'm walkin' down Lake Street with Blind John Davis and Big Bill Broonzy, two of my idols that had recorded with Sonny Boy.

We got to this club and the place was packed. The jukebox was playin', and Memphis Minnie was sittin' at the bar. She was on intermission, too. So we come on in. I knew who Memphis Minnie was, 'cause I had seen her picture out front of Sylvio's and on the posters at the Indiana Theatre, but this was the first time I had seen her in person.

The place was packed, so Big Bill walked to the back and he was talkin' to people, and Blind John was talkin' to different people. Memphis Minnie was sittin' at the bar talkin', and I wanted to meet her. The jukebox was blastin' and there was a lot of people in there, so I was kinda shoutin', "Memphis Minnie! Memphis Minnie! Memphis Minnie!"

Memphis Minnie turned around and looked at me and said, "*Man*, would you get out of my ass!" Man, she was rough!

Memphis Minnie was a good-lookin' woman and she was sharp dressed. She played with her husband, Little Son Joe, and they had great equipment to play on—new guitars and amplifiers. So then Big Bill went up and played the guitar with Minnie. Both of 'em played guitar while she sang. And that was the first time I met Memphis Minnie.

A few months later, I was over at Blind John's house and a drummer friend of his named Lee Shelton came by. He knew me 'cause he'd seen me at John's a lot. Lee told me, "Hey, I'm playin' out at Apex with Memphis Minnie tonight. You got your harmonica with you? Why don't you come on and go out there with me?" I said, "Okay, yeah."

So I rode out to the suburbs with Lee to this club out in Robbins called Apex. Memphis Minnie let me come up and sing a couple of numbers. She and Joe played behind me. Son Joe played rhythm guitar and Memphis Minnie played the lead. That was quite a night.

: : :

I started foolin' around on the guitar when I was about sixteen. I'd play a little bit and then I'd drop it. I talked my younger brother Jerome—I'm fourteen months older than him—into buyin' a guitar when he was about twelve years old. And so he got a white cowboy guitar and put it in the closet. And I'd fool around with it. I had a friend named McGhee. He played harmonica and guitar and he used to hang around with Sonny Boy, and he showed me some stuff on the guitar. And that's how I first got into the guitar. I'd fool around and then I'd stop and then go back to it.

I started workin' harder on my harmonica playin'. I only took two lessons from Sonny Boy, so I didn't get the chance to go into a lot of stuff with him. Even though he showed me the old style of how to use your tongue to play the melody and the chord, I puckered my lips to get each note back then. I didn't really use my tongue on the harp until I got around Bob Myers, Dave and Louis's older brother.[14] Bob played the harmonica, and he idolized Sonny Boy. He used to run with Sonny Boy, and he played the harp just like him. Bob could choke a harp. He could really play. Bob didn't go into music as an occupation, but he was a great harp player. I would pick up little bits from Bob and them, and so I started usin' the tongue like him and Sonny Boy. Little Walter played with and without the tongue, depending on the sounds he wanted.

It was Sonny Boy Williamson that got me started on the harp. And that turned out to be a smart choice, 'cause after Little Walter hit with "Juke" in 1952, a blues band in Chicago couldn't hardly get a gig without a harp player.

---

14. Harmonica players use different techniques to play single notes. Tongue blocking, favored by most of the notable Chicago blues harpists, involves using the mouth to cover three or four holes on the harmonica and then blocking all but one hole with the tongue. Lip pursing, or puckering, involves pursing the lips so that they cover only one hole on the harmonica.

Thanks to the sensational success of "Juke," WGES disc jockey Al Benson (*left*), Little Walter, and Leonard Chess make the cover of *Cash Box* magazine, 1952
Kim Field

4

"Juke"

After Sonny Boy died, you didn't hear much blues harmonica on records. Snooky Pryor made "Stockyard Blues" with Moody Jones, and I thought Snooky was great. I really liked his singin' and playin'. Snooky is one of my favorite harmonica players.

But then Little Walter Jacobs came on the scene when he made that record with Muddy, "Sad Letter Blues" and "Your [sic] Gonna Need My Help." That was the first time I heard his harp playin'. I knew it was Walter 'cause Muddy calls out on that record, "All right, Little Walter!" Walter didn't play amplified harp on that record, but that was the greatest harp playin' I had ever heard. His tone! He had everything. I knew right away that Little Walter was truly the man that could fit into Sonny Boy's shoes. I mean, man, Walter was just a dynamic harmonica player. He was *superior*. And so Little Walter became my new harmonica idol, my main man on the harp.

Little Walter was playin' similar to Sonny Boy, but he had his own ideas, his own tone. "I was in a world of my own all the time," he used to say. I heard him say that many times, and it was true. He knew he was great and original.

When Muddy came out with "Rollin' Stone" and those records he had with Little Walter on 'em—"Louisiana Blues" and all those things, and then "I'm Your Hoochie Coochie Man"—Muddy was the hottest thing in Chicago. He had the hottest band in town, and they really supported him. He was newer on the scene, and he overshadowed all the other guys that was around. Little Walter's harmonica was a huge part of Muddy's sound and sold his records.

There was so much harp on Muddy Waters's records that people thought that it was Muddy playin' the harmonica, 'cause the harp was so dynamic that it made people notice Muddy's records. They would say, "Ooh, that Muddy Waters sure can play that harp!" So Leonard Chess had to start puttin' "Muddy Waters and His Guitar" on the record label, to distinguish that it wasn't Muddy playin' harp. Now, Muddy had talent and power, and his records would have been hits without no harmonica, but nobody could play harp behind Muddy like Little Walter did.

In 1951 Chess put out "That's All Right" and "Ludella" by Jimmy Rogers. They had Little Walter play harp on there, and on those two songs Little Walter stole the show from Jimmy Rogers. I liked Jimmy Rogers's voice—he had a nice, smooth, good voice—and he played some nice guitar. He was real bluesy and everything. But he had a soft thing. Jimmy didn't have the power that Muddy had. Even Walter couldn't steal the show from Muddy, but he really supported Muddy and enhanced the performance and helped sell the records. But Little Walter's harp playin' on those Jimmy Rogers songs was so powerful that he overshadowed Jimmy. In my book, if you subtract the harmonica, "That's All Right" wouldn't have been a hit. It would have been just another blues record with guitar.

Louis Myers told me that Jimmy Rogers told him before his second Chess session, "I ain't gonna use Walter no more. I want to get away from that harmonica." He wanted to get away from the harmonica 'cause that harmonica was kicking him in the ass and stealin' the show! Jimmy got Ernest Cotton on saxophone, Eddie Ware on piano, Big Crawford on bass, and Elga Edmonds on drums. And they made some good records, like "The World Is in a Tangle," "Back Door Friend," and "Money, Marbles and Chalk," which is a great record. Jimmy's guitar playin' and singin' was beautiful on that. Jimmy didn't have a dynamic voice, but it was a good blues voice. And the black people liked it, 'cause lots of black musicians at

Muddy Waters and his band at the Zanzibar in 1954. *Left to right*: Muddy Waters, unidentified, Otis Spann, Henry Strong, Elga Edmonds, and Jimmy Rogers
Bill Greensmith/Blues Unlimited

the time didn't want to be like John Lee Hooker, Muddy Waters, or Lightnin' Hopkins. They wanted to smooth on up like Billy Eckstine. They was tryin' to elevate themselves. So Jimmy's smooth voice got over, but on that second session it was Eddie Ware's piano that stole the show.

Little Walter was on "Money, Marbles and Chalk," but he played second guitar, not harmonica. Walter played guitar on some of Muddy's records, too, like "Still a Fool." Muddy ain't playin' guitar on that. Little Walter's playin' that lead part. That's one of Muddy's greatest records, in my opinion. Junior Wells and Otis Rush used to sing that tune in the clubs, and the women would go crazy.

Louis Myers told me that after Jimmy did "The World Is in a Tangle," Leonard Chess told him, "Hey, man, you'd better get Walter back on the harp. That record didn't sell." They got Walter back on that next session and recorded "Chicago Bound" with him on the harp, and Walter's harp sold the record. Jimmy did a good job, but Walter had so much power and creativity that he overshadowed him. There was just somethin' about him. Jimmy couldn't get away from Walter! Walter just had so much goin' for himself.

Jimmy Rogers was still a sideman in Muddy's band, playin' for twelve dollars a night. After his records came out, he decided to leave Muddy's band and do his own thing. Branch out on his own. He started playin' at a club on Lake Street around the corner from where Blind John was livin'. I saw Baby Face Leroy play there a couple of times. Anyway, I went over to this club one weekend to see Jimmy's group. He had Eddie Ware on piano and Jody Williams on guitar. Eddie and those guys had been after Jimmy to start a band so they could play with him. They was tellin' him, "Man, get yourself a band of your own." But Jimmy wasn't forceful enough to be a bandleader. He was too laid back.

The next week I showed up again, and Jimmy Rogers wasn't there. They had another guitar player. So I asked Eddie Ware, "Where is Jimmy Rogers?" He said, "That chickenshit motherfucker ran back to Muddy Waters!"

I was a big fan of Eddie Ware's. Oh, man, I loved him. He was real *fast* on those keys. He played some beautiful stuff on Jimmy Rogers's records. I don't know if Eddie did much singin'. He was on the scene before Otis Spann showed up in Chicago. Eddie was hangin' out at the Plantation Club when Sonny Boy was down there. I don't know if he was playin' with Sonny Boy, but he and Willie Mabon and Sonny Boy all used to hang out at the Plantation. Billy Stepney, the drummer who used to play with Matt Murphy, was down there, too, and he's the one who told me about the scene there. Sonny Boy was playin' there Wednesday and Thursday nights, and they'd have bands over the weekend. And all the musicians— Eddie Ware, Willie Mabon, Henry Gray, and all of 'em—used to hang out there. Later, Eddie Ware had an accident up in Michigan and lost his hand or his arm or somethin'. But he was a hell of piano player, man, with a beautiful, fluid style.

Muddy Waters and Jimmy Rogers didn't figure that Little Walter was no competition. They knew he was a great harp player—one of the best—but they didn't feel that he was gonna be a star. Muddy wasn't worried that Walter would surpass him. He didn't want to give Walter the credit. Jimmy Rogers and Muddy knew that Little Walter was a dynamite harp player, but they thought they had Walter in their back pocket 'cause they thought that he had a funny little voice. But Walter was a really smart, aggressive person. You couldn't hold him down.

They all thought that you could only go so far with just the harmonica, and that Walter couldn't sing. They would say, "He can't sing, he can't sing." Walter didn't have a powerful voice like Muddy, but they didn't realize that he could sing as good as he could. Walter wouldn't have made it as just a singer. Junior Parker and Junior Wells played harp, but they could have made it just on their singin'. I didn't like Rice Miller's harp style that much, but he was a good singer and a good songwriter who could have made it without the harp.

I first met Little Walter thanks to the Aces. They invited me to a cocktail party at Sam and Gussie's Lounge one Sunday. They said that Little Walter would be there. Sam and Gussie's Lounge was a club on 31st Street near Cottage Grove that was owned by a white lady.

So the next Sunday I went to Sam and Gussie's Lounge. I was really anxious to see this great harmonica player. I met Louis Myers outside. Louis asked me, "You wanna go in and hear the band? I'll tell the guy to let you in. You can just stand against the wall."

I'm only fifteen years old, but I was kind of a tall kid, so I told Louis, "Well, let me put on one of your suit jackets. It'll make me look more mature."

Louis said to the bouncer, "He's with me. Let him stand against the wall."

So I'm just standin' against the wall while Louis played a set with Junior Wells. I remember that Junior Wells's mother and stepfather was there. Sunnyland Slim had his band there, too, with Robert Jr.

Lockwood on guitar. Homesick James was there that day. Jimmy Rogers was in there. He had a new record out—"The World Is in a Tangle." J. B. Lenoir was at Sam and Gussie's, too. He had just put out "Korea Blues."

I was sittin' in a booth, tryin' to blend in 'cause I was underage, and I saw Johnny Jones sittin' with his wife, Letha. I walked over to 'em and said, "Hey, I saw you all up at Sonny Boy's house." He said, "Yeah, yeah, yeah."

I don't know whether he remembered me or not. This was three years later. I think he did 'cause Sonny Boy gave me a lot of attention that day we met. I assumed that Johnny's wife was the same woman I had seen him with at Sonny Boy's—when you're a kid twelve years old and you see a man with a woman, you assume that's his wife—but it wasn't. He had been at Sonny Boy's with some girlfriend. Bein' a kid, I didn't remember exactly what the lady looked like. So I was puttin' Johnny on the spot.

Letha was sayin', "Oh, yeah, I remember you," but she didn't remember me 'cause she hadn't been there. The woman I met at Sonny Boy's was Johnny's girlfriend. Johnny remembered, but he was trying to be evasive 'cause he was married to Letha when I met him at Sonny Boy's.

They took an intermission, and everybody came outside. Muddy Waters walked up with Little Walter. They was comin' from a gig, and they walked up and started talkin' with Louis. And Louis said, "This is Little Walter."

I looked at him and thought, "Man, Little Walter, the harmonica sensation!"

I thought Little Walter would get up and blow some harp that day at Sam and Gussie's, but he went up there and played some guitar. He had a lot of ideas and was real creative on any instrument he would pick up. Walter knew somethin' about the guitar, but he didn't really go into it. What you hear on the records where he plays guitar is pretty much what he had to offer. I only saw him play the guitar that one time.

After Walter played, I ended up sittin' in a booth with him and

"Juke," 1952
Kim Field

Jimmy Rogers. I said I was a harmonica player, and Jimmy pointed to Walter and said, "That's my harmonica player." Blind John had sent me a pamphlet with a picture of him and Big Bill Broonzy on stage in Paris, so I took it out and showed it to Little Walter. He looked at it and put it in his pocket. I said, "Wait a minute, man, that's mine," and he gave it back to me.

:::

In 1952, Chess put out Little Walter's "Juke." I think Walter got that riff from a Snooky Pryor record. "Juke" was Muddy Waters's theme song. Little Walter and the rest of Muddy's band would play it when they would open up or close their show. Junior Wells and the Aces stole it and started usin' it as *their* theme song, too. I never did hear Muddy's band do it, but I heard the Aces do it. In those days, Junior and the Aces would copy everything Walter and the rest of the guys in Muddy's band would do. When Little Walter's "Juke" came out, a lot of people thought that Little Walter had stole Junior's thing, but it was the other way around.

The "Juke" session was supposed to be a Muddy Waters session. Muddy had made that record "Please Have Mercy" at that session. Then they cut "Juke," the band's theme song. Leonard wasn't plannin' on makin' Walter a star, but he probably realized on the spot what he had with Little Walter and "Juke," and decided to get a flip side for Walter while they was in the studio. Leonard was always doin' stuff like that. He would say, "Well, let's get another side," 'cause you never knew which way he'd go.

Bob Myers and Jimmy Rogers was at the session, and they was tryin' to help Little Walter get a quick tune together for the flip side. Bob Myers told Louis later that Little Walter was tryin' to sing Sonny Boy's "Black Gal Blues" that day. Sonny Boy's record went, "Well, I got somethin' to tell you, black gal, that you oughta know / I can get myself a woman most anywhere I go / but Lord knows I'm wild about you, black gal / I'm just as crazy as I can be." That was one of my favorite Sonny Boy songs. Little Walter was singin', "Can't hold out much longer livin' this a way / you know I'm just crazy about you, baby." Jimmy Rogers was helpin' him get the lyrics together.

Leonard Chess said, "I don't wanna put 'Black Gal' on there," 'cause black people was sensitive back then about certain things. Sonny Boy made "Black Gal" in December of 1938. Walter was recording in 1952, and people were a little more sensitive. So that's why they ended up callin' it "Can't Hold Out Much Longer."

So Leonard had "Juke" and the flip side, but he wasn't anxious to put the record out. Blues instrumentals was pretty rare. I read in a book that Marshall Chess, Leonard Chess's son, was at the Chess office one day and Leonard was playin' that record. It was rainin'. There was an older black lady out front, waitin' for the bus, and she could hear the record 'cause she was right in front of the door. And this black lady started dancin'. Leonard stopped the record, and she stopped dancin'. Then he started playin' it again, and she started dancin' again. She was just waitin' for the bus and jammin' with the record. And Leonard said, "Uh-huh," and put it out. And it turned out to be the biggest record Chess had ever had at that time.

Walter and the band went with Muddy to New Orleans. When they got down there, they heard that "Juke" was out. They went to the club to do their gig. Walter went up to the jukebox, and there it was: "'Juke' by Little Walter." And the people in this club in New Orleans kept playin' it, over and over. And you could see why, 'cause it was a hell of a song.

So Little Walter snuck out and went back to the hotel and got his clothes and everything and left. And so when it came time to do the gig that night, everybody was going, "Where's Walter? Where's Walter?" They checked back at the hotel and the lady there told 'em, "You mean that little guy? He left. He went to the airport or somewhere. He's gone. He took off for Chicago."

So Muddy's stranded in New Orleans without a harp player. Walter's harp playin' was so significant in Muddy's band that the two guitars couldn't really make it without Walter, 'cause all of Muddy's stuff was built around that harp. So Little Walter came back to Chicago and took the Aces away from Junior Wells, and Junior Wells hit the highway and joined Muddy Waters down South.

It wasn't a hard decision for the Aces, 'cause Walter had the gigs once "Juke" hit. When they worked with Junior, he was the star of the band 'cause Louis and Dave didn't sing, but officially it was Dave Myers's band. Junior sang and played the harp, but he was just gettin' sideman money. Dave Myers was the bandleader and got the leader's fee, which at that time was eighteen dollars a night. Junior was making twelve dollars a night, like Below or Louis Myers.

Junior was a dynamite entertainer, and he stayed real sharp. Dressed real nice. The women liked him. Dave Myers once told me, "Man, Junior Wells got as many women as Muddy Waters!" He was the star of the show. He was the one singin' all the hits, all the

Little Johnny Jones (*left*) and Junior Wells, 1958
Bill Greensmith/Blues Unlimited

Muddy stuff. But he didn't write no songs. Junior had done a session for States Records, but they didn't even play it on the radio. It wasn't up to the level of Muddy and Walter's stuff. It was a notch down from that. And he was singin' someone else's stuff. Junior didn't make it as an artist, but he was a hell of an entertainer.

Walter would say that he had to get with the Aces 'cause Muddy's thing was a straight-out, bluesy thing, and Walter had some different ideas. He'd criticize Muddy and them to other musicians like Louis Myers. He'd complain, "Man, Muddy and them are playin' all that same slow-ass shit every night." Walter didn't like that, but he backed Muddy and played great harp behind him. But he was young and he wanted to do his thing. When he made "Juke" and got the Aces, Walter came into his own. His ideas started flowing, and he started playin' the type of harp that *he* wanted to play.

Little Walter was a harmonica player, and the harmonica player who was on top at that time was Sonny Boy Williamson, so at first Little Walter was tryin' to imitate Sonny Boy. But bein' his own man with his own ideas and everything, that was just a takeoff point.

Walter had ideas of how to jazz it up to be his thing. Walter grew up in Louisiana, and the black music down in New Orleans was a different thing. It was blues, but it was a different, more progressive type of blues. It had the Cajun influence in it and all that. It was a different thing.

Little Walter got the idea for amplified harp from Sonny Boy. Muddy Waters said that the first guy he heard playin' amplified harmonica was Sonny Boy Williamson. I had heard Sonny Boy play amplified harp over the phone when I was a kid. Junior Wells was playin' amplified harp with the Aces before "Juke." Muddy's first records was made acoustic. I guess Leonard Chess must have told them to do that, 'cause they played through amplifiers when they did those songs live. Leonard finally allowed Walter to play amplified in the studio. I think the first time he did that was the session in 1951 where Muddy recorded "My Fault," "Country Boy," and "She Moves Me." The first time I heard Little Walter play amplified was on those records.

Walter introduced third position on the harp. That's a beautiful sound. It's different from playin' the ordinary way. I don't know if Snooky played third position, but I know Little Walter did. Little Walter plays in third position on Muddy's record "Please Have Mercy," and he plays some third position on the recordings he made with Louisiana Red.[1] I met Robert Nighthawk over at the union office one time.[2] Nighthawk started out as a harp player, and he

1. Guitarist, singer, and harmonica player Iverson "Louisiana Red" Minter (1932–2012) recorded more than fifty albums in his career, beginning with a session for Chess Records in 1949. Minter worked with John Lee Hooker for two years in the late 1950s. In 1964 he hit the charts with his single "I'm Too Poor to Die" for the small Glover label. Minter won the W. C. Handy Award for best traditional blues male artist in 1983, and spent his last years living and working in Germany.

2. Robert Lee McCollum (1909–1967), who recorded under the pseudonyms Robert Lee McCoy and Robert Nighthawk, first made his name as an outstanding harmonica player. Houston Stackhouse introduced McCollum to slide guitar, and over the years McCollum's mastery of this style became his musical trademark. McCollum recorded with Sonny Boy Williamson, Big Joe Williams, and Henry Townsend in St. Louis in 1937. Later that year he made his first recordings as a leader, taking his stage name from one of them—"Prowling Nighthawk." McCollum appeared in

told me, "Them boys over on the West Side"—he was talking about Little Walter and Junior Wells—"is playin' harp in all those different positions." See, Walter could take an A harp and he could play in the keys of A and E—first and second position. But he could play all night in third—in the key of B.

Walter was also the first blues harp player to use the chromatic harmonica—the harmonica with the slide. The first Little Walter on chromatic I heard was Muddy's record "Just Make Love to Me." That was made in 1954, the same year Walter played some beautiful chromatic on Muddy's "I'm Ready." And Walter played chromatic on two of his own instrumentals—"Lights Out" and "Blue Lights." You gotta know how to breathe to handle the chromatic, and Walter had a special way of doin' that. Walter knew how to breathe to sustain those notes.

:::

The first time I heard Little Walter play harp in person was at a show at the Hollywood Rendezvous on South Indiana. The Hollywood Rendezvous was Little Walter's home base. Whenever he'd come back from bein' on the road for a month or two, whoever was playin' at the Rendezvous had to get off that stage, 'cause Walter was back at his home base. And if he was in town for five or six nights, he'd play there every night. He drew crowds to the Rendezvous right away 'cause of "Juke."

When I walked into the Rendezvous that night, Little Walter was on stage with the Aces. Walter always dressed sharp on stage. He was young, and he was a nice-lookin' guy. Back in those days, the musicians sat down on stage, 'cause some of the stages was kinda small. Everybody sat in a chair. Walter sat between the two guitars. One on either side.

Chicago to record for Aristocrat, Leonard Chess's first label, in 1948. After recording some outstanding sides for the United and States labels during the 1950s, McCollum was most often seen playing on Maxwell Street. Norman Dayron recorded a searing set by McCollum there that was released as *Live on Maxwell Street—1964*.

Walter was singin' through an amplifier—I don't remember what kind—and a bullet mic. PA systems and that whole thing hadn't really caught on in 1952. The clubs didn't have speakers all over the place then. They didn't have nothin'.

When I came into the club, I was with two or three other people, and when we walked past the bandstand, Louis and Dave saw me. I heard Louis Myers tell Little Walter, "There goes one of them counterfeit harmonica players."

Walter looked at me, and he kept watchin' me. Walter played one more number and then, to my surprise, he told the audience, "We got a boy here who can blow the sides off a harmonica." He said, "Louis, what's the name? What's the name?" And Louis said, "Billy. Billy." Little Walter said, "We going to get Billy up here. Let Billy come up here. He gonna blow the sides off a harp." I got up on stage and Walter sat down right in front of the bandstand, sittin' on a stool and lookin' at me. I sang one of Sonny Boy's tunes. Probably "Southern Dream," 'cause that one had just come out. They was still releasin' Sonny Boy tunes two or three years after he got killed.

When I came off the stage, I came over and talked to Little Walter. I said, "Did you know Sonny Boy?" and he said, "Yeah, he was the best. He was really good." That's exactly what he said, and that made me feel good, knowing how great Walter was. I never heard Little Walter give too many people compliments, but he really liked Sonny Boy. He said, "Sonny Boy used to tell me, 'You play too fast. You play too fast.'"

Hearin' Walter play in person for the first time was amazing. It was the most exciting thing, for me, to see this big harp player. I was like all the rest of 'em—I wanted to follow the new thing. I still had a lot of Sonny Boy in me. My own harp playin' was kinda dated, 'cause I was doing Sonny Boy's stuff. But Walter was doin' his own thing, and so I was tryin' to get on Walter's kick, too, 'cause Walter was The Man.

That first night I heard him, he was playin' such beautiful stuff. If someone had recorded that show, they would have gotten a lot of good records out of it. Little Walter was just so creative, man,

Hitmaker Little Walter, 1952
Scott Dirks

and that band was cookin'. The Aces—that was some rockin' music. Below was throwin' them bombs in there behind him. Man, it was a swingin' band. Walter could swing on that harp, and he had a lot of ideas. He wasn't repetitious. He wasn't a guy to do a lot of singin', like a lot of guys was doin'. But Walter could play so much harp, he didn't have to sing all the time. The harp carried him. A friend's niece—she was about fifteen at the time—once told me that "Little Walter sounds like a hipped-up Muddy Waters." More modern, you know. The same type of music, but hipped up.

When Walter hit, the harp players started movin' to Chicago from everywhere. I think they all came from the South, 'cause suddenly they was all over the place. Harmonica was *the* thing then. Everybody was gettin' on the harmonica kick. That was thanks to Little Walter and Sonny Boy and all the guys who played harp. They made so much noise with the harp that the club owners would actually ask, "What you got in your band? If you got a harp player, you got the job." 'Cause that's what was happenin', you know. Muddy Waters's records with Little Walter on harp was boomin' all over Chicago. Everywhere.

All kinds of guys was playin' harp in Chicago then. There was P. T. Hayes. There was Little Mack Simmons. And there was Sonny Cooper over on the West Side. He looked somethin' like Little Walter. There was Good Rockin' Charles. George Mayweather, he came around in 1955 or '56, somethin' like that. Snooky Pryor, he was one of the main men. He had played down there on Maxwell Street with Little Walter.

And there was Earl Payton. He was older. He used to run with Sonny Boy and go to Sonny Boy's house and cook for him. He told me that Sonny Boy used to take that harp, throw it up in the air, catch it in his mouth and sing "Caldonia." Earl was Freddy King's harp player. Freddy King was only a year older than me, but he was already a polished guitar player. I used to see him at this place called the Seeley Club at Madison and Seeley. I used to go by and listen to his band, and he'd call me up to do a number or two. We called Freddy King "Big Fred" back then, 'cause he was a big guy who played guitar and sang like B. B. King. Freddy had Jimmie Lee Robinson on second guitar and Payton on harmonica before he started doin' all those instrumental records. See, the harp was the main thing at the time.

Louis Myers was a guitar player, but he played harp, too. And, man, he could come closer to soundin' like Walter than anybody! Louis really had it on the harp. The Aces had been playin' at the 708 Club. Junior Wells had quit the band or got fired or whatever. They brought Otis Rush in to play guitar, so Louis started playin' guitar *and* harp. And, man, Louis was a first-class, top-notch harp player. He could play the closest to Little Walter.

George Smith was hot around Chicago in the 1950s, but he didn't stay here too long.[3] I don't know why they called him "Little" George Smith, 'cause he was about six feet four. I guess they called him that 'cause of Little Walter. He was a hell of a harp player, too. George Smith played with lots of people, including Otis Rush and Muddy Waters. George was such a good singer and harp player that he was upstagin' Junior Wells and everybody else. He was aggressive. George Smith ended up goin' to California with Muddy, and he met some chick and stayed out there in Los Angeles and had a bunch of kids with her. He went out there and billed himself as "Little Walter." And then for a while he called himself "Jimmy Reed." He was a comical guy.

Forest City Joe Pugh was a fine harp player. He lived down on 39th and Cottage Grove, and he used to be out on the street playin' all the time. He was a heavy drinker. Forest City Joe used to run around with Baby Face Leroy. They was both Sonny Boy disciples, and they used to try to sing like him and emulate everything that he did.

3. Blues singer and harmonica virtuoso George "Harmonica" Smith (1924–1983) joined Muddy Waters's band in 1954, about the same time he began recording for the RPM label, owned by Modern Records. Smith moved to Los Angeles in 1955 and continued performing in clubs and recording for small labels. He had an enormous influence on young white harp players in Southern California such as William Clarke, Rod Piazza, and Kim Wilson.

Willie Anderson was around, but he wasn't playin' harmonica then. He used to go down around 31st Street and see Sonny Boy when Sonny Boy stayed down there. Willie had a day job and a wife and some kids, but he was a guy who wanted to get into the harp. He used to go down to the Plantation Club to see Sonny Boy.

But Little Walter was the king. Any record Walter played on as a sideman, he would steal the show. He was just that dynamic. Listen to Memphis Minnie's record of "Me and My Chauffeur" that she did with him. The version she did for Chess with Walter is just like her original record, but his beautiful harp enhanced that newer version. It made it more modern, and his harp sold the record. Baby Face Leroy had a record called "Rollin' and Tumblin'," and Walter's harp sold that record, too. Take Walter's harp off that and you ain't got nothin'. Walter overshadowed it. Listen to John Brim's records with Jimmy Rogers and Walter on there.[4] Jimmy did a good job of supportin' him on the guitar, but a number of guys could have done that. But Little Walter put life to those records, and Walter *sold* the records. When you'd hear Walter on the record, you'd buy it. That was just him. He had that effect on everything he did.

Walter had all those jukebox hits, and he drew a younger crowd. Walter didn't go over at clubs like the 708 Club, where they didn't dance. The younger people liked Walter 'cause he was more swingin' and more lively. And that's why Walter was so popular down South, 'cause the black people down South like to dance.

Ellas McDaniel and I were about to prove that white teenagers in America liked to dance to black music, too.

---

4. Singer and guitarist John Brim (1922–2003) recorded for the Chicago blues labels Random, JOB, and Parrot before doing a session for Chess in 1953 that included his tune "Ice Cream Man." The recording, which also featured Little Walter, remained unissued until it appeared on a Chess anthology in 1969. Van Halen covered "Ice Cream Man" on their debut album in 1978, and Brim used his royalties to finance his own nightclub in Chicago. Brim's 1994 *Ice Cream Man* album for Tone Cool Records was nominated for a W. C. Handy Award for best traditional blues album.

Ellas McDaniel, reinvented as Bo Diddley, 1955
Pictorial Press Ltd./Alamy Stock Photo

5

Bo Diddley

In 1954 I moved out of my folks' place and got a place of my own at 40th and Lake Park. One day, Ellas McDaniel came to my apartment and asked me to join a new band he had put together, Ellas McDaniel and the Hipsters. He said he was goin' to play in the clubs. Ellas had a guy named R. C.—I never knew his last name—playin' harp, but I guess R. C. had a bit of an attitude, and Ellas thought I could beat R. C.'s harp playin'. So he got rid of R. C. and got me to play with him.

Ellas had Jerome Green on maracas, a second guitarist named Buttercup—I don't remember his real name—and a bass player named James Bradford, who was the same age as Ellas and a friend of his. Bradford played upright bass. Some people laughed at Bradford. The joke was that he wasn't *playin'* on his bass, he was *leanin'* on it. So the Hipsters had two guitars, bass, harmonica, and maracas. That was it.

We went into a club called the Castle Rock over on 53rd and Princeton. The Castle Rock was a big club, and the owner had a lot of young, beautiful waitresses in there. They was payin' us five dollars a night.

This girl named Johanna came in one night and said, "Y'all need a drummer?" And Ellas said, "Yeah, we need a drummer." Johanna said, "Well, my brother-in-law plays drums." Ellas said, "Well, tell him to come on down."

So when we come in the next night, here's this young guy, well dressed, sittin' up there behind a brand-new set of drums. This was Clifton James, who lived at 44th and State, right down the street from Club Georgia. He was raised up in that area. Clifton was the same age as me and Jerome. His mother had just bought him a new set of drums. Willie "Big Eyes" Smith, who later played drums for Muddy Waters, was his buddy, and the two of 'em used to just practice drums all the time. We started playin', and Clifton fit in real good right away.

When we played the Castle Rock, Buttercup's whole family—his wife, his kids, his father—they'd all be there. One particular night, Buttercup showed up on crutches. He had broken his foot or his leg or somethin'. Buttercup's old lady got liquored up pretty bad that night. She thought some woman was makin' a play for Buttercup, so she hit the lady with a beer bottle and cut her face. This woman was sittin' there with her face bleedin' and everything. Buttercup's wife went berserk. She started runnin' down the bar, throwin' glasses and bottles and hittin' people. Everyone ran up against the wall. Glasses and tables were all turned over. There was broken bottles all over the floor. Man, she *wrecked* the joint. I mean, she totally *destroyed* it. Finally, the guy who owned the place took out a pistol and fired four shots into the floor to get her attention. *Pow! Pow! Pow! Pow!* Then Ellas came up behind her and got her in a full nelson and carried her out the door. That was the end of Buttercup's music career. I guess Ellas cut him loose. Buttercup never did come back after that.

The owner of the Castle Rock must have been rippin' off all the money, 'cause he'd ask us sometimes, "Can I pay you guys next week?" And I'd say, "Well, I need mine now." He was only payin' us five dollars a night, but he wound up owin' *us* money!

So we left there and went to the Sawdust Trail, which was not far from the Castle Rock, on 44th and Wentworth, I think. This was in the wintertime, and Ellas wasn't workin' construction. In the winter, he would go on relief and draw compensation. We really went over at the Sawdust Trail. Everywhere Ellas played, he went over big. He drew a younger crowd, and they really liked him.

Ellas was a mild-mannered guy. One night at the Sawdust Trail, this girl we called Baby Sister showed up. She was a little, cute girl about eighteen, and she and Ellas was kinda gettin' together. We took a break from playin' and was sittin' on the edge of the stage, and there was quite a few girls tryin' to talk to Ellas and flirt with him. Baby Sister got a little high, and when Ellas got back on the stage, she walked up to him and took his glasses off, throwed 'em down on the floor, and stepped on 'em. If she had done that to anyone else, they would have jumped up and wanted to fight. But Ellas wasn't like that. He just looked at her and said, "Baby Sister, I'm gonna tell your momma on you!"

Ellas was the leader of the band and the star of the show. He was a real gentleman and a ladies' man, and the girls liked him. Ellas's wife, Tootsie, used to get jealous of all the action he was gettin'. We would go by his house to pick him up for the gig, and Tootsie would say, "Ellas ain't gonna play tonight." And Ellas would be sittin' on the edge of the bed, like a little kid. Tootsie would say, "Y'all go ahead. Ellas ain't gonna play tonight." And they'd get to arguin' and everything. About fifteen minutes later, he'd come out. Ellas wasn't henpecked, he was just tryin' to get along with Tootsie.

:::

I had made the record for Cool a couple of years before, but now I was determined to cut a *hit* record. My playin' and singin' wasn't ready, but I thought I was. Little did I know that before 1955 was out, I would have made *two* hit records.

Ellas was good enough to make a record. He was twenty-seven and had a strong, mature singin' voice. He played his own guitar, he was a great songwriter, and he had new ideas. So I told him, "Hey, let's make some records." Ellas was nonchalant about recording. Like I said, he wasn't pursuin' no career as a musician. So I took Ellas to the record companies. We went to them as two distinct artists. I was tryin' to make records, and Ellas was tryin' to make records.

We went to United Records first. Their office was upstairs in this building on 51st and Cottage. Leonard Allen owned that label, and they had artists like Memphis Slim and Tab Smith. I had known Memphis Slim since I was fourteen, and he had told 'em a couple of years before that I played like Sonny Boy, but, of course, they didn't record me then.

We talked to a guy named Smitty—I don't remember his real name, he was Allen's son-in-law and partner—and he said, "Well, go over to Al Smith's house and rehearse."

Al Smith was an upright bass player and a producer. He was a very good friend of Leonard Allen and the folks at Vee-Jay Records. Al had a nice bungalow over in Hyde Park, past Drexel. So we went over to Al Smith's basement—that's where United recorded their stuff. We rehearsed for two weeks, and Al Smith was right there for all of it. Al Smith was a savvy guy, and he and Smitty was listenin' while we worked on things. They didn't know what to do with the stuff Ellas had, 'cause it wasn't straight-out blues like Muddy Waters, Howlin' Wolf, or Sonny Boy.

After two weeks, Smitty came up to me and Ellas and he said, "You guys really want to make a record?"

We said, "Yeah."

Smitty said, "Well, go up to Mr. Allen and say, 'We want a record, but we don't want no money.'"

We cracked up laughin'. At least, I did. And I said, "What the hell?" I'm thinkin' that we were in the business of tryin' to better ourselves financially and in other ways, too.

So, of course, we didn't go back *there* no more.

Ellas had one of those home disc makers—a machine where you could record your own acetate dubs. He would record stuff at home for fun. Just for himself, you know. He had recorded this dub with just him playin' and singin'. The dub had "I'm a Man" and a song called "Little Grenadier" on it. "Little Grenadier" was about some barmaid and he had put a strong guitar riff to it. Ellas would always make up songs about girls to that riff.

Ellas and I took Ellas's dub and went over to Vee-Jay Records, which was right across the street from Chess Records. Vee-Jay was a black-owned label that had only been in business about a year. They

The Vee-Jay executive team. *Left to right*: Jimmy Bracken, Ewart Abner, Vivian
Carter, and Calvin Carter
Bill Greensmith/Blues Unlimited

had just hit it big with Jimmy Reed. The owners were Vivian Carter,
a disc jockey with a real popular radio show in Gary, Indiana, and her
husband and manager, Jimmy Bracken. The "Vee" was for Vivian and
the "Jay" was for Jimmy. Ewart Abner was running the label for 'em.
He's the one who got Vee-Jay on their feet. Vivian's brother was Calvin Carter, the A&R man. He sang in the doo-wop group the Spaniels
and wrote their big hit, "Goodnite Sweetheart, Goodnite." He also
wrote "Eldorado Cadillac," which I later recorded as "I Ain't Got You."

We walked in the door at Vee-Jay with Ellas's dub. The secretary
there was named Sharon. She was headed out to lunch, so she said,
"What you guys want?"

I said, "Well, we got a dub here." She put it on the turntable and
listened for about a second.

She said, "I don't like that," and she walked on out.

So we went across the street to Chess Records, the strongest record company in the area. Everybody was in awe of Leonard Chess,

the owner, 'cause he was the man who made Muddy Waters and Little Walter. Everybody wanted to record for Chess 'cause they had all those hits out for Muddy and everything and 'cause Leonard was the type of guy that tried to get as much as possible out of every record that he invested in.

When Ellas and I walked into the Chess office, Leonard wasn't there. But Little Walter was in there. Leonard had to go up to the bank that day, and he had asked Walter, who was gettin' ready to go out on the road, to help him pack up some records while he was gone. So when we walked in the door, Little Walter was in there packin' some records.

Walter had seen us around, in the clubs, so he recognized us.

He told us, "Hey, man, we don't need nothin' today. Come back in a couple of weeks." He was tryin' to shoo us off.

Just as Walter said that, Phil Chess came out of the back room. He knew me—I was that teenager back in the stock room blowin' the harmonica and singin'—but he didn't know Ellas yet. If Phil hadn't come out of that room, we'd have left, 'cause Walter was shooin' us out the door.

Phil said, "Hey, man, what's up?"

I said, "We got a dub here."

He said, "Well, let me hear it."

Phil put on the dub, listened to the songs, and then said, "Can you guys come back here tomorrow around two o'clock? I want my brother Leonard to hear this."

After getting' nowhere with United and Vee-Jay, this was promisin'.

So the next day at two o'clock we was back at Chess, and here comes Leonard Chess. Leonard Chess was like a movie star. Everybody was in awe of him, 'cause he was the strongest record producer. I had met Leonard two years before, when I talked to him about distributin' the record I made for Cool.

When Leonard came in, we played the dub for him. Muddy Waters and Howlin' Wolf and Little Walter was goin' in and out of the office when we played the dub for Leonard.

When Little Walter heard "Little Grenadier"—the song that had a strong guitar riff in Spanish tuning—he said, "Man, I want that motherfucker," and he went on and started talkin' to Leonard.

And Muddy heard "I'm a Man" and *he* said, "I want that motherfucker. I want that."

They thought that Leonard was gonna shoo Ellas away, give him a few dollars, and give 'em the songs. But Leonard listened to the dub and he knew that Ellas had somethin', somethin' different. I could tell he liked "I'm a Man." He said, "Can you guys come by and rehearse tomorrow?"

So the next day we showed up with our equipment. It was me, Ellas, James Bradford, Clifton James, and Jerome Green. We started workin' on this hambone groove that Ellas had. He was playin' that hambone beat on an acoustic guitar with a pickup stuck under the strings that gave him a tremolo sound—an organ effect—and Leonard liked that. Leonard wanted that beat. He knew that if he did somethin' around that beat and that tremolo guitar, he'd have a hell of a record.

Ellas didn't walk into that rehearsal with a song with all the music and words to it. He just came in there with this beat, and he was singin' "Hey, Noxzema" and these different words and things—all kinds of crazy, made-up stuff. Ellas didn't have any verses to this thing. See, on the street he would have sung somethin' like "Dirty Motherfuyer"—derogatory words—to that beat. Ellas knew that wouldn't work on a record, and so when we was rehearsin' with Leonard at Chess that day Ellas was singin' "Hey, Noxzema" instead of "Dirty Motherfuyer" or whatever. Ellas was singin', "Papa gonna buy you a Sunday coat and hat" and "Papa gonna buy his baby a diamond ring."

Leonard told us, "We got to get a story together on this. We gotta get a story on this song." Leonard was the type of guy who was always lookin' for ideas and tryin' to pull the best out of the artist. He was askin' for ideas, and nobody in the studio was sayin' anything.

Somethin' popped into my head and I said, "Why don't you say *Bo Diddley* gonna buy his baby a diamond ring?"

See, four years before that, in 1951, Ellas, Roosevelt, and me was walkin' down 51st Street near Cottage Grove. We had just played on one corner and we was goin' down the street when Roosevelt said, "Hey, Ellas, there goes Bo Diddley!"

He was talkin' about a little bitty short guy about four feet tall and extremely bow legged, goin' by on the opposite side of the street.

And man, I cracked up. I had never heard that word before, and I just laughed, laughed, and laughed. I was fifteen years old, and I thought that was the funniest word I'd ever heard.

The little short guy who had walked by was a comedian at the Indiana Theatre that they called Bo Diddley. The Indiana Theatre was on 43rd and Indiana. It was a great big theater. Every Saturday night, after showin' motion pictures all day, they would have the "Midnight Ramble." They would clear the theater after the last movie, 'cause you had to buy a separate ticket to see the Midnight Ramble.

On the Midnight Ramble they would feature a major blues artist. Sonny Boy Williamson played there, Big Bill played there, Memphis Minnie played there. Butterbeans and Susie. You would pass the theater and they'd have a life-size picture of Big Bill and his guitar, or Memphis Minnie. And at the Midnight Ramble they had this comedian, Bo Diddley. Roosevelt and Ellas knew him, 'cause Ellas used to go and do the amateur show at the Indiana Theatre to make a few bucks.

So that's how the name "Bo Diddley" came into my head at the rehearsal with Leonard.

Leonard said, "Wait a minute, hold on. What does 'Bo Diddley' mean? I don't want to put nothin' on the record that's gonna offend the black audience." 'Cause his records was made for black people. Nobody else was buyin' 'em in those days.

I said, "No, that just means a little, short, extremely bow-legged guy. Bo Diddley is a comedian at the Indiana Theatre—four feet tall." It had nothing to do with bein' derogatory to black people. And so Leonard decided he was okay with it.

Now, if we had been at United Records or Vee-Jay Records,

I never would have spoken up. The folks at those labels had no ideas. They wouldn't have been askin' no questions and they wouldn't have inspired me to say anything.

I made up some other verses to the song, right there in rehearsal. I came up with "Mojo came to my house with a black cat bone, to take my baby away from home," "Asked mojo where you been, up to your house and gone again," and "Bo Diddley, Bo Diddley, have you heard, my baby said she was a bird." I wrote those verses right on the spot, and Ellas started singin' 'em.

I was young. I was nineteen. I should have said, "Wait a minute, man, I should be gettin' writer's credit out of this." But I didn't say nothin'. Leonard's not going to say nothin' about a writer's credit. Ellas is not going to say nothin'. So I never did get any credit for it.

When we played the hambone thing on the street, I didn't play harp on it, so we never talked about havin' me play harp on this tune in the studio that day.

So that's how that went down. That's how the hambone song became the song "Bo Diddley."

After we rehearsed a couple of times, Leonard said, "Be at Universal Recording tomorrow night," which was a Friday. This was in February of 1955.

Leonard recorded all those Chess hits at Universal Recording. Vee-Jay and United recorded their stuff there, too. It was the best studio in town, and the engineer, Bill Putnam, really knew what to do.[1] All of Chess's great records was recorded at Universal with Bill Putnam. When it came to recording studios in Chicago, Universal was *it*.

---

1. Milton Tasker "Bill" Putnam (1920–1989) revolutionized the recording industry by designing the first modern recording studio and pioneering techniques like multitracking, overdubbing, stereo, equalization, compression, and reverb. Putnam founded Universal Recording, one of America's first independent recording studios, in Chicago in 1946. The Chess and Vee-Jay labels recorded many of their now legendary sessions at Universal. In 1957, Frank Sinatra and Bing Crosby backed Putnam in founding the United Recording Corporation in Los Angeles, which soon became one of the preeminent recording facilities in the United States.

I told Leonard that I knew Blind John Davis and that he might fit our sound. So I had Blind John come out to the rehearsal and play on "I'm a Man." And Blind John couldn't play the stuff 'cause his style was from back in the 1940s and dated. But bein' a kid, and Blind John being my friend and everything, I had asked him to be there. Finally, Leonard walked up to me and said, "Look, we can't use him." And he gave me twenty-five dollars to give to Blind John for his time in comin' out to the studio. Muddy Waters and his band were playin' their regular Friday night gig at the 708 Club that evening, and Leonard pulled Otis Spann off that gig to play piano on the session with us.

The four tunes that Ellas McDaniel and the Hipsters did at that first Chess session was "I'm a Man," "Bo Diddley," "You Don't Love Me," and "Little Girl." Ellas played guitar and sang, I blew harp, Jerome was on maracas, Clifton James was the drummer, Bradford was on bass, and Spann played piano.

"I'm a Man" was cut before Muddy Waters recorded his tune "Mannish Boy." That came out a couple of months later. That's where Muddy got that, from Ellas. That was Ellas's song. And black people related to it, 'cause they wanted respect: "Look, motherfucker, I'm a *man.*"

Leonard was really involved in that session. He worked with that record. He arranged it. The reason the "Bo Diddley" record came out the way it did is because he was involved in it. He was tellin' us where to play. He said, "You don't have no song," and he was right. We didn't come in there and say, "This is a song called 'Bo Diddley.'" Leonard first heard that name from me that day.

Leonard was a smart man. He knew how to put together a record that would make sense. Leonard was the kind of guy who saw potential and could make somethin' out of it. He knew Ellas had his own style. When I said, "Sing 'Bo Diddley,'" Leonard knew that name was somethin' different. I guess he liked "Bo Diddley" for the same reasons I did—'cause it was funny and unusual.

While we was recording, Leonard would be standin' in front of Ellas while he was singin' and playin', and he'd point when it would

Leonard Chess
Bill Greensmith/Blues Unlimited

be the singin' part or when he wanted Ellas to play the guitar. Leonard wanted that guitar in a lot of parts. When you listen to that record, everywhere where Ellas is playin' the guitar, that's where Leonard pointed at him to play. He kept tellin' Ellas to turn up that tremolo.

After we finished Ellas's four sides, I told Leonard, "Hey, wait a minute. What about the songs I was doin'?" and Leonard said, "Okay, all right, man. Let him do his two songs."

And that's how I recorded two songs at the end of Ellas McDaniel's first session: "Sweet on You Baby" and "You Got to Love

Me." "Sweet on You Baby" was my song. It was a Sonny Boy type of kick that I had already recorded on the dub I did with the Red Devil Trio. "You Got to Love Me" was a song that Ellas gave me. Otis Spann was playin' the piano, and at one point while we was recording "Sweet on You Baby" I called out, "All right, Otis Spann!" I was tryin' to do like what Sonny Boy did when he would say "All right, Blind John!" on his records. And Leonard Chess looked at me and shook his head. He didn't want me to say that. But I *had* to say that, 'cause Otis Spann was my favorite piano player and blues singer, and it thrilled me that we was recording together.

But Leonard wasn't interested in what *I* had, he was interested in Ellas. My stuff was a little dated compared to what he was lookin' for. He was lookin' for new ideas, and Ellas had 'em. Chess never released those tunes of mine that I recorded that day. They came out on an LP years later.

So that's the way it went down that night at Universal. And that's the way it came *up*, too!

We left the session thinkin' that the record was gonna come out as "Bo Diddley" by Ellas McDaniel and the Hipsters. But, to our surprise, when the record came out two weeks later, the label said "Bo Diddley" by the artist "Bo Diddley."

The name "Bo Diddley"—that was a shocker. Everybody laughed: "*Bo Diddley*, man!" And that tremolo guitar—if you listen to the record, the words weren't all that clever, but the tremolo and that drum beat on the back of it made that record *different*. And the flip side, "I'm a Man," had that riff: da *da* da da. That was different, too.

That "Bo Diddley" record with "I'm a Man" on the flip side was sensational. It was a smash hit. It went all over. Ellas McDaniel was Bo Diddley now, and he was on his way.

∶ ∶ ∶

When the "Bo Diddley" record came out, Essex Records wanted to have this white girl singer, Jean Dinning, cover it. They wanted to use the Bo Diddley band. Leonard wasn't too keen on givin' his smash hit to somebody else so they could do it, but he was tryin' to

Left to right: Jerome Green, Bo Diddley, and Clifton James
Michael Ochs Archives/Getty Images

be a nice guy or somethin', and he would still make money on the publishing. He was definitely not gonna let 'em record Bo Diddley with his guitar, but he helped 'em arrange a session in Chicago with Willie Dixon on bass, Clifton James on drums, and me on harmonica to cut a cover of "Bo Diddley" with Jean Dinning. We made union scale for sidemen—$41.25.

We ended up goin' down to New Orleans a week later, 'cause we got booked on a tour to play a couple of shows with Howlin' Wolf. Jody Williams was Howlin' Wolf's guitar player, so the Wolf brought him, too. I was anxious to go down there, 'cause I had never been down South, and I wanted to see what it looked like. Chess gave Ellas some money to buy a carry-all DeSoto. That's a big, long car. Howlin' Wolf said he wasn't gonna be ridin' up and down the road in no coffee pot, so he flew down to New Orleans. Jody Williams and the band and all of us, we went in the DeSoto. On the drive down South, the "Bo Diddley" record was burnin' up the airwaves.

The black audiences down South wanted to dance. If you played music they could dance to, they liked you. They liked blues, but they didn't want to hear the real slow blues. You could play blues, but it had to have a dance beat. That's one of the features of black people—we can dance. If you see black people in the Caribbean or in Chicago or in Africa, they all got that same movement, 'cause that's where they came from. Rhythm, for black people, is in everything they do. They do it more aggressive than most other people, and that's why other people look at black people and marvel, "Ooh, yeah. I'd like to be able to do that, too." It's not actin'. They're just bein' themselves.

Howlin' Wolf's records was on the jukeboxes down there. The "Bo Diddley" record was big in New Orleans—you could hear it ringin' all up and down Rampart Street. But when we played live, the black people looked at us real strange, like we was crazy. Smiley Lewis was on the bill in New Orleans. He was a local artist who they knew, and he was playin' blues in a New Orleans style. But when Bo Diddley came on stage and played "I'm a Man," our hot new record, they didn't get up and dance. They just stared at us. The Wolf came up and did his best act, and the people just looked at him like he was from outer space. The next night we played in Homer, Louisiana, and the reaction was the same.

That's when I realized that even though blues music *came* from the South, the black audiences down there was gettin' away from Muddy Waters and the original blues that Big Bill and all of them played. They was gettin' away from that way before we went down there. They was sorta like movin' up to what you might call a higher class of music. What appealed to 'em were artists like Louis Jordan and Roy Brown and B. B. King, who had big bands with horns and everything. The black people down South looked at that as bein' progressive.

Ellas's hometown was McComb, Mississippi, and we visited there on that trip. It was a little town. You could stand on a corner and look down the street three blocks and you're out of town.

When we were tourin' down there, Jean Dinning's version of

"Bo Diddley," that I had also played on, was blastin' all down on the radio. So when we got back to Chicago, me and Clifton James went in to Chess and said, "Did the money come in for the session we did for Jean Dinning?" And they said, "No." Word started goin' around that we had come in there bein' pushy and askin' about money. Bo Diddley told me that Leonard told him, "Your harmonica player came in here and asked for a bunch of money." Well, hell, we did the session, you know? I did some work and deserved that money.

See, the musicians from down South was different. They wasn't goin' to show up at Chess askin' for royalties and not be with the program. Down South, they was sharecroppers on the plantation. If you walked up to the white guy you was sharecroppin' for and said, "Boss, we had a pretty good year this year," he'd get mad. Maybe whup you. Cuss you out. No matter how good it was, he wasn't going to tell *you* that. He'd tell you, "Motherfucker, you owe me five hundred dollars!" And if you wanted to leave the plantation, you had to slip off.

When I asked Chess for my session money, I was only makin' twenty-five dollars a night in the clubs. And Leonard got mad. Little Walter, Muddy Waters, Bo Diddley, and those guys, they was buildin' somethin' with Leonard. If they came up and asked him, "Hey, what about a royalty check?" or "How many records did we sell?" he might get mad. They knew the system, you know. You know your record is a hit, 'cause you're workin' all over the country, but you don't ask nothin' about no royalty. You just go to Leonard and borrow some money. "Hey, can I get eight hundred dollars?" And Leonard, as long as he's got records on the shelf and all that, he might lend you that money. If you needed a car, he could get you a car, but don't go down there askin' for your right amount of money or to bring in an accountant. That could be the end of your career.

Muddy treated his band the same way. They was scared to ask how much the next gig was payin'. And Muddy had a guy named Bo who was raised up with him who kept the guys in line. Bo was a big, strong guy, and if he got mad, he was gonna whup your ass. "Get in the goddamn car!" And you'd drive to Boston.

Now, Leonard didn't do everybody like that. He didn't do Chuck Berry like that. Chuck was raised in St. Louis, and he had a different attitude. After he had that smash, "Maybellene," it was a different deal. Chuck Berry set up his own publishing company. Leonard was no fool. He wasn't gonna miss out on more money by fallin' out with Chuck over the publishing.

When Ellas and the band got back to Chicago from our road trip down South, Chess got Ellas in—Ellas lived around the corner from Chess—to play guitar on a Little Walter session. Walter had heard the stuff we recorded, and he wanted to use some of Ellas's licks in that special tuning of his for background. Ellas played the same guitar part he had played on "You Don't Love Me," and Walter put new words to it and turned it into "Hate to See You Go." Ellas's song "Little Grenadier" became Little Walter's "Roller Coaster."

: : :

I was always tryin' to write songs. I started writin' songs when I was fourteen. I knew that Sonny Boy wrote his own songs. Tampa Red was a prolific songwriter. And Big Bill, Sonny Boy, and Memphis Minnie was, too. I knew that you couldn't go to Chess and sing one of Little Walter's songs. They would have said, "Hey, man, what's this?" 'Cause they was lookin' for people with new ideas. Even if it's a gimmick song, as long as it makes a million dollars. If it makes 'em a million dollars, they gonna give you some. And it was worth it.

Those other guys, they was tryin' to play like Muddy and Little Walter and them. Junior Wells, now he was a dynamic harp player and a good singer. But he didn't write no songs. He was singin' Sonny Boy songs on his States records, and he wasn't doin' nothing dynamic with 'em.

At this time I was goin' with a girl who had a little daughter about three years old. We called her "Diddy." I had made up this song that I called "Diddy Diddy Dum Dum," and I came up with a harp lick for it. I can't remember the lyrics now, it's been so long. I started doin' the song with Ellas, and he put a guitar part to it.

I played a big show with Ellas at the Trianon Ballroom with Ruth

Brown. I sang "Diddy Diddy Dum Dum" at the Trianon show. Leonard Chess was there that night, and he told Ellas, "That's your next record." Leonard said, "Let Billy sing and play the harp on it."

But I didn't know if Leonard really wanted me to do it, 'cause Ellas had already told me that Leonard didn't particularly like me. He said that Leonard had told him when he first met me that "I don't like your harp player." Leonard thought I was a smart-aleck know-it-all. Ellas told me, "Leonard don't like you." I thought maybe he was bullshittin' me about Leonard, but he didn't usually exaggerate. So I told Ellas, "Well, if he don't want to record me . . ." and Ellas said, "Well, I'll go with you to another company."

I didn't need him to take me to a record company. I'm the one who took *him* to the record companies. My feeling was that I didn't work for Ellas McDaniel. My main goal was to make my own records. My attitude was if Leonard didn't like me, then the hell with him, I'm just gonna go record for somebody else. I wasn't gonna stay where there wasn't no grass under my feet. That was my attitude from the beginnin'. My goal wasn't to be Ellas McDaniel's harmonica player or anybody else's. I wasn't no Little Walter, but I was young and had ideas. I wasn't even ready—I realize that now—but I had the ambition. I guess, in the end, I believed Ellas when he told me that Leonard didn't like me more than I believed Leonard when he said he wanted to record my song.

So I went to Vee-Jay and said, "I'm Bo Diddley's harmonica player and I've got a song called 'Diddy Diddy Dum Dum' and Leonard don't want me to record for him." Jimmy Bracken told me, "Come by tomorrow and talk to Calvin Carter."

I went by the next day and talked to Calvin. I didn't really play "Diddy Diddy Dum Dum" for him, I just told him how it went. He said, "Well, okay, we got a session comin' up."

I brought Jody Williams over to Al Smith's house and showed him how the song went. I told Jody what to play 'cause Jody had never heard it. I sang him the guitar part that Ellas had put to it. I told Jody, "That's what I want," and he did it. The guitar part that Ellas had been playin' on it was real slow and a little dull, but Jody put a little more pickup and rhythm into it. Jody, being a different kind of guitar player than Ellas, he played the same kind of riff, but his version of it had more appeal.

The Bo Diddley record had just came out and was takin' off. We played the song for Vee-Jay, and they knew it was somethin' different on the Bo Diddley kick. I told Vee-Jay about the connection between "Diddy Diddy Dum Dum" and Ellas and Chess.

Calvin told me, "Well, then, write another lyric on it, 'cause we don't want no conflict with Leonard." So I went home and wrote "I Wish You Would" right on the spot.

Before the session, we talked about me doin' a song of Jody's called "I Was Fooled." Vee-Jay convinced Jody to let me sing that number as the flip side of "I Wish You Would." Al Smith told him that, style-wise, I had a voice more suited for that type of song, and Jody went along with it. He said, "Well, okay."

That Vee-Jay session was a split session—Morris Pejoe did two sides, I did two sides, and the drummer Earl Phillips did two sides and played behind me and Pejoe. Henry Gray was on the piano—he was in Morris Pejoe's band—and Milton Rector was on bass. I knew Milton. He lived right across the street from Ellas, a couple of blocks from Chess Records, and I would sometimes see Ellas talkin' to him. But I didn't know that Milton was a musician 'til we got to the studio and there he was, sittin' out there with a Fender bass. That was the first time I had ever seen an electric bass, and the first electric bass that was in Chicago, that I know of.

The only person I brought to that session was Jody Williams. We had played on the streets with Ellas, but at that time he and Hubert Sumlin were both playin' with Wolf. Jody's guitar playin' *made* my Vee-Jay record. Jody played with a lot of feeling, and he had a lot of ideas. He was young. He had fire in his playin', you know, and he would always come up with these swingin' solos.

When you get with a great musician, a lot of people say, "Hold on to that guy," but you don't want to hold on to that guy, 'cause he ain't *you*. If you got a solo artist in your band that out-stars you, well, then, it's his record and not yours. If that guy decides that he wants to go his own way, then you're lost, and you gotta go get somebody else. So you can't really lean on anybody.

We recorded at Universal Recording, where I had done the Chess session with Ellas. I don't remember whether they used headphones or not in the studio in those days. I know they had me in a little isolation booth with the vocal mic and my amplifier, and the rest of the musicians was out in the main room. Bill Putnam, the same engineer that did all the Little Walter and Chuck Berry hits for Chess Records, was the engineer. He was in another room, but he could talk to us. He would sometimes come out of the booth where I was and adjust things. I guess they got the recording levels set before we started playin', but he would come out and do a couple of little things if somethin' needed adjustment. We played live in the studio. I don't remember doin' any overdubs at Universal.

The session was kind of rushed. See, Vee-Jay was mostly into doo-wop. They had the Moonglows and they had Dee Clark and people like that. They also had Snooky Pryor, Jimmy Reed, Eddie Taylor, and two or three other blues guys. But the Vee-Jay folks looked at blues like all you had to do was plug in the amplifiers and start playin' and do a blues song. They would bring Snooky and them in there and Snooky would just start playin' and jammin', and they would make a record. They looked at the blues as somethin' that they wouldn't put that much effort into.

: : :

While I was at Universal recording "I Wish You Would" for Vee-Jay, Ellas came to my house to get me so we could record again for Chess. Leonard had told him, "Go get Billy Boy." He held up the session for two days until they could find me, 'cause he wanted me to sing "Diddy Diddy Dum Dum" and play harp on it.

When they finally found me, they took me to Leonard's back room there at Chess for the second Bo Diddley session. We didn't record at Universal this time. Leonard had a little recorder in the back there at Chess, and he was doin' some of his own recording there in his back room. And that wasn't cool, man, 'cause Universal was *it*.

Leonard, Little Walter, and the Moonglows was there waitin' when we showed up. Leonard wanted to record "Diddy Diddy Dum Dum" first.

I had the signed contract with Vee-Jay for "I Wish You Would" in my pocket.

I said, "I can't make the record."

And Leonard said, "What do you mean, man?"

And I said, "I just recorded it for Vee-Jay."

And Leonard said, "Goddammit! Oh, man, I've had this happen to me before."

And then Ellas got mad. But he was the one who told me that Leonard didn't like me, and so that's why I went to Vee-Jay in the first place.

Lookin' back on it, "Diddy Diddy Dum Dum" and "I Wish You Would" ended up bein' different songs, so I probably could have recorded "Diddy Diddy Dum Dum" for Chess. What I recorded for Vee-Jay was different. I could have gotten two different songs out of it. I got hung up on the fact that I had the same harp riff on both songs. I was sorta puttin' the cart before the horse. I didn't realize that I was inexperienced. When you're young, you're tryin' to do somethin'. I hadn't done much singin' and had no stage experience. I was just caught up in one of those things. I guess Little Walter wasn't so polished, either, at that age. It takes time to develop. But I was young, and I told Leonard I couldn't record "Diddy Diddy Dum Dum" for him.

Leonard said, "You know, when I first saw you, I didn't like you. When I first saw Little Walter, I didn't like Little Walter."

I think he told me that 'cause I was a smart-alecky kid and he was used to different type of guys. Most of the black guys that Leonard worked with came from the South and was kinda docile, and he knew how to handle 'em. He'd ask you, "Where you from? What different area are you from?" I wasn't docile and I wasn't from the South, so Leonard thought I was kind of cocky. Little Walter was younger, too, and he wasn't as humble acting as most of the musicians Leonard dealt with. I took what he said to mean that he must have changed his mind about me—that at one point he had accepted me, but then I sort of crossed him and recorded for somebody else. He didn't hit the ceiling, but he was mad 'cause I wouldn't do the song.

Little Walter and them that was in the studio thought I had stabbed Ellas in the back. I didn't stab him in the back. It was *my* goddamn song that the man liked.

Little Walter was tellin' Ellas, "Man, if it was me, I'd tell him to hit the goddamn road," and blah, blah, blah. Shootin' off at the mouth, you know.

Leonard decided to try to come up with a different song on the spot. Harvey Fuqua of the Moonglows happened to be there at Chess that day, and he jumped in and started writin' some lyrics and background vocals for a new tune that ended up bein' called "Diddley Daddy." I told 'em I wouldn't play harp on "Diddley Daddy," 'cause I didn't want to play my riff from "I Wish You Would" on there. Walter said, "Well, give me the harp and the amp, man. Let me play it." And so on "Diddley Daddy" you have the Moonglows singin' the background and Little Walter playin' my harp through my amplifier.

Then we recorded one more side back there in that back room, "She's Fine, She's Mine," and I played the harmonica on it. We just cut those two songs that day.

: : :

Ellas and I played one or two gigs after that second session. I was stayin' with a girl at that time, and one day when I wasn't there he brought my amplifier by and dropped it off. I knew that was goodbye. Ellas was goin' on the road to New York, and he went out and got Lester Davenport to play harp with him. Lester was a great harp player. He and Big Smokey Smothers was cousins. As far as harp on the Bo Diddley records goes, I'm the one playin' harp on "You Don't Love Me (You Don't Care)," "Little Girl," and "I'm a Man." Lester played harp on "Pretty Thing." Willie "Big Eyes" Smith says that he played harp on "Diddy Wah Diddy." But Ellas really didn't need harp on the stuff he was doin'. Ellas played the blues, but he had his own way of doin' it. He was a prolific songwriter with his own style, so eventually he stopped usin' the harp.

Me and Ellas didn't have a fallin' out. It didn't make me mad, 'cause my thing was not to just play harp behind Bo Diddley. I don't know whether he was mad at me. He might have thought that I did a disservice to him, but I didn't feel that way. I was the one who took him to Chess, and when we walked in there, it was *me* that Phil Chess knew—he didn't know Ellas McDaniel. When Phil said, "Hey, man, what you got?" he was talkin' to me.

But I knew Ellas was a star. I knew he was the one that had what people really wanted. I was just sort of a youngster tryin' to get started. I was tryin' to make records, and I had already *made* a record before I got *him* interested in tryin' to make records.

So my thing with Bo Diddley ended up with a big mix-up, but that's exactly the way it went down, word for word. I ain't put nothin' new in this story or taken nothin' out.

If Ellas had recorded for United Records or Vee-Jay, he never would've become Bo Diddley and he never would've been a star. They would've just stood there and recorded whatever he played. They would've just recorded "I'm a Man" just the way he had it down and released it as Ellas McDaniel and the Hipsters. They would've made *their* money, and Ellas would've had one record and still been doin' construction work.

The black record companies was fast-buck artists. They wanted to get a record out, cover two or three states, and make *them* some money, but they were not out to build no artists. You wouldn't necessarily get a better deal with a black-owned label.

One day in 1955, I was at Vee-Jay Records sittin' with the owner, Jimmy Bracken, in his office, and I heard him say, "Leonard Chess is gonna give Chuck Berry two cents a record. I wouldn't give *nobody* two cents a record." And records at that time was sellin' for seventy-nine cents. That's why he went down the goddamn drain. That was Jimmy Bracken's attitude.

Leonard Chess wanted to make money, of course. But he

saw somethin' that he could make bigger than it was. The other companies—now, I hate to say this too, again—make 'em a little money and buy themselves a Cadillac and everything, and that's it. But Leonard wasn't into that. He gave the Cadillac to Muddy, and he would drive a station wagon, 'cause Leonard was in for the thrill of buildin' somethin'.

Me and Ellas was never really conscious that we was pioneerin' a new kind of music. A couple of months after he recorded "Bo Diddley," Leonard did his first session with Chuck Berry. Chuck had a song called "Ida Red." Leonard said, "No, change it to Maybellene." And Chuck Berry came in with a singer. The singer was gonna sing the song, and Chuck was gonna play the guitar. And so, when they was rehearsin', Chuck Berry was singin' it to show the singer how to sing it. And Leonard said, "Wait a minute, hold it." He told Chuck, "Let me hear *you* do it." And that's how Chuck Berry got started.

Ellas ended up makin' about twenty albums for Chess, and he wrote about 99 percent of the songs. He turned out to be very successful and very prolific. Ellas McDaniel and Leonard Chess are gone now, God rest their souls. They should be forever grateful to me for sayin', "Why don't you say, 'Bo Diddley gonna buy his baby a diamond ring?'" and rememberin' the little short comedian from the Indiana Theatre whose stage name was the funniest thing I had ever heard.

"I Wish You Would" wasn't the smash that "Bo Diddley" was, but it was a good-sellin' record, and it was a rock-and-roll record. Vee-Jay told me, "You hit the charts. You sold fifteen thousand records in Detroit the first week." They said that Leonard was tellin' the disc jockeys not to play "I Wish You Would" 'cause he saw it as competition against Bo Diddley.

Vee-Jay told me, "We changed your name." See, on the Cool record I was called "Billy Boy Arnold." Vee-Jay said, "We just called you 'Billy Boy.'" At that point, I didn't have any feelin' about that at all, one way or the other. You know, Muddy Waters had his nickname down South as a kid, comin' up, and so Leonard and everybody called him Muddy Waters. And they called Little Walter that

"I Wish You Would," 1955
Bill Greensmith

'cause he was small in stature and young. Sonny Boy got Eddie Boyd a deal with Melrose and RCA Victor, and when they put his records out, they called him "Little Eddie Boyd." Eddie resented that 'cause he *was* little. And so later, when he signed with Chess, he told them, "Man, I don't like that shit, 'Little Eddie Boyd,' 'Little Walter.' Little this, little that. I ain't no goddamn midget! My name is Eddie Boyd!"

We used to call Junior Wells "Little Junior," but Junior didn't have no complex about it. We called him "Little June" and "Little Junior." Little Walter was small—he was about five-eight, an inch or so taller than Junior Wells—and when he came to Chicago he was a young kid, seventeen years old. A little, skinny kid. He wasn't built robust. And so people said, "Hey look, there's little Walter blowin' the harp." And he was young. People call you that 'cause you're a kid under them. But that nickname didn't bother him. At least, he didn't say anything about it.

Vee-Jay gave me a three-year contract. They signed me for two years with another year option after that. But they was sorta lookin' at the blues as somethin' that they wouldn't put that much into.

I never made any money with Vee-Jay. Every time Vee-Jay would send me a royalty accountin', they would say there was so much money outstandin', you know. Like, "we didn't make any money on it." You knew damn well they was makin' money off it, but the publishing was different.

I don't know whether I'd have gone a different route if I could have done it all over again. I probably would have got more experience playin' with different people before I recorded. I missed out on a chance to have my own record on Chess. I'm not bitter about that, but I would rather have recorded for Leonard Chess. When you recorded with him, you were on your way somewhere.

But it didn't come out too bad. Ellas got to be Bo Diddley, and, with the help of my song "I Wish You Would," and Eric Clapton and the Yardbirds and David Bowie, who covered it, I got to be Billy Boy Arnold.

It was a hell of a start, really. There were tons of harp players in Chicago tryin' to make records, but they didn't have "I Wish You Would." When that record came out, the guys was jealous, you know. They figured I didn't have no experience. But I was writin' songs and they wasn't. That record put my name on the map, even overseas. It got all over the world. One thing about Vee-Jay, their records got overseas, just like Chess's records did. "I Wish You Would" came out in '55, and two years later I was playin' at Sylvio's opposite Muddy's and Wolf's bands, and I had Syl Johnson on guitar. That record put me up there, with those guys. I had made a name for myself.

Vee-Jay recording artist "Billy Boy" Arnold, 1955
Billy Boy Arnold

6

Bluesman

After "I Wish You Would" hit, things happened fast for me. Vee-Jay gave me money to buy an amplifier, microphones, and a PA system. A black guy named Fleming who worked for Shaw Artists agency came out to see me after "I Wish You Would" became a hit and said, "We'd like to sign you up," so I signed with them. I had to put a band together. I was a nineteen-year-old kid out there tryin' to make it, and then Vee-Jay just put me out there. I just kind of stumbled out there and one thing led to another.

When I was playin' with Ellas McDaniel, I was the harp player. I didn't do hardly any singin.' So when Vee-Jay launched me, I had to come up with an act and an entire repertoire. I knew all the blues songs—the Bluebird stuff, all of Muddy's songs, Little Walter's tunes—but I'd never sung them in public. I had never fronted a band in public as a leader. And I was tryin' to play harp like Little Walter, too. Junior Wells told me, "You're supposed to play in the clubs and *then* make a record."

I didn't have no sound of my own. First, I'm a young kid, tryin' to be like Sonny Boy Williamson and tryin' to make a record. And then I'm a guy with a popular record, but I didn't really have my own sound.

And all these harmonica players around Chicago, like Little Mack Simmons and all of 'em, they didn't have "I Wish You Would."

They would go to Vee-Jay and say, "Hey, I want to make a record," you know. And Vee-Jay would say, "Well, let us hear what you got." And they would sound like Muddy Waters. They'd have a regular blues sound. And Vee-Jay would say "Naw, right now we don't need somebody." And then these guys would say, "Well, you got Billy Boy Arnold, and *he* can't sing too good!"

These musicians was all older than me. I didn't have the seasonin' or experience that Muddy and Wolf and them had. Little Walter was young, but he had been through the mill. And Junior had been playin' with the Aces two or three years. He could play the harmonica and he had a hell of a voice, but he didn't write no songs. I think Junior wrote one song. That was "Come On in This House," which was a great one. But I had my own material.

I had to put a whole act together from scratch. I got a guy named Bobby Lee on guitar. He had played with Little Mack Simmons and was a great guitar player. Jimmy Walker played piano with me for a while. Bo Diddley had fired James Bradford, so I hired him to play bass. Bradford told me, "I know a drummer," and he brought Billy Davenport into the picture.

Billy Davenport was older than Bo Diddley. He was in his early thirties. Davenport wasn't a blues drummer. He played mostly jazz. Billy wasn't playin' with no blues people before he played with me. He was kind of a weird guy. He was very quiet. Never did talk much. You never knew what he was thinkin'. Didn't drink. Didn't smoke. Billy was livin' up over a garage. I went over there once. You'd go in the alleyway and park your car, and Billy was livin' upstairs in this garage with his girlfriend. She was a nice-lookin' girl. I remember there were five or six of those little, small cans of sardines layin' around on the table.

Kid Rivera's Barrelhouse was a real swanky, brand-new club in Chicago. They had called the union and said, "Little Walter's coming in on Wednesday and Thursday, but we need a band for Friday, Saturday, and Sunday. What about Billy Boy?" And so they hired me in there.

Kid Rivera, the owner, was a black prizefighter. He was a great, big, powerful-lookin' guy. All the guys that worked at his club were Italian and black gangsters or ex–prize fighters—thugs and stuff. Bouncers. People affiliated with gangsters and fightin'. The club had tables with tops that were made to look like barrels with candlelight in the center.

When I first started there, one of the Barrelhouse guys told me, "Billy Boy, you ain't nothin' but a goddamn kid. You ain't even supposed to be in here." I was only nineteen, but I had a hot record.

We played the Barrelhouse for about three weeks. We went over good, but then they got Freddy King to come in with his band. Freddy was a sophisticated singer and a great guitar player, and his band was more experienced. He was soundin' great, as he always did. But he played there about three weeks and then the Barrelhouse hired me back. The guy there said, "Those other guys can play better than y'all, but they didn't have the charisma that y'all had. They didn't have the class that you got."

That's what they said, but the only person in the band that had class was me. I was young and well dressed. I always was a dresser, from a kid all the way up. I was always conscious of how I looked, and I always dressed that way. I didn't have a special place to shop for stage clothes. They had lot of different stores in Chicago. I didn't pattern myself after nobody. I just liked to look *good*. See, one thing about black people: if you're young and black and good-lookin' and sharp, then that's how they want you to look. They don't want you to look like you just crawled off a freight train, 'cause they came to Chicago to better themselves. They came out to see somebody playin', and they want you to look like somebody.

Audiences liked me in general, and the young women liked me in particular. We drew a younger crowd at the Barrelhouse. I had those pretty girls comin' in. The Barrelhouse put my Vee-Jay promo photo up in all the windows.

That's how I met my future wife, Mary. She and her girlfriends stopped by the Barrelhouse and saw my picture plastered all over

Billy Boy Arnold and his wife, Mary, New Year's Eve, 1964
Billy Boy Arnold

the windows, and one of 'em said, "Ooh, let's come and see him." 'Cause I was around their age, you know. And they came and saw me and flipped. I kissed Mary on the cheek on her way out the door, and the rest is history. I was nineteen when I met Mary. We got married a few years later, when I was about twenty-two, and we're still together. We have two sons, Gregory and Angelo. Gregory was born in 1959 and Angelo was born in 1970.

In 1955, when I got started, blues artists was doin' better record-wise and gettin' more recognition, 'cause Muddy Waters was pretty popular with the black audiences. Everybody was tryin' to make records. At first there were three independent record companies in Chicago: Chess Records, United Records, and States Records. And then Vee-Jay came on, and there was Chance Records, too—that was owned by Art Sheridan. Chance was around the corner on 47th from Vee-Jay.

I got my own gigs. The Shaw agency didn't have nothin' to do with club gigs in Chicago, they focused on road gigs. I had steady work in the clubs. I was pretty popular 'cause I had a record. My picture was in the *Chicago Defender* every week.

In 1955, after I made "I Wish You Would," I heard that they needed a band over at the Zanzibar, the place where I had seen Junior Wells and the Aces play and where I first laid eyes on Little Walter. So I got a guitar player—Big Smokey Smothers—and a drummer and everything and I called the guy up.

He said, "How much you want?"

I said, "Well, give me thirty dollars."

And he said, "*Christ*, man! Goddamn! Muddy only gets eighteen dollars!" That was union scale for a leader in those days. I ended up goin' down for the eighteen dollars, 'cause I was in the union. Things was cheaper back then, it's true, but that's what the deal really was.

On our first night at the Zanzibar, Little Walter was in there, sittin' at the bar. So I'm singin' like Sonny Boy and playin' like Sonny Boy—phrasin' the harmonica like him and everything, 'cause I was still on the Sonny Boy kick. And Walter's sayin', "You're playin' wrong, man! We play different now."

A lot of guys was jealous of Little Walter. I wasn't. I was his *fan*. I was in awe of him.

Little Walter was aggressive when he was young. He had aggressive ideas. He'd hear somethin' and he would try to play it on his harmonica. Walter was hip to jazz, but I don't think he hung out with the jazz guys in Chicago. Walter was from Louisiana. There was a lot of horn players down there. But Little Walter still played that hard-core blues.

Walter came to Chicago as a kid. He was bummin' around Arkansas with Honeyboy Edwards when he was a boy. When you're out there on the road like that, drinkin' was what musicians did, and so Walter started drinkin' young. He was mainly a whiskey drinker, but he also smoked pot. At that time they called it "blowin' gage." Sonny Boy made a record called "Mellow Chick Swing," and he sings on there, "She's kinda fine / she changed my mind / I know you was kinda slick / but I'm hip to this mellow chick / I got away / been blowin' gage." Most of the blues musicians didn't smoke marijuana. The older guys like Big Bill, Blind John, Memphis Slim, and Muddy was all whiskey drinkers. They was drinkin' that hard liquor—Old Crow, Old Grand-Dad. Ninety-proof this and one-hundred-proof that. But Little Walter, Sonny Boy, and James Cotton—the younger, hipper guys—they was blowin' gage *and* drinkin'. I don't know if Little Walter ever got into any other kind of drugs. At that time there wasn't all the drugs that's around now.

Walter was an assertive guy whose harp on his records spoke for him. He had the determination to do his own thing. He didn't leave Muddy and then run back, like Jimmy Rogers did. He did his own thing, and he surpassed Muddy in terms of record sales and popularity. He did a lot of steady travelin' with his group. They'd be on the road for three or four months at a time.

All I know about Walter is that he was a great artist. I didn't know Walter's personal business. He wasn't real friendly with everybody. I knew some of the guys who socialized with him. Walter had an entourage—certain people he liked. He liked Willie Anderson. He liked Luther Tucker, who was his guitar player. He was friends with George Mayweather. Different harp players would be with him, tryin' to learn his licks and stuff, I guess.

It seemed to me that Walter thought that all the harp players was out to get him and was tryin' to overthrow him. Which was strange, 'cause he was light years ahead of all of 'em. I mean, they didn't have a ghost of a chance. But Walter was insecure. I was at the union office one time and Walter came in. He was pretty drunk. The union man asked him, "You know Billy Boy, don't you?" And he said, "Well, he might know *me*." If you could sing pretty good, Walter could be a little leery of that. Walter had a good voice. There was somethin' special about it. But I think he had a complex about his singin'. But he was a star with all those hits out there, and he didn't have nothin' to worry about. He went over real big on the road. He stayed out there on the road in those days. Muddy didn't go out on the road until he started doing the concerts for the white kids.

Walter was a good-lookin' guy who dressed well. I never saw him when he wasn't lookin' presentable. He had a lot of different women. Walter was a kick-ass artist and kinda rough. He had a group of prostitutes, women over on Maxwell Street that he knew from when he was comin' up, who would give him money. Maxwell Street was where Walter hung out, at this club over there. You'd see his Cadillac parked out front. When he was in town, that Cadillac would be there, every day, all day. And these chicks was sweet on Little Walter. They saw him come up to fame, and they liked him and they was his girlfriends. Three of 'em came out to see me, Walter, and Junior Wells one time when we costarred at McKie's Disc Jockey Show Lounge. I'd be playin' or Junior would be playin', and these women would be yellin', "We want Little Walter! We want Little Walter!" Walter got too high that night and passed out. Later on, his friends came out and put him in the back seat of his Cadillac.

When I played at the Happy Home Lounge on Madison, these two prostitutes—one was light skinned and the other was real dark—would come in every night, 'cause the club stayed open until 4 a.m. When I sing I kind of shake my leg, and these two prostitutes liked me and they would come in and buy me drinks and give me money to shake my leg. Now, I wasn't the pimpin' type. That wasn't my thing. I don't like to degrade women, I like to make love to 'em.

Little Walter got shot in the leg in 1958. Some people said that

Walter accidentally shot himself when he was pullin' his gun out or somethin'. Other folks said a girl shot him. I don't know the real story. After Walter got shot, Willie Anderson would chauffeur Walter all around in his 1957 Cadillac. Willie had a day job, but after he got off work he'd drive Walter all around town and buy him drinks. Walter was laid up for several months, and he ended up with a limp when he walked. He had to use a walkin' cane or a crutch for a while. Walter had a real cool, cocky walk before he got hurt, but after that he never could walk like he used to.

Walter would come into the Happy Home Lounge limpin' on one leg or on a crutch, and these women would party with Walter and go with him over to Maxwell Street, where he'd park his car and sit all day drinkin' and everything. They told me they went to his house, too. Walter had an apartment near there. This was right after Little Walter had gotten shot in the leg, and he wasn't workin', so Luther Tucker was playin' guitar with me.

Willie Anderson idolized Walter so much that he imitated all of Walter's special ways. Willie would get on the bandstand and he would make all the gestures that Little Walter would make on stage, like squeezin' his nose. After he got shot, Little Walter would come off the bandstand walkin' crippled, so Willie Anderson started walkin' crippled when *he* came off the bandstand. He was limpin' like Walter, and everybody would crack up. I guess Willie figured if you did everything like Walter, it might rub off on you.

Little Walter had an uncle named Louis who played the harmonica and looked like he could be Walter's twin brother. If you saw him, you could tell they was relatives. Everybody thought he was Walter's brother, but he said he was Walter's uncle. Louis Myers knew Louis, and he said that Louis was Walter's uncle *and* his brother. Louis was around Walter's age. Maybe a couple of years older. I don't know what Louis's last name was. He was a good harp player and was tryin' to get into it. When Walter made "Juke," Louis was livin' in Chicago with Walter, so he'd be wherever Walter was. And Walter had a cousin, Latelle Barton, who lives in Los Angeles now. Latelle is built like Walter and looks like Walter, and he's no slouch on the harp, either. Walter had two sisters who lived in Los Angeles at one point, but then later they was livin' up around Oakland. After Walter became famous, his sisters would come visit him in Chicago. Walter had a girlfriend named Alma Lee. I would see her out and about with Walter. She had a baby girl who looked just like Walter.

When he didn't drink, Little Walter was a dynamic performer. He could do the same things he did on records. He could do that and *more*. I heard him play stuff in the clubs that you never heard on a record. If they had put it on a record, it would have been smash hit after smash hit.

::::

The first time I saw Big Walter Horton was in 1953.[1] He was playin' with Muddy Waters at the Zanzibar. I remember that Muddy had that song "She's All Right" out then. I went to the Zanzibar and there was Big Walter, sittin' at a table. Muddy had sent for him to come from Memphis, and he blew the shit out of the harp that night.

Big Walter wouldn't stay in Chicago long. He'd come here and play for two or three weeks, and then, once the weather would get cold, Muddy and them would look up and Walter would've gone back to Memphis.

Big Walter was a dynamite harp player. When you heard him play, you knew that he wasn't no run-of-the-mill harmonica player. Big Walter used his tongue to do all his stuff. He had somethin'

1. Harmonica genius Walter Horton (1921–1981) was recording in Memphis before he was out of his teens. Horton did sessions for Sam Phillips's fledgling Sun label in the early 1950s and alternated between Memphis and Chicago during the next decade. Horton had a brief stint with the Muddy Waters band in 1953, and his spectacular gifts made him a sought-after session player in Chicago. He recorded his own LP for Chess, *The Soul of Blues Harmonica*, in 1964. Alligator released a brilliant album featuring Horton and his protégé Carey Bell in 1972, and another stellar Horton release, *Fine Cuts*, appeared on Blind Pig Records in 1977. Walter Horton recorded with Johnny Winter and Fleetwood Mac and had a cameo appearance in the 1980 film *The Blues Brothers*. He was inducted into the Blues Hall of Fame in 1983.

special on the harmonica, but he just didn't have the style or the charisma.

One time me and Johnny Shines was playin' at 43rd and Greenwood. It wasn't no big deal, just a little Monday-night thing. And Big Walter came in there while we was playin'. Big Walter and Johnny Shines worked together quite a bit. And so Big Walter came in there and said, "Boy, let me show you how to blow that harp." And he grabbed the harp and started blowin', and Johnny said somethin' like, "Wait a minute, you're interferin' with what we're doin'." Big Walter said, "I'll kick the motherfucker's ass!" and Johnny Shines said, "You won't kick *my* motherfuckin' ass!"

I got to know Big Walter pretty well. We played on shows together. He was an interesting guy. Big Walter loved to drink. He liked that whiskey. One time, when I was doin' a little drinkin', too, we was down at this club on 39th and Cottage. Big Walter had a half a pint, and he had his old lady with him. And she said, "Give Billy Boy a drink." He looked at her and said, "I got to give Billy Boy some?"

The two Sonny Boys was gifted poets who played the harmonica, and the two Walters was instrumentalists. Little Walter was a great singer. Big Walter wasn't much of a singer. But neither of those guys had to sing to get over. They could really jam on the harmonica.

I asked Big Walter one time about the harmonica, and he told me, "If I show you, then I won't have no goddamn job!"

: : :

Rice Miller came to Chicago in 1963 to make that record "Help Me." He was playin' up on Madison and he was lookin' for a bass player. I told him that my brother was playin' bass for Howlin' Wolf, so Rice Miller ended up usin' Jerome on some gigs and we became kind of friendly for a while.

I went into this club one time and Rice Miller was sittin' at the bar, and we talked. He said, "You think I can't play, but ask Leonard Chess." I knew he could play, but I didn't like his singin' or his style.

Now Rice Miller, he was a great harmonica player and a good singer and everything, but I never would have wanted to play the harmonica and sing the blues if *he* had been the Sonny Boy on those records I heard when I was a boy. Rice Miller didn't move me. He went over big and made a lot of money and made a lot of records and everything, but to me he just didn't have that feelin'.

When Rice Miller was down South, he was singin' Sonny Boy Williamson's songs 'cause he didn't have no songs of his own. But Rice Miller had the ability, and after he took the man's name and claimed his fame and started writin', he found out that he was a good songwriter and he wrote in his own style.

Rice Miller could drink, drink, drink, and steady play. He'd keep a half a pint in his back pocket. He'd be drinkin' all the time, but he could still take care of business. I recorded one of his tunes, "Trust My Baby," on an album I made over in France. I liked a few things he did, like "Help Me." I ain't takin' nothin' away from him. To each his own.

:::

After "I Ain't Got You" came out, I got booked at the New Era Club in Nashville. Kid King's Combo was the house band there, and they backed me up. They were a great band. They recorded "Chocolate Sundae" and a bunch of other instrumentals for Excello Records. The New Era Club was one of the top black clubs in Nashville. All the great recording artists played there, like Jimmy Witherspoon. Jody Williams and Memphis Slim played there a few months before I came in.

I played the New Era Club for two weeks. Joe Tex came in there for my last two nights at the club and did two weeks there after I left. Joe Tex was a real hot act. He was only two or three years older than I was, and he didn't have hit records yet, but he was real polished. I mean, he was *dynamite*. Joe Tex was from Texas. I think he came up with some of the gospel groups. I really like Joe Tex's music and style and everything. I do a lot of his songs. If I get the opportunity to record again, I'd like to record Joe Tex's "Anything You Wanna Know."

There was a black university in Nashville named Fisk University. A lot of fine, beautiful chicks went to that school. Man, that gig was like a holiday.

: : :

"I Wish You Would" didn't turn out to be a smash hit, but it was a good-selling record, and Vee-Jay had me come in for another session in October of 1955, so they could get a follow-up record out.

We used pretty much the same band as we used on the "I Wish You Would" session. Jody Williams was on guitar, Henry Gray played piano, and Earl Phillips was on drums. Instead of Milton Rector on electric bass, we used Quinn Wilson on upright bass. Quinn Wilson was a jazz bass player. It would have been better if we had used an electric bass on that session. That upright didn't have no weight on it and didn't add nothin' to the record.

At that second Vee-Jay session, we cut four tunes: "You've Got Me Wrong," "I Ain't Got You," "Don't Stay Out All Night," and "Here's My Picture."

Jesse Cryor wrote "You've Got Me Wrong." He was an older guy. Cryor was one of those guys who would go down to Vee-Jay and pitch their songs, and then Vee-Jay would tell their artists, "Here's a song we'd like you to do on your next session." I met Cryor at Vee-Jay.

Calvin Carter wrote "I Ain't Got You." Vee-Jay had already recorded that song with Jimmy Reed, but they didn't like his take on it. Jimmy Reed was one of those guys who had his own style. He didn't do other people's songs as good as he did his own songs. Jimmy made the record in his style, but Calvin wanted more of a swingin', upbeat thing, so Vee-Jay asked me and Jody to do it. They released Jimmy Reed's version twenty years later on an LP. Some people prefer Jimmy Reed's version to mine, but Calvin Carter and the people at Vee-Jay didn't, and so they didn't release it. My version had that signature guitar part that Jody Williams put in there.

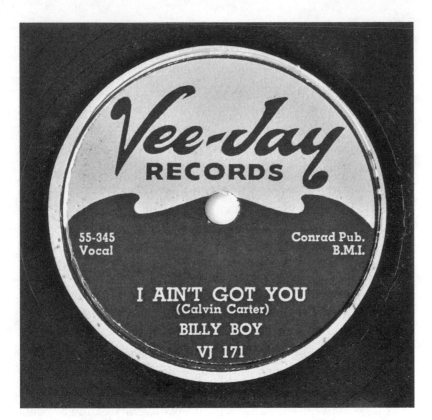

"I Ain't Got You," 1955
Bill Greensmith

It was my version of "I Ain't Got You" that the English rock groups like the Yardbirds heard and covered in the 1960s.

Vee-Jay put out all four of those tunes on two singles. "I Ain't Got You" had "Don't Stay Out All Night" as the flip side, and "Here's My Picture" was released with "You've Got Me Wrong" as the B side.

If I had made my first few Vee-Jay records with any of the other guitar players around Chicago but Jody Williams, they wouldn't have went nowhere, 'cause those other players wouldn't have had the ideas that Jody had.

Jody was young, the same age as I was, and he had his own ideas. Jody would create stuff, like that guitar intro on "I Ain't Got You" and those swingin' solos of his. He played some dynamite guitar on Bo Diddley's "Who Do You Love." He had fire and a lot of feelin' in his playin'. There was somethin' about Jody. He had that magic touch. Jody was awesome. He could add so much to a record. He knew how to really put you over if he was playin' behind you.

Jody Williams was the genius behind "Love Is Strange," the big hit record that Mickey and Sylvia had in 1956. That's Jody. Jody created that. He didn't write the song, but it was his guitar playin'—his music—that made that record what it was.

Bo Diddley wrote "Love Is Strange" and recorded it for Chess Records. In 1956 Jody Williams went out on the road with Bo to New York. Jody had just played a cool guitar riff on a record by Billy Stewart called "Billy's Blues." When Jody played "Love Is Strange" with Bo Diddley on a show at the Apollo Theater in New York, he put his "Billy's Blues" riff in there.

Mickey and Sylvia was on that show, and they heard Bo do "Love Is Strange" with Jody's guitar lick and asked Bo if they could cover it.[2] Mickey was Mickey Baker, the famous guitar player. He had played on lots of sessions with people like Ray Charles. The average guitar player couldn't have played Jody's guitar lick on "Love Is Strange," but Mickey Baker was an advanced player and he could do it. Bo was in awe of Mickey, 'cause Bo felt that Mickey was so advanced over him as a guitar player. So Bo Diddley told him he could do it.

Mickey and Sylvia recorded their own version of "Love Is Strange" with Mickey playin' Jody's guitar part from "Billy's Blues." It came out on one of RCA Victor's subsidiary labels and it was a

2. Mickey Baker was a prominent session guitarist and music teacher when he formed a duo act called Mickey and Sylvia with one of his students, Sylvia Vanderpool, in 1954. Their 1956 version of Bo Diddley's song "Love Is Strange" hit number one on the R&B charts and sold more than a million copies for RCA. After a two-year hiatus, Mickey and Sylvia reunited to record for RCA and launch their own label and music publishing company. Sylvia Vanderpool helped found the Sugar Hill rap label in 1979 and died in 2011. Mickey Baker moved to France in the 1960s and died there in 2012.

smash hit. It's just my opinion, but I will tell anybody that if Jody's guitar lick hadn't been on that record, it wouldn't have sold that big, 'cause it was no ordinary boogie lick or B. B. King lick or Jimmy Reed lick. It was unusual. It was different. It was Jody's, and it got taken away from him.

Bo Diddley made money from Mickey and Sylvia's version of "Love Is Strange," and he deserved that 'cause he wrote the song. He didn't put his own name on there, he used the name of his first wife, Ethel Smith—we called her Tootsie—'cause he thought that Leonard Chess didn't want him recording for anybody else or that he should be loyal to Leonard. Bo and Mickey Baker made a lot of royalties from that record at the time. But Jody got nothing, from either Bo or Mickey and Sylvia. No money, no recognition at all. Jody created that riff. It was his thing. If you listen to that record, subtract the guitar and see what you got.

You know that story *The Phantom of the Opera*, about the guy who wanted to kill another guy for stealin' his music? Jody was all mad over "Love Is Strange." He was seethin'. He felt like he got a dirty deal and a slap in the face. Bo Diddley didn't *have* to give Jody money, 'cause he wrote that record, but all Bo or Mickey had to do was put Jody's name on there and Jody would have gotten his just reward.

"Billy's Blues" was released on Argo Records, which was owned by Leonard Chess. Leonard sued RCA Victor over "Love Is Strange," and won, but Jody got nothin' out of that, either, 'cause the court said that you can't copyright a lick. That's what they still say, even today. Like that song "Pinetop's Boogie Woogie" from 1928. All the boogie-woogie piano players from that time on have used some of Pinetop Smith's licks. Or the "Hoochie Coochie Man" riff. You can't copyright those riffs.

Jody was so disgusted that he quit the music business. He didn't touch a guitar for thirty years. Jody was a dynamic musician who felt that he'd been wronged. But he was a genius and very creative, and he could do other things. He had a lot of other talents besides music. He worked in electronics. Jody made art. He fixed clocks. He had his own business installing burglar alarms. If you wanted your home wired up, he could do all of that.

And then in 2018, just before Jody died, it turned out that after all that worldwide airplay over the years, there was ten million dollars in accumulated back royalties for "Love Is Strange." And that money was divided between Mickey Baker's family and Bo Diddley's family. Bo Diddley's family got two million of it. Jody got nothin'. Jody was in poor health, and he and his family could have used that money. So the only person that got screwed in all these deals—*really* screwed—was Jody Williams. He didn't get a dime. Even today, I really feel bad for Jody.

:::

In January of 1956, I was playin' with my band at a place on 43rd and Oakenwald. Big Smokey Smothers had replaced Bobby Lee on guitar. Earl Hooker came in one night around New Year's Eve.[3] He had just come back from Oklahoma, and he was lookin' for a new band to take down there. Junior Wells had been down there with him, but Earl said that Junior had been actin' crazy and talkin' to himself. Earl asked if we wanted to go to Oklahoma with him. He asked for my phone number, so I wrote it down for him. Earl couldn't read or write too well, so he took the pencil and drew a harmonica under my name so he'd remember whose number it was.

Earl would take a band out of town and work 'em for a couple of weeks, then he wouldn't pay 'em right and they wouldn't play

---

3. Earl Zebedee Hooker (1929–1970) moved to Chicago from his native Mississippi with his family in 1930. Hooker contracted tuberculosis as a child and endured frequent hospitalizations throughout his life. Hooker taught himself how to play the guitar and was profoundly influenced by the technique and showmanship of T-Bone Walker and slide-guitar master Robert Nighthawk. Hooker recorded extensively as a front man and a studio guitarist for many labels, including King, Rockin', Sun, Argo, Vee-Jay, States, United, Cuca, Arhoolie. Blue Thumb, and Bluesway. He died at age forty from complications of tuberculosis.

with him no more. He wouldn't keep no band too long, 'cause he'd promise you one thing and then, when you'd get down there after a week or two, the money would be different than what he had said it would be. So you'd quit and then Earl would come back to Chicago—he lived with his mother—and look for a new band.

Earl said that down in Oklahoma we would get fifteen dollars a night and play six nights a week. All I had goin' in Chicago was this little gig, two nights a week, so I told him I would do it. Earl hired me 'cause I had the three pieces and at that time I was mostly a singer. I could sing everybody's records. And that's how we ended up going to Oklahoma with Earl Hooker for about three or four weeks.

Earl, me, Smokey Smothers, and Billy Davenport—he was tryin' to get away from this woman he was livin' with—left Chicago in Earl's car the day after New Year's, around midnight. We was headin' for East St. Louis, where Earl was goin' to get a piano player. It was snowin' like mad all over the highway. Earl had bad tires, and we was havin' flat tires all the way down there.

So Earl is drivin' down the highway on these bad tires, and he's drivin' fast. Earl was a roadmaster. He had been on the road for years. I was sittin' up front, and Smokey and Billy was in the back seat. Billy was scared to death by Earl's driving. He's in the back seat, faintin' and havin' blackouts and fallin' out. And he was sayin', "Stop the car! Stop the car!"

Earl used to stutter, and he was lookin' back at Billy and sayin', "Say, m-m-man, what's wrong with that m-m-motherfucker?"

Billy was so desperate that he offered to drive. Earl was kinda tired, so he pulled over to let Billy take over the drivin'. I was half asleep and not payin' attention.

We found out right away that Billy was a terrible driver. He was all over the highway.

Earl said, "Man, p-p-pull the goddamn car over and get the fuck outta that d-d-driver's seat!" And he got back behind the wheel.

We found out later that Billy had never drove a car before in his life. He was so scared of Earl's drivin' that he pretended that he could drive a car. It's a wonder we didn't get killed.

We got to East St. Louis that morning, and Earl drove us to a little house. There was maybe a hundred musicians in there. Pinetop Perkins was livin' there. All kinds of bass players and drummers lived there. Any kind of musician you'd want. Earl went in there lookin' for a piano player.

After a while Earl came out with Johnny "Big Moose" Walker, the great singer and piano player. Moose had on a nice maroon suit. He had just gotten off a tour with Lowell Fulson, and that was the uniform he wore in Fulson's band. Earl and Moose knew each other, 'cause they had played together before, but that was the first time I met Moose. And we lit out for Lawton, Oklahoma.

When we got down to Missouri, Earl stopped, and I went into this place to get somethin' to eat. There was nothin' but white people in there. I was standin' there and nobody would ask me if I wanted somethin'. They was ignorin' me. I guess they thought I was crazy, 'cause I didn't know what was goin' on. And when I went back outside Earl said, "You can't go in there!" I said, "Why in the fuck didn't you tell me? Why didn't you say somethin'? Shit!"

We finally got to Lawton. Earl went over *big* down in Oklahoma. Everybody down there was waitin' for him to come back. Everybody liked Earl everywhere he went. The whole town would be sayin' "Earl Hooker, Earl Hooker."

Lawton was right next to Fort Sill, and there was an air force base near there, too, so that's how the town made its money. Earl had worked with a musician named Earl Prindell. Prindell's father was a soldier stationed in Lawton and got him gigs down there. That's how Earl Hooker got established in Lawton—playin' gigs there with Earl Prindell.

There was a lot of prostitutes in Lawton, and Billy started talkin' to one of 'em. When Billy met a woman, he would latch onto 'em like a baby. You ever see a little baby cryin' and grabbin' when its mama walks away? That's what Billy would do with women. He latched onto this girl, and he would follow her to the bathroom. She'd go to the bathroom, and he'd be right behind her. Everybody was sayin', "Man, what's up with that?"

Earl was a master guitar player. He was way out ahead of his time. He would come up with all kinds of great stuff. Like the guitar riff on that Ray Sharpe song "Linda Lu"—Earl was playin' all that stuff way back there. He would jam on that guitar, and the guitar would be talkin' for itself. Anything that could be played on the guitar, Earl could play it. He used to play country and western music down in Oklahoma. Earl used to go all through Texas and places like that, and a lot of them guys down there stole a lot of his beats. Earl just couldn't sing. Or he didn't like his voice. If he'd been a fairly good singer, he would have been much more in demand as an artist.

Earl's sister, Earline, was a *great* singer. After we got to Lawton, Earl told the guy at the club we was playin' at about his sister and told him he should send for Miss Earline Hooker. So they sent for her to come down there, and she came down and showed up in blue jeans. The club owner's wife owned a dress shop, and she gave Earline three or four nice gowns to wear on stage and everything.

The guy that owned the club also owned a hotel. The guitar player Lee Cooper, a piano player named Cookie, and several other musicians was stayin' there.[4] They had come down there with Earl, and when they fell out with him about the money they stayed down there in Lawton and lived for free in this guy's hotel. We was all stayin' in rooms upstairs from the club. Earline had the room right next door to Earl, and I had the room on the other side of Earl's.

One day I heard some racket and went out in the hall. Earline was out there with a paring knife in each hand, and she was bangin' on Earl's door. She was sayin', "Open this door, Zebedee!" His

4. Echford Lee Cooper Jr. (ca. 1925–ca. 1966) was well known by his musical contemporaries in Chicago, but because his brief career was spent as a sideman, he is little known today. Cooper was an early master of the electric guitar, and during the 1950s he found steady work at Chess Records, recording with Big Bill Broonzy and Washboard Sam, among others. Cooper succeeded Willie Johnson as Howlin' Wolf's guitar player for a period in the mid-1950s.

family called Earl "Zebedee." Earline was sayin', "Open this door, motherfucker! I'll cut the shit out of you! I'll cut your motherfuckin' throat!" Earl just hid in his room, and Earline eventually gave up and went on back to her room.

Earline was supposed to be the star attraction, so the plan was for her to stay upstairs until later in the show and then make a big entrance dressed in one of these new gowns that the owner's wife had fixed up for her. But on her first night Earline walked in too early in her blue jeans when Earl was jammin' on the guitar, so they took her upstairs to wait for her entrance. And then, when it was time for her to appear, she didn't come down for showtime, so the club owner went upstairs lookin' for her. He found Earline in bed with a soldier, a customer. She was drunk, and she cursed him out. "Who the fuck is that at the motherfuckin' door? You dumb motherfucker, can't you see I'm in here? Motherfucker, don't come in here!"

When Earline finally made her entrance that night, she didn't come down wearin' one of the dresses the club owner's wife had given her. She was wearin' blue jeans and a blouse. She just walked up on the bandstand, grabbed the mic, said, "All right, motherfuckers, play such and such," and started singin'.

Earl knew he made a mistake, 'cause when Earline would get crazy and everything, he'd just run and hide from her. He'd get embarrassed and would just stay in his room. Earline would get drunk and want to come downstairs and fight with her brother and call him all kinda names. But she had a beautiful voice and she could play a little bit on any instrument. She could play the harmonica and play some on the guitar and play a little piano, but she didn't go in for them that much. She had a hell of a voice, though. If Earl had had the voice his sister had, with his guitar playin', he would've *really* went over.

So in the end, after four or five weeks, I left Earl for the same reason everybody left him. And that blues station in Gallatin, Tennessee, that broadcast all over the South and north to Chicago, was

Left to right: Earl Hooker, Billy Davenport, and Billy Boy Arnold, Lawton, Oklahoma, 1956
Billy Boy Arnold

playin' my new record.[5] I heard 'em announce, "Here's a new one by Billy Boy—'Don't Stay Out All Night.'" And then they played "I Ain't Got You." So I said, "Man, I'm goin' back to Chicago. My record is out." And so I left.

5. WLAC was a fifty-thousand-watt AM radio station in Nashville that became famous in the 1950s for blasting black rhythm and blues throughout the South and much of the Midwest. Colorful disc jockey Gene Nobles hosted *The Midnight Special*, a rhythm and blues show sponsored by Randy's Record Shop in Gallatin, Tennessee. The shop became a thriving mail-order business, thanks to the program's popularity, and owner Randy Wood used his profits to start his own record label, Dot.

Earl Hooker was a genius on the guitar, like Little Walter was a genius on the harp. He played some real great stuff, but he didn't know how to coordinate it and make it into a three-minute song. Earl played from inspiration. He'd forget it as soon as he played it. Maybe he'd play it again some other time, and maybe he wouldn't. But the other guitar players studied his records. Freddy King got most of his stuff from Earl.

Earl was from Clarksdale, Mississippi, Muddy's hometown. He moved to Chicago with his mother when he was young. Earl was a famous guitar player when he was just a kid. In 1946, when Earl was sixteen or seventeen, Sonny Boy Williamson took him and a friend of Earl's named Vincent Duling, who also played guitar, from Chicago to Jackson, Tennessee. One night in Theresa's, I showed Earl and Vincent a picture of Sonny Boy, and they said, "That's Sonny Boy. We went to Jackson, Tennessee, with him. Carried him down there." Earl went down South when he was just a kid and played with a lot of bands. He played with Rice Miller and all of 'em. I saw a photo of him playin' on the *King Biscuit* radio show when he was about twelve years old. A little kid with an acoustic guitar.

When Earl was in Chicago, he lived with his mother and Earline right around the corner from where Sonny Boy lived, in a basement apartment at 32nd and South Parkway. Muddy Waters used to come to Earl Hooker's mother's apartment and get her permission for Earl to play behind him in the clubs when he was underage. Earl's mother was a nice lady. She tried to deal with Earline, but she would say that she couldn't do nothin' with the girl. Earline's mother told me once, "That girl is dangerous. Be careful, 'cause she'll cut you and all that stuff." Earline would stay with her mother when she wanted to stay there, or when she was through with a boyfriend. Everyone knew Earline. She'd get drunk and come in the clubs, and she'd run up on the bandstand and grab the mic and start singin'. And everybody would like it, 'cause Earline had a beautiful voice.

Everybody thought that Earl and Earline was twins 'cause they looked so much alike, but Earl was older than Earline by two or three years. Earl called Earline "Grandma." "Man," he'd say, "Don't mess with Grandma. Grandma's *crazy*." I don't think Earline ever made any records, given the kind of person she was. She drank and clowned and she'd bite. Earline was a wild woman.

Earl didn't drink and he didn't smoke. He was a guitar freak and a musician, that's what he was. His whole life was about playin' that guitar. While we was stayin' in that hotel in Oklahoma, I'd wake up in the morning around seven or eight o'clock, and I could hear him in his room on that guitar, playin' all kinds of great stuff. He was real creative, and he loved to play his guitar. He had a lot of women, everywhere he went. The women was crazy about him. Earl had a lot of kids. He had kids all over the country.

Earl didn't care about a regular band, 'cause he didn't need one. He could pick up a guitar player and a bass player and a piano player and that's it. And if you stayed with him two or three weeks, you were gonna fall out about the money, 'cause he was gonna cut the money he promised you almost in half.

Earl was tricky with the money, but he was basically a nice guy. Earl was a road runner, a wanderer type of a guy. He wouldn't stay in no one place too long. Runnin' up and down the road like he did, you don't eat proper or take care of yourself. That's a bad life. Earl had caught tuberculosis when he was real young, and he couldn't stand still long enough to try to get himself cured, 'cause he had to play. He just went on and on until the end. Earl was in the hospital just before he died, but he snuck out of there. If he had stayed in the hospital, he might have got himself together, but he just couldn't stay off the bandstand. Earl was only forty years old when he died from that tuberculosis.

: : :

When me, Smokey Smothers, and Billy Davenport got back to Chicago from Lawton—we left Earl Hooker and Big Moose Walker down there—Billy brought Delores, the girl he had been seein' in Oklahoma, back with him. Then he disappeared. We didn't know

Left to right: Reynolds Howard, Billy Boy Arnold, Jerome Arnold, and Jody Williams, Rock and Roll Lounge, ca. 1959
Billy Boy Arnold

where he went. We didn't know if he was gonna drop Delores and go back to that woman he'd been livin' and eatin' out of sardine cans with.

Right after we got back to town, I ran into Shakey Jake on the street. "Hey, Billy Boy," he said. "Y'all need a band? 'Cause I got two bad boys who can play the guitar—Syl Johnson and Odell Campbell." And they *were* good. I wanted to do stuff like "Blue Suede Shoes" and Ray Charles's hits, and they could handle that material. They had been workin' with a drummer named Duke Tyson, so the four of us started workin' at Club Alabam at 2711 Wentworth.

The lady that Billy Davenport had left behind in Chicago showed up at Club Alabam one night. She knew we had come back from Oklahoma, 'cause they was advertisin' me on the radio and everything. So she came down there, and she said, "Where's Billy?" and I said, "I don't know." Like I said, he was kind of a weird guy.

Several years later I was visiting a friend at St. Luke's Hospital in Chicago, and I passed this guy and said, "That's Billy Davenport." Billy saw me, but he didn't want to talk. He was wearing a green cap and gown and everything. He was assistin' in the operating room at St. Luke's Hospital!

:::

Vee-Jay called me in for a third session in November of 1957. I had been playin' in the clubs with Syl Johnson—his real name is Sylvester Thompson—on lead guitar and Odell Campbell on rhythm guitar, so I used them. Henry Gray played piano again, which was great, and I called up Fred Below and got him to come down and play drums. Below was not only the greatest blues drummer of 'em all, he was a great guy with a lot of interests—he was a good photographer—and enjoyed things and got along with everybody. We didn't have a bass player on that session. At that time, there still wasn't nobody playin' electric bass but Milton Rector. Everybody had two guitars in their bands in those days. Muddy had two guitars. Little Walter had two guitars.

I was busy playin' at Sylvio's at that time, so we didn't do a lot of rehearsin' for that third session. We recorded four tunes: "My Heart Is Crying," "Kissing at Midnight," "Heartache and Trouble," and "How Come You Leave Heaven." Those were all original tunes of mine. There was nobody around writin' songs for blues in those days but Willie Dixon, and he was just writin' for hitmakers like Muddy, Little Walter, and the Wolf, you know. I don't think that we ever played any of those four songs we recorded on the bandstand before the session.

The session went fine, but when I think back, I didn't take the time to really work on the material as hard as I should have. Not enough time was spent on it. When we worked up "Kissing at Midnight," I asked Syl Johnson to play somethin' different on the guitar, and he came up with that riff he played on the record. He heard that riff down in Mississippi. He had heard different guys down there play that lick. It really added to the record, so I gave Syl part of the writer's credit on that song.

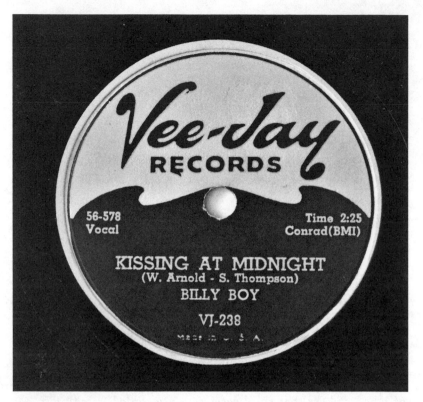

"Kissing at Midnight," 1956
Bill Greensmith

Vee-Jay ended up releasin' "Kissing at Midnight" with "My Heart Is Crying" as the flip side. They never released the other two tunes we did. I don't even remember how they went. "Kissing at Midnight" did all right.

When "Kissing at Midnight" came out, Vee-Jay wanted me to go out on the road and tour behind the record. If you had a hot record, those big New York talent agencies like Shaw would hire you and put you on the road. I was with the Shaw agency then. Little Walter was with them, and I think Ray Charles was represented by them, too. There was also the Gale agency. Jimmy Reed was with Gale. If you had enough hits and there was a demand for you, you could stay with one of those good agencies. Shaw got me some gigs, but I couldn't keep those hit records goin' to have them book me steady.

The way it worked was the agency would book you a gig and sign a contract with the promoter sayin' that so much money would go to you and so much money would go to the agency. But it got to the point where if you played a dance or somethin', the local promoter would disappear with all the money a half hour before the show. They'd get in their car, or sometimes they'd just run. Bo Diddley told me that he had to chase some of them promoters down South through the cornfields to get his money.

So the Shaw and Gale agencies stopped that. They changed it to where if a local promoter wanted a name artist to do a show, the promoter had to send half the money to the agency in advance. When the band got to the gig, the local promoter had to give 'em the other half before the artist played a lick.

The Shaw agency got me a spot on a southern tour with Fats Domino and Johnny "Guitar" Watson to support "Kissing at Midnight." The tour would start in New Orleans and go all the way through Louisiana, Texas, Alabama, and Arkansas. For the first two weeks, we would be goin' out with two bands—Fats's band and Joe Jones's band—playin' big auditoriums, and then we would part company with Fats and go on for another couple of weeks with Joe Jones's band, through Texas and thereabouts.[6]

I needed to bring my own guitar player. Syl Johnson was my regular guitar player, but he was in the National Guard, so he couldn't travel. I had been workin' with Big Smokey, too, but he wasn't playin' much guitar, and his timin' was bad.

6. New Orleans native Joseph Charles "Joe" Jones (1926–2005) was a Juilliard-trained talent who could cover all the musical bases—writing, arranging, playing piano, and singing. His band, the Atomic Rebops, backed singer Roy Brown on his 1947 hit, "Good Rockin' Tonight." After working as B. B. King's pianist and arranger, Jones began recording as a singer. His 1960 hit "You Talk Too Much" reached number three on *Billboard*'s Hot 100 and number nine on its Hot R&B chart. After his recording career ended, Jones worked in music publishing and production.

Howlin' Wolf had just fired his great guitar player, Willie Johnson. He and Wolf had fallen out. Willie was just hangin' around, so I decided to take Willie Johnson with me. Syl Johnson let me borrow his guitar, 'cause Willie Johnson didn't even have a guitar.

The Shaw agency sent me and Willie Johnson to New Orleans on the Panama Limited. Up until the 1940s, black people couldn't ride on the Panama Limited. It was a special, high-class, high-speed train for white people only. There was a big-time black preacher in Chicago named Reverend Clarence H. Cobbs. My grandmother went to his church. He tried to ride the Panama Limited, but they refused him. Cobbs was friends with President Roosevelt's wife, so he talked to her, and Mrs. Roosevelt told the railroad to let Reverend Cobbs ride the Panama Limited. And that's how they broke the color barrier down so blacks could ride the Panama Limited.

The Panama Limited went straight from Chicago down to New Orleans. It was a nice trip. We had our own compartment and everything. We got to New Orleans on Mother's Day, 1957. We was supposed to meet Johnny "Guitar" Watson and Joe Jones and his band there.

When we checked in to our hotel, the lady there said, "Another guy on the show with you all just checked in. He just went across the street to the restaurant." So me and Willie went over to the restaurant to get somethin' to eat, and we met Donnie Elbert, a young singer from Buffalo, New York, who was also on the show. He had a record out called "What Can I Do." He recorded for Deluxe, which was a subsidiary of King.

Donnie said, "I'm gonna play my record for y'all," and he went over to the jukebox and put on a record. We thought it was a lady singin'. We thought that he had played the wrong record. When Donnie came back, I said, "I thought you was gonna play your record." He said, "I did. That *was* my record." Donnie was a straight guy, but he sang in a real high falsetto.

Donnie had conk hair. In Chicago we called that a "process." This was common with black musicians up North, but black people down

Left to right: Unidentified, Willie Johnson, unidentified, Billy Boy Arnold, and Donnie Elbert, 1957
Billy Boy Arnold

South didn't wear no processes in those days. And when acts from up North like the Five Royales who had their hair all done up would go down South, the blacks down there thought they was weird. If you had a conk, they thought you was a sissy or a female impersonator or somethin'.

The first show was in New Orleans. Donnie Elbert sang his song, which was real big in New Orleans 'cause it was a doo-wop type of song. It wasn't a blues. The people down South, they didn't like blues as much as the people in Chicago.

Donnie was down on his knees in front of the audience singin' "What Can I Do" in that high voice of his. And this woman in the audience—she was high and had a bottle in her purse—came down to where Donnie was and started hollerin', "Sing, bitch! Sing, bitch!" And she hit Donnie with that purse with the bottle in it, and it staggered him. Almost knocked him down. And she's yellin', "Sing, bitch!"

We left New Orleans and went all the way through Louisiana, Texas, Oklahoma, Georgia—all down through there. Fats Domino had a big record out at that time, and we did about two weeks with him. This was a big show with two bands, and we was playin' these great big auditoriums to large audiences of whites, blacks, Mexicans—everybody.

Down South, the races wasn't supposed to mingle. Sometimes they would have the white kids upstairs in the balcony. Other times, they'd have a big rope that would divide the auditorium—the blacks on one side and the whites on the other. They would have a lot of policemen and security there, but when the music started playin', the white kids would run over the police, throw the rope down, and come over and start dancin' with the black kids, 'cause this was two black bands playin' black music.

Some of us traveled by car, but most of us was travelin' in these big buses. We stayed in black hotels, of course, 'cause of Jim Crow. In certain places down South, a white guy and a black guy couldn't even be on the same stage together. Once, when we were in Tupelo, Mississippi—we were on our way to Alabama somewhere—we stopped to get some hamburgers, and we had to go around to the kitchen and come in through the back door, 'cause blacks couldn't go through the front door.

We played Dallas on that tour, and one afternoon while we was there, I decided to go see a movie. I'm a big movie buff. Ever since I was a little bitty kid, I just loved the movies. I asked around, and somebody said, "Well, the movie theaters are down the street there, about four or five blocks."

So I'm walkin' down this street, and cabs are passing me every three or four seconds, so I said to myself, "Well, I'll grab a cab." I'm flaggin' these cabs, and every time I flagged one the white cab driver would look at me with a frown on his face like, "Are you crazy?" or, "Where are you from?" They didn't say nothin', they just kept movin'. I must have flagged about ten cabs goin' that way. I'm not aware, see, that cabs don't pick up blacks in Dallas.

It was only a few blocks, so I kept on walkin' and I finally got to the movie theater. I walked up to the ticket window, and the lady in the booth said, "You have to go around the back." So I went around the side, and there was another ticket window for black people. After I paid for my ticket, I had to go up an elevator to the balcony on the second floor, where the black people had to sit. You couldn't sit down on the main floor where the white people was. So I went up there, and there was a glass partition in front of the balcony. You're sittin' in the balcony, and there was a big plate of glass there between you and the movie, so you couldn't throw nothin' on the white people or anything like that. So *that* was an experience.

After the movie was over, I started walkin' back to our hotel. I passed by this great big tent where they was sellin' slices of watermelon. They must have had thousands of watermelons, and there was about three or four hundred white people hangin' around there. I decided to get a piece of watermelon. So I walked up there, and none of those white people ever said anything to me or asked me what I wanted. So then it dawned on me: *Damn! This is another one of them prejudice things. They don't serve blacks.* I finally got the message and went on back to the black hotel we was stayin' at.

So that was another experience. I'm learnin', you know. As far as I'm concerned, the only good thing about the South is the weather.

Willie Johnson played some dynamite guitar on that tour. He was known as a drinker, but during that two-week tour he might have had a beer or somethin', but he didn't get drunk. Everybody on that tour—including Fats Domino's guitar player and Johnny "Guitar" Watson—was amazed at how much guitar Willie knew and could play. He was a hell of a musician. Willie could play all kind of blues styles and all kinds of modern styles and in all kinds of tunings, whatever you wanted.

When we got to Atlanta, we ran into Jimmy Rogers and his band. They were down there to do a tour with Ann Cole, a singer who had a hot record with the original version of "Got My Mojo Working." Muddy Waters got that song from her. Some booking people in New York arranged for Jimmy and his band to back her up on this southern tour, and they sent Ann Cole to Atlanta to rehearse 'em.

So Ann Cole gets down to Atlanta with her horn charts and all that. Jimmy Rogers didn't have no bass player—just him and Poor Bob Woodfork on guitars. Jimmy Rogers couldn't play no lead guitar, and Poor Bob Woodfork couldn't play no more lead than Jimmy Rogers could. Jimmy didn't want a great guitar player showin' him up, so he's got *two* guys up there playin' bumpty bumpty on the guitar.

Jimmy had Big Walter Horton on harp, S. P. Leary on drums, and Henry Gray on piano. Ann Cole hands Big Walter a chart, and he says, "What the fuck am I supposed to do with this?" If they had had a lead guitarist—somebody like Willie Johnson, Syl Johnson, Matt Murphy, or Jody Williams—they could have been a solid band for Ann Cole. Henry Gray could read charts, Big Walter could have played with swing on the harp, and S. P. was a damn dynamite drummer. But she called New York and said, "I can't do nothin' with this band," so they sent Jimmy Rogers and them back.

Jimmy Rogers wanted to be a star. You sure can't blame him for that. He had a good voice and he made some really nice records. But Leonard Chess didn't have to worry about Jimmy Rogers, 'cause Leonard knew that Jimmy was just a supportive act. Jimmy Rogers didn't really have the personality for a bandleader. He wasn't forceful enough. He was shy and laid back. When they put him on the road after he had the hit "Walking by Myself," they had to send him back 'cause he didn't know how to take charge. And he didn't write no songs, just copied other people's stuff. He got a lot of his stuff from Sonny Boy Williamson.

I played with Jimmy at Sylvio's around the time Jimmy had that

"Going Away Baby" record out that had some beautiful harp on it by Little Walter. They had Muddy Waters's band, Jimmy Rogers's band, my band, and Howlin' Wolf's band. And one weekend we had Jimmy Reed over there, too.

One night I asked Jimmy to play his record "Going Away Baby." But without Walter on the harp, or another harp player who could play it, it wouldn't have been effective, so Jimmy didn't play it. So when I went up on the stage, *I* played it. Later he said, "I wonder why you did that?" And I said, "Well, *you* wouldn't play it!" I didn't know at the time that it was Sonny Boy Williamson's song. If I'd have known that, I'd have said, "Well, that was Sonny Boy's song, anyway!"

:::

I did my fourth and last session for Vee-Jay in November 1957. I brought Sunnyland Slim in to play piano on the session. Syl Johnson was on guitar. I wanted Odell Campbell on that session, but I couldn't find him, so I got Syl's brother Mack Thompson to play the other guitar. Reynolds Howard played drums. He was playin' with me in the clubs at the time.

We cut four tunes that day: "Prisoner's Plea," "Rockin' Itis," "No, No, No, No," and "Every Day, Every Night." "Prisoner's Plea" was written by a guy named C. L. Hawkins. That's an old song that goes way back to the 1920s. Vee-Jay asked me to do it, and I liked it pretty good. "Rockin' Itis," "No, No, No, No," and "Every Day, Every Night," weren't my tunes. A young guy named Ted Twiggs who wrote for Vee-Jay wrote those.

We had some problems on that session. Mack Thompson lost the beat on "Prisoner's Plea" and "Rockin' Itis." Reynolds Howard wasn't really a blues drummer, and he had never been in the studio before. The session would have gone better if we had had Odell Campbell. And we did "Prisoner's Plea" in a key that made my voice too high, so I never really liked my vocal on that tune.

Vee-Jay never did release "No, No, No, No" and "Every Day,

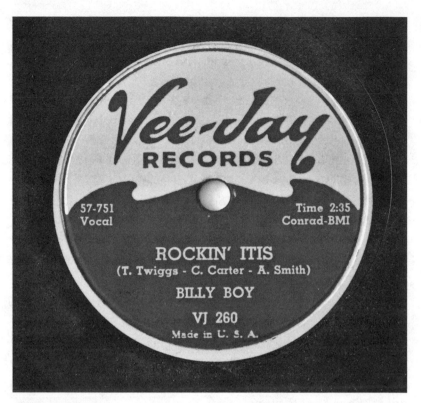

"Rockin' Itis," 1957
Bill Greensmith

Every Night." Those tunes came out years later on an LP from England. Vee-Jay put out "Rockin' Itis" with "Prisoner's Plea" on the flip side. That record was a hit in Pittsburgh and in different places.

My deal with Vee-Jay ran out after that fourth session. Leonard Chess pushed his records, but Vee-Jay didn't really put any effort behind theirs. They didn't have to do nothin' on Jimmy Reed, 'cause Jimmy Reed would come in and he had his songs, and it was just him on guitar and harmonica with a bass player and drummer behind him, and that was it. Vee-Jay was lookin' mostly for doo-wop and stuff like that. Like most black people at the time, they wasn't really interested in blues.

Startin' in March of 1957, after "Kissing at Midnight" came out, I played Fridays, Saturdays, and Sundays for three or four months at Sylvio's, on the same bill with Muddy Waters and Howlin' Wolf. When Sylvio found out how old I was, he asked me, "Well, how old was you back in 1951, when you used to come in with Big Bill and all those guys?" He had thought I was a man then, but I was only fourteen or fifteen.

Muddy, the Wolf, and me each used our own band on those shows. I had Syl Johnson on guitar. Wolf would play for an hour, then I would play for an hour, and then Muddy would play for an hour. One band would stop and the other one would come up, and then we'd rotate all over again. We'd start at nine o'clock and go until two in the morning. They was only chargin' a dollar at the door, but at that time people thought that was a lot of money.

One night when I was playin' on that triple bill, Syl Johnson couldn't make the show, so I got Matt Murphy and Jody Williams on guitars. Matt Murphy would work with me when he wasn't giggin' with Memphis Slim, and sometimes, when Memphis Slim wanted a night off, he'd have me front his band. Anyway, when Wolf's road man came in that night and saw those two giant guitar players, he dropped the stuff and ran back out there and said, "Man, he got Matt Murphy and Jody Williams!" So Wolf and his band came walkin' in and saw all these top guitar players, you know, and they knew they had to work that night. When we got through playin' our set, Muddy went into a huddle with his band, like they was football players. I got the impression that Muddy was tellin' 'em, "Get up there and play. Them young motherfuckers is kickin' ass!"

I was the young upstart, but that gig put me up there with those guys. One night the Wolf was on stage and Muddy's band and my band was sittin' at the bar. I asked Muddy, "Muddy, do you remember when I met you on 53rd and Cottage Grove in front of the Pershing Hotel? You was gettin' out of a black convertible Buick."

And he said, "Oh, yeah, I remember you. You was that little piss-tail boy!" I told Muddy that I wanted to go out on the road, and he said, "You keep makin' them good records and you'll go out on the road."

I got along with Muddy and the Wolf. I respected them and they treated me nice. These guys comin' along now, they're jealous. If you're an older musician, they want you to get out of the way and make room for them. I look at it like this: ain't nobody in nobody's way. I respected Sunnyland, Blind John, Big Bill. I wasn't challengin' them. I didn't think they was in my way. I was tryin' to get to where they *was*. I knew that I had to pay my dues and that it would take time.

Muddy Waters made it 'cause he had the talent, the voice, and a good strong record company behind him. Leonard had to build a band around Muddy. Lester Melrose didn't build no band around Sonny Boy Williamson. The session players either had it or they didn't. Sonny Boy was the kind of guy who could play with anybody. He could play with jazz bands and everybody. Muddy's thing was heavy, but Muddy was more limited.

Muddy was a nice guy, and a real professional in every sense of the word. Muddy let his band play. Once he got James Cotton, Muddy'd be sitting at the table with his girlfriend. Muddy stopped playin' guitar, and Cotton would be up there doing all the singin'.

James Cotton was a good friend of mine. I liked him, and I had the highest respect for him. He was a dynamite harmonica player and a great showman. He could sing all types of different songs and everything. Cotton was a real friendly guy—gregarious, outgoin'. He was the kind of guy you couldn't hold down. He had a lot of personality and a lot of drive. He had that powerful energy. Cotton wasn't no great singer, and he didn't have the creative qualities that Little Walter had on the harmonica, but he was a great showman and he had that push.

Cotton grew up in Mississippi, and he used to hear Rice Miller down there on the *King Biscuit* show. Rice Miller didn't have no records out at that time. He didn't record until 1951. Cotton says that he had some of John Lee Williamson's records, and that he thought he and Rice Miller was the same guy. I don't understand how he could possibly have thought that, 'cause they sound so different.

When Cotton was with Muddy, Muddy would let him get up there and sing all night, 'cause he didn't think of Cotton as competition. Muddy would stand back and say, "He can't sing, he can't sing," and laugh about it, you know. Cotton wouldn't sing Muddy's stuff. He would sing all the latest songs that people wanted to hear, like Bobby Bland's tunes. Cotton would sing all the bluesier rock-and-roll songs, and that gave him a lot of experience. When Cotton went out on his own, he got the right band—Matt Murphy and those guys—and they built a thing. So there are all these different ways to get to the same point.

When Otis Spann was in his band, Muddy Waters never let him sing. And I know why, 'cause he would have overthrown Muddy. Otis Spann was a *dynamite* vocalist. Oh, *man*. When Little Walter became a star and left his band, Muddy knew that Spann was his key man. Muddy didn't want Spann to get away, 'cause without Spann his sound wouldn't be what it was. And Leonard Chess wanted Spann to stay with Muddy. He knew that Spann was Muddy's backbone. That's why he wouldn't record Spann. He made one record with Spann, but he wasn't anxious to make a star out of him 'cause that would have been another star gone from Muddy. Spann didn't have that forceful personality, and he went along. Muddy held Otis down, with the help of Leonard Chess. Little Walter was more aggressive. He took off and did his own thing.

Otis Spann is the greatest blues piano player that I *ever* heard. The greatest in the world. Man, oh man, Spann was dynamite. I really loved Otis Spann. Spann was too heavy, man. He could tear 'em up. Every time I'd see Spann, I'd say, "Otis Spann—Muddy Waters's right-hand man." He was a dynamite guy, too.

Spann was a motherfucker on Muddy's records, but in the clubs you couldn't even hear his piano playin'. The main clubs had all those big old upright pianos that Memphis Slim and Johnny Jones and all of 'em played. When the guitars started bein' amplified, Sylvio bought Johnny Jones an electric piano, and guys like Sunnyland

Otis Spann and James Cotton rehearsing in Muddy Waters's basement, 1965
Photograph by Raeburn Flerlage; Chicago History Museum, ICHi-106051

Slim started gettin' 'em, too. But Spann wasn't assertive enough to get his own amp. When Spann was playin' with Muddy, they wasn't makin' that much money, so he didn't have an electric piano or an amplifier for his piano. You couldn't hear Spann at all when he played with Muddy in the clubs. You know that beautiful intro he played on the recording of "I Just Want to Make Love to You"? You didn't hear that live. Spann's playin' sold those records. They couldn't hold him down in the studio.

Howlin' Wolf was one hell of a showman. Howlin' Wolf *was* the show. The Wolf had that power. He was just a natural-born musician. He had a lot of personality. Wolf wasn't scared of people. He wasn't timid at all. Wolf had everything that people like. He was a crowd pleaser. That boomin' voice and that aggressiveness that he had on records was the same thing he put out when he was on the bandstand.

Wolf was the hardest workin' musician in Chicago. Little Walter would just sit down and play the harp. Muddy might have his moments on stage when he would get up and dance, but mostly he would just be cool. Muddy got to the place where he'd just sing a few numbers sittin' down, but Wolf was a drivin' kind of performer who worked hard for the people. And that's why even the blacks who didn't like blues would follow him wherever he played. Wolf could play *anywhere*, and he could always draw a black crowd.

When he first came to Chicago, Wolf had Hubert Sumlin and Jody Williams on guitar. Then Jody quit about the money. Wolf went down South to get a second guitar player who would do him justice, and he came back with Willie Johnson. Willie and Hubert had played together with Wolf down South before he came to Chicago, so they was reunited with the Wolf in Chicago. The first time I saw Willie Johnson with the Wolf, he was sittin' on the stage with a pair of blue jeans on.

But no matter who came through Wolf's band, Wolf was the star. He'd let Henry Gray or someone else do a song or two, but couldn't *nobody* outdo Wolf. Wolf didn't rely on the piano, the saxophone player, or the drummer. He had that unusual voice. That *power*.

Howlin' Wolf and band at Sylvio's, 1964
Photograph by Raeburn Flerlage; Chicago History Museum, ICHi-11043

Howlin' Wolf was a creative artist. He was progressive. He was always tryin' new stuff. That's why he had all them big hits. Wolf played a more versatile style of blues—his music had a beat to it. He had a *sound*, and that's what made him so powerful. *Nobody* had a voice like that. The Wolf was a great harp player, too. He had his own style on the harp.

Wolf was an operator, man. Wolf didn't do like a lot of musicians. He didn't drink or smoke pot. He wasn't that type of guy. Wolf was all business and all about the music, and that's what he did. If you played in his band, he expected a certain amount of respect for what he wanted you to do. He'd buy his band their stage clothes, and he'd fine you if you didn't have on the right socks or the wrong tie. He'd pay your Social Security, so if you quit or he fired you, you could draw unemployment compensation. Wolf was a good businessman. He didn't have to go to Leonard Chess to borrow money like those other guys. Leonard only had to give him the money he owed him.

Elmore James with a fan
Bill Greensmith/Blues Unlimited

Wolf went to night school! On the intermission, he'd be sittin'
down at a table over in the corner with his specs on, goin' over his
lessons.

Howlin' Wolf was really somethin'. He was just a unique person.
I don't know nobody comin' along that's doin' a thing like what Wolf

did. He was a nice guy, too. When I would sit in with him, Wolf would tell me, "When I'm gone, you gonna be a big star one day. Just keep on doin' what you doin'."

: : :

Sylvio's was Elmore James's home base in Chicago. Sylvio's was like a cabaret. It was only open on Thursday, Friday, Saturday, and Sunday. Elmore played those four nights every week, and he'd pack the house. I used to see Elmore there all the time, and he would always get me up to do a couple of numbers.

Elmore James was one of my favorite artists. He just had it all goin' on. Man, he was somethin' else. That voice and that slide! He was a great singer and a great guitar player. His voice was really dynamic. He had the talent, the gifts, and he could sing a whole lot of different stuff. He was an amazing performer. He had the charisma to draw the people, and they just really went for him. Everybody liked Elmore.

Sylvio said that Elmore was the greatest blues guitarist he had ever heard. Elmore was a nice guy, too. All the musicians had the highest regard for him, 'cause he was a master on that slide. Elmore could take that one signature slide lick of his and do so much with it. He was a guitar master without the slide, too. And Elmore was a great songwriter. Elmore James was a bad boy!

Elmore came to Chicago in 1951 and made that big hit, "Dust My Broom." Rice Miller played some great harmonica on that record. "Dust My Broom" was a huge hit. It went over so big that the record companies just wanted to keep that thing goin'.

Sylvio's was a music club, so there wasn't a lot of business during the day. For a while, Sylvio had Elmore open the club and tend bar in the daytime. So Elmore was sort of like runnin' the club two or three days a week, until in 1954 he got homesick for down South. He put a couple of cases of whiskey in the trunk of his car and went back to Mississippi. Against Sylvio's wishes, you know.

When Elmore came back to Chicago a year later, Homesick

James started playin' rhythm, the background guitar, with him. Homesick claimed that he was Elmore's cousin, but Homesick was *everybody's* cousin. If you was famous, you was Homesick's cousin. He was Elmore James's cousin. He was Sonny Boy Williamson's cousin. He used to call himself Homesick James Williamson! Homesick James was from Brownsville, Tennessee, about thirty miles from Jackson, where Sonny Boy was from, so he knew Sonny Boy growin' up.

Elmore drank, but I never saw him as a heavy drinker. In the clubs, you know, he'd be drinkin' all night, but it wasn't the drinkin' that got him. His heart gave out on him. Elmore had a heart attack, and after that he couldn't play. He'd just sit at the door with Sylvio, when he was well enough to do that.

But over time Elmore got stronger and everything and started back to playin'. That's when he went to New York and made those hit records for Bobby Robinson on the Fire label, "Bobby's Rock" and "The Sky Is Crying." Elmore did some things for the Chess brothers, but they didn't like him 'cause they couldn't control him. He was the type of guy that was smart and a guy who knew about the business, so he didn't like their system, I guess.

Elmore was around Muddy Waters's age, but he died in 1963. The last time I talked to Elmore, he told me, "Billy Boy, you just keep on blowin' that harp, man. You gonna be bad."

: : :

My brother Jerome started spendin' more time with me around 1958. When I was learnin' to play harp, Jerome didn't pay all that much attention to it, but by about 1958 he started gettin' interested in music. He saw Syl Johnson's brother Mack play bass, and he said, "I think I can play that." So he went and got himself a bass, and Jerome started playin' with Byther Smith and some smaller, unknown bands. He didn't sing, but he learned the bass real fast. He decided he wanted to get into music, and he was dedicated. When he got good, he started playin' with me, and then he got better and left me and went with Otis Rush, and then he moved up to playin' with Howlin' Wolf, Muddy Waters, Little Walter—everybody. Jerome could play all kinds of stuff.

All the while I was workin' in the clubs, I kept workin' on my music. I picked up the guitar again and started to learn how to play the bass. I started takin' lessons from Reggie Boyd around 1957 or '58. He's the one who started me into readin' music.

Reggie Boyd was a great guitar player who knew a lot about music. He was from Jackson, Tennessee. He knew Sonny Boy when he was a young kid down there, 'cause Sonny Boy's wife used to babysit him. Reggie came to Chicago when he was a teenager, and he met the Scott brothers, who also knew Sonny Boy. Later, Reggie joined the Army and became a paratrooper. When he came back to Chicago, Reggie went to music school on the GI Bill and learned to read, write, and arrange music.

Reggie was a great musician and a great teacher. Howlin' Wolf and Hosea Kennard, his piano player, took lessons from Reggie. Otis Rush took lessons from him, too. Reggie was the man in Chicago. He knew how to put it together. But he was an alcoholic. He drank and messed up a lot of times. He'd get high and not show up.

Reggie really didn't like blues. He wanted to play jazz. Reggie was doin' a lot of writin' and arrangin' for Chess Records. He worked a lot with Willie Dixon, and Dixon said, "Man, that Reggie Boyd, he wants to read everything." They'd be workin' on a song, and Willie would say, "We're gonna do this," and Reggie would write the parts out. Most of the blues musicians couldn't read or write music, and Reggie would show 'em how to do it.

A lot of the black musicians that came out of the South—especially the guitar players, and they was all from Mississippi—wanted to escape from the blues. They wanted to come to Chicago 'cause there wasn't much happenin' down South. You wasn't making no big money playin' those juke joints. But when they came to Chicago, they started bendin' those strings like B. B. King and stuff, you know. These guitar players would come to Chicago and say, "Man,

I want to get away from them blues. I don't wanna play no goddamn blues. I wanna play some *jazz*."

But you can't play jazz without a foundation. It would be like goin' right into college when you never went to kindergarten or grammar school. You need a foundation to play jazz. The blacks who played jazz went to school and they learned to read music.

The black jazz clubs in Chicago was wilder than the blues clubs. The Sutherland Lounge was in the Sutherland Hotel on South Drexel Boulevard, and that was a special place where the jazz musicians played. The jazz scene on the South Side was centered around Oakwood Boulevard, over near Lake Michigan. It was a fast pace on Oakwood Boulevard. That was where you'd find all the pimps and drug addicts and the fast, fast livers. There was a big hotel there called the Morocco, and there was the DuSable Hotel across the street, and that's where you would hear a lot of jazz. It was a drug neighborhood. They were into cocaine. They was snortin' that white powder. And heroin was a thing on Oakwood Boulevard. There was a lot of prostitution out of these fast hotels and a lot of fast pimps. There were all kinds of prostitutes there—white, oriental, black. It was the only place in Chicago where you could find all kinds of different races and whatnot.

Leonard Chess had a club, the Macomba Lounge, over there on Drexel Boulevard in the 1940s, before he got into the record business.[7] Tom Archia and Andrew Tibbs, who both recorded for Aristocrat Records, and a lot of other jazz musicians lived at the Morocco.

There wasn't really any mixin' between the jazz musicians and the blues players. The jazz guys looked down on the blues guys, and the blues guys couldn't play with the jazz guys. And, actually, the jazz guys couldn't play with the blues guys! Take Kenny Burrell,

7. Leonard Chess bought the Macomba Lounge on Chicago's South Side in 1946. He was introduced to black music when he decided to hire jazz bands to play at the after-hours club. Saxophonist Tom Archia, who led the house band at the Macomba, recorded for Aristocrat Records, and Chess became a part owner in the label. The Macomba burned down in 1950.

for instance. He's a great jazz guitarist, but he couldn't play guitar the way John Lee Hooker plays it to save his life. And John Lee Hooker couldn't play with Kenny Burrell. There were a few guys like Reggie Boyd who could cover both grounds, but for the most part it was two separate worlds.

The blues audience was not large. There wasn't a whole lot of blues clubs back in the 1950s compared to all the clubs that was in Chicago, 'cause they was all all-black clubs on the South and West Sides. The blues hadn't branched out to the North Side or the suburbs and places like that. But there was always somethin' happenin'. You had the Friday, Saturday, and Sunday spots on the South Side that had the bigger-name entertainers—the bands that would draw. Musicians would be playin' at different clubs on the West Side. There was all kinds of music clubs up and down Madison Street. And there was blues clubs out in Gary, Indiana.

In the 1930s and '40s, the heavy hitters like Tampa Red, Big Bill, and Sonny Boy lived on the South Side. Later, Muddy Waters, Little Walter, and Howlin' Wolf all lived on the South Side. Otis Rush played a lot on the West Side, but he always lived on the South Side. Magic Sam was livin' on the South Side, too, before he got old enough to play in the clubs. Me, Buddy Guy, Dave Myers, Otis Rush, and Junior Wells all lived within a few blocks of each other on East 72nd Street. Otis Rush and Dave Myers lived on one corner, Buddy bought a house in that neighborhood, and Junior was livin' down the street at a place about a block or two from Buddy. It wasn't somethin' that was designed. When the neighborhood started changin', the black people moved further out where it wasn't a black area before, you know, and they started buyin' houses. I was livin' over on 1837 E. 72nd. Corky Siegel used to live out there when he was a kid.[8]

8. Mark Paul "Corky" Siegel (b. 1943) is a harmonica and piano player who began his professional career in 1964 when he teamed up with guitarist and Roosevelt University bandmate Jim Schwall. The white duo became the house band at Pepper's Lounge, a blues club on Chicago's South Side, and musicians like Willie Dixon, Muddy Waters, and Howlin' Wolf would often sit in. In 1965 Sam Charters

Patrons at a South Side blues club, 1964
Photograph by Raeburn Flerlage; Chicago History Museum, ICHi-113079

I lived on the South Side and played at Sylvio's, which was on the West Side. There was all kinds of clubs and music there, up and down Madison Street. There would be two or three bands on every block during that time. There wasn't really a difference between the blues music on the South Side and the blues music on the West Side. The music was the same.

Because of Jim Crow and everything, black people in Chicago *didn't make no money*. The blues audience didn't have a lot of money. They was workin' in factories and different things like that, so they

---

signed the Siegel-Schwall Band to Vanguard Records, and they toured widely. They were the first blues band to perform with a symphony orchestra when they debuted William Russo's "Three Pieces for Blues Band and Symphony Orchestra" in 1968. When the band broke up in 1974, Siegel formed the Happy Year band with drummer Sam Lay and continued his interest in classical music by forming the Chamber Blues ensemble in 1988.

did better than they did down South—they wasn't makin' *nothin'* down there. But black people didn't make a lot of money.

The blues clubs didn't even charge a cover until the mid-1950s, 'cause the people would have balked at a dollar to get in, you know. The clubs paid the bands from the money they made on liquor. I don't know what a bottle of beer cost in 1945, but let's say it was twenty or twenty-five cents a bottle. Well, the club would charge twice that much. The higher price was to make money to pay the band. So there wasn't a lot of money involved in the music. Even the black jazz musicians wasn't makin' a livin'. I guess the jazz clubs might have paid a little more than blues, but maybe not. 'Cause their audience was all black people, too, so their bases was about the same.

If you wanted to be a blues singer, it wasn't about the money. You had to love it. It was somethin' you *wanted* to do, or somethin' you was *born* to do. In the late 1940s, big blues stars like Sonny Boy and Big Bill was makin' fifteen dollars a night. In the 1950s, musicians wasn't makin' nothin' but union scale, and union scale then was twenty-five dollars a night for the leader and fifteen dollars a night for a sideman.

There was two musicians unions in Chicago. They had a black union, Local 208, that had an office at 39th and State. And then they had Local 10, what the black musicians called "the white union." That was downtown, on Washington Street. The black musicians from the South Side and the West Side, they was in Local 208.

Most of the black musicians, like the blues singers, didn't know nothin' about arrangin' and readin'. If you was a black musician who read music and arranged and all that, you could play for white audiences and still be in the black union. Blind John Davis could play "Tea for Two" and "September Song" and all that kind of stuff, so he worked a lot of the time in white clubs out in the suburbs. During the gangster era, in the 1920s, Blind John used to work for Al Capone. And black musicians could get gigs through the white union if they could read or were in a band or were recording. Guys like Nat Cole. The white union didn't bother handlin' the black musicians, 'cause they had their hands full with all the big-time musicians comin' in from New York and everywhere to do recordings. The black union was handlin' their thing and the white union was handlin' theirs. Lots of black musicians felt more comfortable working with their own local, but Petrillo's American Federation of Musicians owned both unions.[9] After the two unions merged together in 1966, the black union was put totally out of business.

I joined the union when I made my first record, in 1953. Before then, singers and harmonica players didn't have to be in a union.[10] Singers didn't have to be in the union to make a record, but all the musicians that played behind 'em had to have union cards. But it wasn't mandatory for harp players. They could get nonunion gigs, and the union guys would come in and turn their heads like they didn't see what was happenin'.

After Little Walter and players like that made the harmonica a real thing, the harp players had to be in the union to work in the blues clubs in Chicago. Once I joined, every gig I had, I always got union scale. Every musician that played with me got union scale, 'cause all my gigs was contract gigs and you had to be in the union to get those. For instance, if I was workin' at Sylvio's, I signed a union contract with him. That meant that Sylvio would have to give me a two-week notice if he wanted to change the contract. I'd play there on Friday, Saturday, and Sunday, and Sylvio would pay me every Sunday night. I was the bandleader, so I got twenty-two fifty a night, and the guys that played with me got fifteen a night. As the bandleader, I had to pay a tax to the union. The sidemen didn't have

9. James Petrillo (1892–1984), a Chicago-born trumpet player, began working for Local 10 in 1919, serving as union president from 1922 to 1963. Petrillo was elected to lead the national American Federation of Musicians in 1940, and he instituted recording bans for all union members twice during the 1940s to compensate musicians for live gigs lost to recorded music. He opposed merging the white and black musicians unions in Chicago, and in 1958 he stepped down as AFM president after integration gained the support of its members.

10. Before World War II, unionized harmonica players and singers were members of the American Guild of Variety Artists (AGVA). The American Federation of Musicians did not officially accept harmonica players until 1956.

to pay no union taxes out of their fifteen. And there were union dues, too. You paid union dues every three months. I think they was somethin' like fifteen dollars. It wasn't too much. That's the way it was. You really weren't makin' a whole lot of money playin' music in the clubs. The union had what they called "walkin' delegates." They would come around the clubs and check to see if the musicians had union cards and make sure that the union was gettin' its cut.

It wasn't any better on the road. If you was a piano player or a saxophone player tourin' with Count Basie or Ray Charles or whoever, you got twenty-five dollars a night. I don't care how big the name was, the goin' price on the road was twenty-five dollars a night. And you had to pay for your own hotel out of that. So two or three of the musicians would get a room together, and that's how you got by on twenty-five dollars.

When Muddy started out, he was drivin' a truck during the day, deliverin' venetian blinds, and workin' five or six nights a week in the clubs. He quit that day job when his records started gettin' popular around Chicago. Leonard Chess told me, "Muddy's got a family, so I don't want Muddy to have to go out of town for those twenty-five-dollar gigs." So that's why Leonard bought Muddy a two-flat building over there on 43rd and Lake Park. See, Muddy was married, and his wife, Geneva, had two sons. They wasn't Muddy's sons. They was his stepchildren. I guess Geneva came from Clarksdale with Muddy. I guess he married her down South. Leonard didn't want Muddy to have to scuffle. Muddy was a good guy, and Leonard knew that those guys had had a hard time in the South and everything.

Now when Howlin' Wolf came to Chicago, he had money. Wolf was always independent. He didn't lean on Leonard for any money. Wolf bought himself a brand-new car. He didn't go to Leonard for it. But Leonard bought Muddy a Cadillac. It wasn't a charity thing. It wasn't welfare. Muddy's records bought that car. Leonard was in with people, and he knew these different guys and could get deals on stuff. If you was makin' money for him, Leonard could probably get you a car for cost. Leonard treated Muddy well.

The blues clubs in Chicago in those days was pretty dangerous.

I used to play the Happy Home Lounge over on Madison, and every Friday and Saturday night four or five fights would break out. The waiters there was bouncers *and* waiters, 'cause I'm talkin' about some ruthless fights.

Black people drank hard whiskey. In those days, all the black clubs that had bands sold "setups." A setup might cost you four dollars and fifty cents. You'd get a bowl of ice, three glasses, and a half a pint of whiskey, and you'd pour your own drinks. People usually drank Old Grand-Dad, Old Taylor, or Old Crow. People would come in the club to drink and listen to a couple of sets by the band. Two or three people would pour themselves a good shot of whiskey in there, and that's the end of that half-pint. They'd drink that and ask the waitress for another setup. That's the way it went down. There wasn't no shots. There wasn't no whiskey sours or Manhattans. Nothin' like that. Just straight whiskey or gin or vodka or whatever they was drinkin'.

When they would drink that hard liquor, man, look out. People would come in as a couple, or two couples. Sometimes you'd have two, three, or four women come in. If a woman liked somebody in the band, she might come in by herself to get next to him. Everybody would be in there dancin' and everything. The guys would be drinkin' and talkin' to the women. "Can I have this dance?" And they'd drink and they'd get on the floor and dance all night. And somebody would step on somebody's feet or whatever and the fight would break out. *Boom! Boom! Bam! Bam!* And the tables would start flying. I mean hellish fights. Fist fights. Fights where, when they got through, the tables was torn down. Three or four fights a night like that.

The bandstands was usually kinda high above the floor, and when there was a fight, people would run up on the bandstand, where we musicians was. They would have two or three bouncers and the man that owned the joint, and they would break the fight up and get 'em under control. If some guy was unruly and drunk, they would put him out of the club, and everybody else would keep rollin' on.

Left to right, seated at table: Unidentified, Howlin' Wolf, Little Hudson, and B. B. King; *rear*: Lane, the security guard, 708 Club, 1957
Bill Greensmith/Blues Unlimited

And then they started havin' uniformed security at a lot of the clubs 'cause so many fights would break out. Muddy Waters played the 708 Club from 1951 up until around 1958. The guy that owned the place was named Ben Gold, and he had a security guy there named Lane to keep order. Lane was a little short guy, but real powerful built. Real husky. And he was a rough guy, man. Mean. They didn't have no fights in there, 'cause if you got out of hand, he would say somethin' to you one time. If you did it again, Lane would hit you and knock you down. If you got up, he'd knock you down again and throw you out the door. Sometimes he'd go out there into the street and knock you down two or three *more* times.

There was always a possibility that you could get robbed on the way home. You've been drinkin', and you're staggerin', and you're by yourself. There's always some shady guys who might follow you and try to rob you or somethin'.

Black people always tried to look their best. When black audiences came out to hear a band or out to a club to hear music, they wore their very best. It was like they was goin' to church. The musicians dressed, too. When I saw Sonny Boy, he always had on a shirt and tie and suit. That's the way most of the musicians dressed. Muddy Waters always wore a suit and a shirt and tie. In the 1950s, we was all wearin' shirts and ties and suits. See, black audiences look at a lot of things. They look at you the way you're dressed, and you got to look presentable, 'cause black people are very fashionable about clothes. You got to come in there lookin' good, and you should be gettin' out of a real nice car, 'cause you're a big star, you know what I mean? It started loosenin' up when people started dressin' more casual, but in those days, most musicians wore shirts and ties. Sport coats or whatever.

Some of the clubs had girls runnin' what they called the "twenty-six game." They'd have a girl at the door, lookin' kind of glamorous, and she'd have a little stand there, like a table. And you'd put your money in there and bet on a number, and she'd shake the dice up and throw 'em out and see if you won somethin'—a drink or a few bucks or somethin'. They called her the "twenty-six girl."

They'd have photographers in the clubs. The 708 Club had their own photographer. He had a room in the back. If you went to the 708 Club and you wanted your picture taken, you could get it taken and developed and put in a frame with "708 Club" on there. Eugene Lyons was a drummer who played with the Aces. He quit playin' drums to be a photographer who went around to the different clubs.

As far as the South Side blues clubs go, there was Club Georgia on 45th and State. Sonny Boy played Friday, Saturday, and Sunday there for about two years, up until the day he died.

The Plantation Club was out on 31st Street. That's where Sonny Boy played the night he got killed. Sonny Boy played there on Wednesdays and Thursdays for about a year and a half before he brought Lonnie Johnson in there to costar with him.

Muddy Waters, Howlin' Wolf, Junior Wells, Otis Rush, and Fenton Robinson all played at Pepper's. Pepper's was where Charlie Musselwhite and Paul Butterfield used to go when they was first startin' out.[11]

Smitty's Corner was at 35th Street and Indiana. The only time it got any recognition that I know about was when Muddy Waters was playin' there. He played weekends there for quite a while. There might have been other people that was in there before that, but I don't know about that.

Club DeLisa was a sort of a supper club or show club. T-Bone Walker would play there. I didn't really go there myself. That was a little bit before my time. Rhythm Willie played there.

When I was a kid, Theresa's Lounge was a candy store. The streetcar ran down the street, and there was a little candy store down in the basement. Later on, over the years, Theresa made a lounge out of it. I didn't do many gigs at Theresa's Lounge. That

11. Charlie Musselwhite (b. 1944) fell in love with the blues as a child in Memphis, where he got to know black bluesmen like Will Shade and Furry Lewis. In 1962 Musselwhite moved to Chicago, where he worked as an exterminator, lived in the basement of Delmark Records with Big Joe Williams, and began sitting in at local blues clubs, playing regularly with guitarist Mike Bloomfield at Big John's on the North Side. Musselwhite's first album, *Stand Back*, was released on Vanguard Records in 1966 and established him as a top blues performer. Since then Musselwhite has recorded more than thirty albums and been nominated for more than a dozen Grammy Awards, winning one in 2013 for his album *Get Up!*

By his late teens, Paul Butterfield (1942–1987) was not only haunting the blues clubs on the South Side of his native Chicago but sitting in with musicians like Muddy Waters, Howlin' Wolf, Little Walter, and Otis Rush and developing a soulful and dynamic harmonica style. In 1963 Butterfield teamed up with guitarist Elvin Bishop, bassist Jerome Arnold, and drummer Sam Lay, and the group became the house band at Big John's. Paul Rothchild signed the band to Elektra Records and convinced Butterfield to bring guitarist Mike Bloomfield into the band. Keyboardist Mark Naftalin was also added to the group. Two recording sessions were shelved before Elektra released *The Paul Butterfield Blues Band* in 1965. The album had an enormous influence on a generation of young listeners and musicians. Butterfield added a horn section to later versions of the band, which broke up in 1971. He formed a new band, Paul Butterfield's Better Days, and performed and recorded with Muddy Waters and The Band. Butterfield was inducted into the Blues Hall of Fame in 2006 and the Rock and Roll Hall of Fame in 2015.

was Junior Wells's home club. Theresa worked with Junior Wells's mother at R. R. Donnelley, the big publishing company, at 22nd and Calumet. They was good friends, and that's how Junior got the spot workin' down there at the lounge. He could do anything he wanted in that place. Junior would come in there, sit at the bar and drink all night, and then get up and do two or three numbers a half hour before closin' time. He'd get drunk and go up there and blow and they would turn the lights on to stop him. He got away with it 'cause he had charisma and the people liked him. I had a lot of respect for Junior. He was a great harp player, but he got to the place where he was playin' so little harp that he didn't have much to add to it. But Junior earned his way up there.

The Wagon Wheel was on 63rd Street. When I was a kid, that street was all white people and hillbilly clubs. You'd see country and western bands in the window of the Wagon Wheel. Little did I know that I would be playin' in that same club in 1959. But by then the neighborhood was changin' over. The whites was movin' out and the blacks was movin' in. It was a mixed neighborhood in 1959, when two Arab guys bought the Wagon Wheel and renamed it Club Columbia. Willie Dixon played there first, then Birdlegs and Pauline played there.[12] Then they brought me in there, and I stayed there for a couple of years.

From 1951 up until '60 or so, Muddy would be playin' at the 708 Club on Friday, Saturday, and Sunday. I remember seein' Memphis Slim and Matt Murphy—they was both based out of St. Louis—play at the 708 Club. Little Walter was there that night, and Matt Murphy was *smokin'* on that guitar. The bandstand at the 708 Club was behind the bar and was kind of higher up. People didn't dance at the 708 Club, so people like Little Walter who drew a younger, dancing crowd didn't go over at the 708 Club. Muddy and them

12. Sidney "Birdlegs" Banks (b. 1929) and Pauline Shivers Banks (b. 1933) were a married performing duo from Illinois. Their biggest success was their 1963 single on Vee-Jay Records, "Spring." This led to national tours with an excellent band that included Matt Murphy and his brother Floyd on guitars. After the couple divorced in the 1960s, Pauline Shivers made several soul recordings for Chicago's O-Pex label.

went over, 'cause the people that came there wanted to sit and listen to the words and the music.

Cadillac Baby had a club at 47th and Dearborn.[13] Earl Hooker played there. Little Mack Simmons played there for a long time—longer than he wanted to. Cadillac was kind of the sponsor for Little Mack. Cadillac started a record company, and they recorded Mack. And that's where Detroit Junior made that record "Money Tree." See, Detroit Junior—his name was Emery Williams—came to Chicago, and Mack was makin' a record, so he hired a band and Detroit Junior was the piano player. When they went in to do the session, Mack cut both of his sides. At the end of the session, Cadillac Baby let Detroit Junior do a couple of numbers, and Detroit Junior did "Money Tree." It was a good record. Detroit Junior had that blues voice, and he was a great songwriter and entertainer. Anyway, "Money Tree" was a Chicago hit, and Mack's record didn't do nothin'. So Little Mack said, "Ain't this a goddamn shame? I go in there to cut a record, and *he's* the one that gets the hit." That's the way it is in the music business, you know. So a week later, Little Mack bought a brand-new Nash station wagon, and he had "St. Louis Mack" painted on there. He had changed his name from Little Mack Simmons to St. Louis Mack. I laughed when I saw that.

Club Alibi was at 27th and Wentworth. Tiny Davis and her band played down there. I think she owned the building. I played Club Alibi. George Smith and Otis Rush used to play there, too.

The Rhumboogie featured a lot of the travelin' show bands. T-Bone Walker, Pee Wee Crayton, and Rhythm Willie played the Rhumboogie.

As far as the West Side is concerned, there was a lot of blues clubs on Madison Street, even before my time. Between Madison and Lake

13. Songwriter and producer Narvel "Cadillac Baby" Eatmon (1912–1991) owned several South Side blues clubs and founded Bea & Baby Records, which released titles by top-flight blues artists such as Earl Hooker, Little Mack Simmons, Robert Jr. Lockwood, Sunnyland Slim, and James Cotton. The label's biggest hit was Bobby Saxton's "Trying to Make a Living," released in 1960.

Street, there was clubs all up and down there. There was Ralph's Club, the Purple Cat, the Seeley Club, and the Happy Home Lounge. Me and Jody Williams was playin' at the Happy Home Lounge when Jody went into the service in 1958 or '59. Memphis Slim played at Ralph's Club. The Purple Cat was a place on Madison down the street from Ralph's Club. Sonny Boy played there five nights a week for a couple of years. Then, when Little Walter was comin' on the scene, they hired him to play there. Some people say he took Sonny Boy's gig. I think Snooky Pryor played there, too.

The original Sylvio's was at Lake Street and Oakley. It was a great big cabaret that Sylvio and his brothers started in the 1920s. Blind John knew Sylvio and his brothers when he was a kid comin' up. It was the main club in Chicago for blues in the 1940s and '50s. All the big stars played Sylvio's. Big Bill, Memphis Minnie, Sunnyland Slim, Memphis Slim, Roosevelt Sykes the Honeydripper—all of 'em played there.

When Sylvio sold that place or lost that place—I don't know what happened—he moved to a little, small place down on Lake and Kedzie, which was nothing like the original Sylvio's. I played the second Sylvio's for several months on the weekends in 1957 with Muddy Waters and Howlin' Wolf. That was where Magic Sam started playin'.

Ruby Lee Gatewood's club was a great big club in the '40s, a little before my time. It was two blocks west of Western and about three blocks west of the original Sylvio's, on the south side of the street. Blind John lived not too far from there. Ruby Lee was a black woman, and her husband owned the club. Big Bill, Sonny Boy, and Memphis Slim played there for a long time in 1939 and '40. I had heard Louis Myers and Bob Myers and Blind John talk about Ruby Gatewood's club, so one day, when I was sixteen or seventeen— I really wasn't old enough to get in—I went in there. Big Bill had a record out called "Willie Mae," and I played it on the jukebox at Ruby Lee Gatewood's.

The Tay May Club was on the West Side. Later it was known

as the Alex Club. That's where Magic Sam played.[14] He went over real big at the Tay May Club. He recorded *Magic Sam Live* there. Sam loved the West Side. I think he liked it 'cause it was run-down and reminded him of his native Mississippi. I think he felt more comfortable on the West Side 'cause there was a lot of people there that related to down South. Shakey Jake hung out at the Tay May Club a lot, too. He was an older guy, and he was married to Magic Sam's auntie. Wherever Sam was playin' at, Shakey would be there, too. He would come up and play some numbers on the harp, but he was really a gambler. His thing was gamblin', and he was a heavy drinker. Shakey Jake was a con artist, and he was a hustler. He went out to California and met a white woman out there and took over her house. He was stayin' there and runnin' the house and chargin' rent. He was a character. When he'd get drunk, oh man, he'd go *crazy*. He wasn't violent or nothin', he would just act up, you know.

The 1815 Club on Roosevelt Road was owned by Howlin' Wolf. I only played there one time. Eddie Shaw, Wolf's saxophone player and bandleader, took over that place when Wolf died.

All the big-time musicians played at the Zanzibar, but the Zanzibar was Muddy's hot spot. The Zanzibar was at 14th and Ashland and was owned by two white guys. Muddy played there every Friday, Saturday, and Sunday for a long time. Little Walter played there when he was with Muddy, and Junior Wells played there, too. Later Howlin' Wolf played there on the weekends after Muddy. I played the Zanzibar in '55 or '56. I had made "I Wish You Would" and they needed a band. They called me and Big Smokey Smothers and a drummer named Junior went over there.

McKie's Disc Jockey Show Lounge was right down the street

14. Samuel Gene Maghett (1937–1969), a.k.a. Magic Sam, scored a hit with his very first record, "All Your Love," released by Cobra Records in 1957. Magic Sam, Buddy Guy, and Otis Rush became identified with a new blues style known as the West Side sound. Magic Sam recorded two outstanding albums for Delmark, *West Side Soul* (1967) and *Black Magic* (1968), and built a reputation that continued to grow after he stole the show at the 1969 Ann Arbor Blues Festival. His promising career was cut short when he died of a heart attack at the age of thirty-two.

from the Pershing Lounge on 63rd and Cottage Grove. It was a jazz
club that featured Jack McDuff, Jimmy Smith, and all the jazz organ
players. McKie Fitzhugh was a disc jockey in Chicago. He played all
the doo-wop songs and stuff. McKie decided to feature blues two
nights a week at his club. He called it "Blues-O-Rama."

Me and Junior Wells just happened to show up there on the
same night in 1959 to see Little Walter's show. Me, Junior, and
Little Walter ended up talkin' with McKie that night, and he told
us, "Hey, what about all three of you guys playin' some shows together? We'll have the Muddy Waters band on Tuesday nights and
you guys and Walter can play here on Wednesday night. We'll call it
'Landlady's Nite.'" Then me, Junior, and Little Walter went outside
the club and they took a picture of the three of us.

We used Walter's band when we played together on those shows at McKie's. I'd go up and do three or four numbers, Junior would go up and do three or four numbers, and then Walter would play. Little Walter's band at that time was Luther Tucker on guitar, Freddy Robinson on second guitar, and George Hunter on drums.

That was an excitin' gig, you know, bein' on the bill with Little Walter, the king of the blues harmonica players. Walter got too high sometimes, but he had a lot of mystique about him. Everybody was just glad to see him, 'cause he was the top guy. All the harmonica players around Chicago would come down there to see Little Walter in action. And they'd see me and Junior, and they'd figure, "Well, you guys is up there with Walter." There was a lot of harmonica players that maybe made one or two records or somethin' or was playin' in bands, but they didn't have the recognition that Junior and I had. Junior and I both had records out, and at that time I was playin' most Fridays, Saturdays, and Sundays at the Rock and Roll Club on West 63rd Street.

One night at McKie's, Little Walter had to drive in from St. Louis, and he and his band showed up about a half hour late. They drove up, and Walter sent Luther Tucker inside to tell me to get him two half-pints of Gordon's gin. Then Walter came in with a lady and the rest of the band. Walter and I talked that night, and he asked me, "How would you like to go out on the road with me?" Walter played a lot of dances, and he needed an extra piece or an extra singer to go up and kick off his shows. A lot of times he'd take a piano player like Johnny Jones or Henry Gray, or sometimes he'd take a saxophone player on the road with him. It wasn't about coverin' for him when he got too high, 'cause Walter had been gettin' high all of his career. It was about addin' somethin' to the show. I didn't take Walter up on it, 'cause I had been workin' regular at this club for about a year.

Luther Tucker told me that sometimes Walter would get a little high and forget the lyrics to his songs. Walter learned a lot of his songs on the spot in the studio, so when he'd go out on the road, he had to learn his own songs off his records, just like we did. He'd blow a lot of great solos on his records, but he would never play those solos again in person. He might play somethin' even better than that. If you heard him play "Juke" on a show, you wouldn't hear him play it like he played it on the record, 'cause he had so many variations to put in it. But the rest of us harmonica players had to learn that song note for note.

Some of the nights we was playin' at McKie's, Memphis Slim would come in, 'cause he was stayin' at the Pershing Hotel then, which was only a half a block from McKie's. One night Memphis Slim came in with two other guys, and they sat at the bar. I was singin' Junior Parker's latest record, "Pretty Baby," and this guy who was with Slim at the bar was watchin' me and noddin' his head in approval. When I came off stage, somebody pointed at him and said, "That's Junior Parker." And the other guy who showed up with Memphis Slim turned out to be Bobby Bland. That was a great moment.

Billy Boy Arnold and band on stage at a South Side club, 1964
Photograph by Raeburn Flerlage; Chicago History Museum, ICHi-124883

7

The Blues Breaks Out

What some people don't understand is that the blues was an all-black thing back in the 1940s and '50s. The type of music we was playin' and recording was for the consumption of black people. The blues was played on black radio for black people on the South Side and the West Side of Chicago. It was black musicians playin' in black clubs for black club owners, mostly.

The other races didn't even know about it. There wasn't no white people involved. They didn't buy the records. They didn't even *hear* the records. Every now and then a white person would come into one of the blues clubs, but they didn't know nothin' about it.

During Lester Melrose's time, in the 1940s, they didn't play his records on the radio for the black people. The first black disc jockey was a guy named Jack L. Cooper. He mostly played jazz. He wasn't broadcastin' the real, authentic blues.

Then, in 1947 or '48, WGES-AM in Chicago brought in a black disc jockey named Al Benson. WGES's audience was black people, and they had blues music goin' all day long, and Benson was the main disc jockey. If you made blues and had a blues record that you wanted to get played in Chicago, all you had to do was get in touch with Al Benson. Leonard Chess and Vee-Jay and all the independents was tight with Al. I'm sure they was payin' him. Slippin' him some money, you know.

Al Benson was on the air playin' blues records three or four times a day. He would play Muddy Waters and Lightnin' Hopkins and everybody, so black people in Chicago started hearin' that kind of blues. They would hear it on the radio and then they'd go out and buy it.

Leonard pushed his records all over the country. He wanted his artists to make money, and he wanted to make money, too, so he was really on top of that stuff. He got his records played so that his artists got gigs with agencies and everything. And when he got Chuck Berry and Bo Diddley, those were two artists that were different from Muddy and Wolf and the rest of the blues guys he was dealin' with. And they sold more records than the regular blues guys. And he had the doo-wop groups. Chess had the Moonglows and Vee-Jay had the Spaniels, so doo-wop was goin' strong, too.

Most white people didn't know blues music existed, 'cause of Jim Crow. It was not allowed to be played on the radio for other races. White America wouldn't publicize anything that made black people stand out. They didn't want the world to know what black people had. They didn't want the white culture to hear black music. They called the records made by black artists "race records." A few whites knew about it. Charlie Musselwhite heard the blues as a kid down South 'cause his mother had Walter Davis's records, and when Charlie was a teenager he hung around with black guys like Bobby Bland. And Elvis Presley was listenin' to the blues as a kid in Memphis. But most white people didn't know nothin' about the real blues or about Muddy Waters or B. B. King or Sonny Boy Williamson or Howlin' Wolf. The disc jockeys wouldn't play those records 'cause they thought white audiences wouldn't accept 'em. It was racism.

Four musicians are responsible for black blues and rhythm and blues bein' played all over the world: Fats Domino, Bo Diddley, Chuck Berry, and Little Richard. Before these artists broke out, the white kids didn't know who B. B. King or Muddy Waters and Little Walter and Howlin' Wolf was. They didn't know nothin' about those people.

In 1955, some of the white disc jockeys started to play Fats

Domino's records. He was the first crossover artist. About a year later, Bo Diddley hit. A few months after that, Chuck Berry broke out, and then came Little Richard. The big breakthrough was when this white disc jockey Alan Freed started playin' black artists on his radio show in New York City and promotin' shows with black artists in theaters. He and Leonard Chess was tight. Leonard put Alan Freed's name on Chuck Berry's "Maybellene" as a writer without Chuck's knowledge. So Freed started playin' Bo Diddley and Chuck Berry. I don't think that Freed only played "Maybellene" 'cause he got a cut. Nobody knew that that record was gonna be as big as it was. For Leonard Chess, blues was his business, and he was pushin' his artists. But he liked the blues personally. I could tell that just by bein' around him.

The white kids had heard Pat Boone's cover of Little Richard's "Tutti Frutti," but when they heard Little Richard's original version, they said, "This is the original guy who made that song. *That's* what I want to hear." 'Cause Pat Boone couldn't deliver it like Little Richard could. One thing that black people have is soul. We got so much soul and feelin' that other people can feel it. They didn't want people to feel our soul, but once our music broke out, it was too late.

At first, the white teenagers thought that everything started with Fats Domino, Bo Diddley, Chuck Berry, and Little Richard. But when they went to the record shops to buy their music, they found out where Fats Domino and all this music really came from. There was more than rock-and-roll blues, there was *real* blues. They found out how deep the blues really went. They found the gold mine of where the music came from, and once they heard it, they wanted to hear more. They *demanded* it. The radio and the record stores was where they discovered B. B. King and Muddy Waters and Sonny Boy Williamson.

It was Elvis Presley that made black rhythm and blues acceptable to white people. Elvis was popular with black audiences, too. Oh, yeah, definitely. They liked what he was doin'. He was popular with both sides. When he made that first record, a lot of people didn't know he was white until he made those personal appearances. After he got famous, somebody put out a rumor that Elvis didn't like blacks. If Elvis had really felt that way, he would have shunned the music, period. He liked the music. He *loved* the music. And he did a hell of a job on it. He was a great singer, and he had all the ingredients. He had the looks, he had the style, and he knew what to do with it. Pat Boone was doin' "Tutti Frutti" and stuff like that, but he didn't have what Elvis had. So I'd say that Elvis and Alan Freed really got this music over to the white audience. Black music started to sell all over the world, in every country.

It worked both ways. A lot of black people listened to the Grand Ole Opry, too. Ray Charles listened to country music as a kid. I was a big fan of Hank Williams. I got his albums and his book. I like his music. Hank could really get down, you know.

At the same time the white teenagers was discoverin' the blues, it was phasin' out in Chicago. The big era for blues in Chicago started in 1950 when Muddy Waters made "Rollin' Stone" and went all the way up to '57 or '58. Around 1960, that scene started waning. B. B. King was still big, but the country blues had been around for a while and was phasin' out. Pepper's went down. The 708 Club started playin' out. The black audiences stopped supporting traditional blues—them black-bottom goodies, you know. Blues just kind of petered out as far as the blacks was concerned. I guess that they had heard so much of it that they decided to go in a different direction. They started listenin' to Ray Charles and Aretha Franklin and James Brown and artists like that.

I didn't lose faith in the blues, even though it was windin' down. I didn't try to escape into another music. I was into it and I was workin' in the clubs and everything. I was giggin' all around town. I was pretty popular around Chicago. I had a big, strong name. I was popular 'cause I could sing all different kinds of styles. Black audiences wanted to hear you sing the latest songs—the hits. And I could sing Chuck Berry's stuff, Ernie K-Doe's stuff, Fats Domino's stuff, some of Jerry Butler's stuff. The bluesier hits.

Wolf was the strongest blues guy still doin' it in Chicago in the

'60s. He was still bringin' in the black audiences. Wolf maintained his popularity and was still in demand. He was still workin' five or six nights a week. Black people like to dance, and Wolf's music had a beat to it. And Wolf kept comin' up with strong records, "Shake for Me" and all that stuff with Hubert Sumlin. Wolf was able to pack a house on Monday, Tuesday, and Wednesday from the time he first came to Chicago, and he maintained his popularity with black people.

Wolf had a consistent following, but Muddy Waters could hardly get a job. My brother Jerome was playin' bass with Muddy then, and there would be times when they'd be out of work. And when they *did* work, Muddy was only payin' twelve dollars a night. Johnny Pepper told me about Muddy askin' him for a job at his club around this time. Johnny said, "Man, I can't afford you." Johnny was shocked by the low price that Muddy settled on, just to keep his band workin'. Muddy had a strong record with "The Same Thing" by Willie Dixon, but he wasn't makin' many singles.

I always did have a regular band. Mighty Joe Young was playin' with me on guitar. I had my brother on bass. And I had a drummer that I had for quite a while. Syl Johnson played guitar with me. Luther Tucker played with me a little while, and Jody Williams played with me occasionally.

Me and James Wheeler worked a lot together. To me, James Wheeler was one of the top guitarists around Chicago. James was one of my all-time favorites. He was two years younger than me. James was from Georgia. His older brother was the harmonica player Golden Wheeler. I met Golden Wheeler in 1962, and he introduced me to James. James played with Joe Carter—Carter was another Georgia guy, I think they all knew each other down there—in 1959 or '60, and after that James sorta freelanced, playin' with whoever had the gigs. I always had gigs, and I paid union scale. And when I got a gig, I usually held it for six months or more.

Me and James started playin' together around 1962 when I got a gig at Club Arden out on 63rd and Dorchester, around the corner from where I was livin' at the time. McKinley Mitchell had played out there before us.[1] He had a few hit records out. Club Arden was owned by an older white guy named Buddy. It wasn't a hard-core blues club like Pepper's. They wasn't into the typical Muddy Waters or Howlin' Wolf stuff at Club Arden. They wanted more of the latest hits. That worked for me, 'cause I was doin' Ray Charles's "Hit the Road Jack" and "Unchain My Heart," Chuck Berry, and the bluesier stuff by Jerry Butler. All kinds of different stuff. James Wheeler was the type of guitar player who could play anything he wanted to play and work with any type of singer. He'd learn a song and know it right away. He could follow you into whatever bag you wanted to go into. James wasn't really into harmonica stuff and that type of blues. He was a young guy tryin' to move up. He wanted to branch out and play more sophisticated stuff. There were a lot of girl singers around 63rd Street, and James could play behind all of 'em.

At Club Arden I had Wheeler on guitar, Willie Chaisson—he was from Louisiana—on bass, and Sam Burton—we called him "Savage Boy"—on drums. We played there for a few months in 1962, until Buddy changed things up.

James Wheeler went down South and got stranded down there. And then he went to Rockford, Illinois, to work with Birdlegs and Pauline, and then he came back to Chicago. He had a band called the Jaguars, and they backed up people like B. B. King and Otis Clay. If James wasn't workin' and I had a gig, we would work together.

Blind John Davis called me one day and said, "There's a guy comin' over to my place to do a recording thing," and he invited me over. So that's how I met Pete Welding. Pete was a writer for *Down-Beat* magazine, and he was recording an interview with Blind John. Me and Pete was born in the same year. One night, Pete Welding came down to Club Arden and caught one of our sets, and he wrote

1. McKinley Mitchell (1934–1986) began his musical career singing with gospel groups in his hometown of Jackson, Mississippi. He moved to Chicago in 1958 and switched to rhythm and blues, signing a contract with Boxer Records in 1959. His 1962 record for the One-derful label, "The Town I Live In," reached number eight on *Billboard*'s Hot R&B chart.

an article in *DownBeat* about us. Me and Pete became good buddies after that. He was a really nice guy and a great writer. Pete lived on the South Side, in Hyde Park, just a few blocks from where I lived.

: : :

Until the early 1960s, white people hardly ever came into the blues clubs in Chicago. I remember one time when I was playin' out on 63rd Street when that neighborhood was changin' over. The whites was movin' out and the blacks was movin' in. A white guy I knew came in the club, and all of a sudden everybody in the band wanted to sing a number. "Let me sing! Let me sing one!" They thought this white guy must be some big-time producer and this might be their big break, you know.

I first saw Paul Butterfield and Charlie Musselwhite when they started showin' up at Pepper's in the early 1960s. They was there a lot. Corky Siegel was comin' around Howlin' Wolf and gettin' into it. I first met Corky when he was fifteen years old, when he was playin' saxophone.

The Wolf would be on stage and he'd say, "Some of my white friends has come down to see the Wolf. They wanna hear the Wolf sing somethin'." Then Wolf would call one of them on stage to blow some harp or sing.

At first, some of the black people was shocked. "What are they doin', tryin' to play the blues?" you know. I remember one time when Paul was on stage and there was this black guy in the audience who was drunk and kept hollerin', "Out of place! Out of place!" He figured a white guy tryin' to play the harmonica and sing the low-down blues didn't fit.

Muddy Waters and Howlin' Wolf and a lot of the black musicians was very supportive of those guys. They was glad that these white guys liked our music, that they wanted to play it, and that they *could* play it. And so it was like, "Hey, man, that's great!" The black musicians respected Paul and Charlie 'cause they could really play and sing the blues, and so they were well received and accepted.

After the shock wore off, the black audiences embraced 'em, too.

They saw that these white guys wasn't up there messin' up—that they could really play. And the black people was amazed that they knew all those songs. "Man, what's goin' on? You mean white people like the blues?" The black audiences was in awe. They thought, "Wow, man!"

When I look back at Charlie Musselwhite and Paul Butterfield and myself in those days, we was all young guys who had a calling. Playin' blues is what I was meant to do, and that's what Charlie Musselwhite was meant to do, and that's what Paul Butterfield was meant to do. When I saw Paul Butterfield and Charlie Musselwhite playin' in those clubs, I wasn't surprised at all. It's just like anything else. It's like food. If you get some food and it tastes good, it don't make no difference what nationality you are. What's good is good. If someone gives you a coconut pie and you like it, they'll say, "Hey, he likes it, too!" That's the way I looked at the music, so I wasn't surprised at all to see Charlie Musselwhite and Paul Butterfield and Corky Siegel. I felt comfortable with them. I thought that they were just like me. We was about the same age. Whatever drove me was drivin' *them*. And it didn't have nothin' to do with race. It's about what's in *you*.

I thought that Paul Butterfield was a great harp player and a good singer. He was assertive. And he was a nice guy, too. He was a friendly, outgoin' guy. Paul had a lot of personality. He just acted regular, like he was just one of the guys.

:::

I got back into the recording studio in early 1964. I did a session for Sam Charters, who was producin' for Prestige Records at that time. Sam came to Chicago to record Homesick James. He asked Bob Koester who else in town he should record, and Bob said, "Well, Billy Boy Arnold or Junior Wells." So Sam did an album on me and another on Homesick James.

I had Lafayette Leake on the piano, my brother Jerome on the bass, Mighty Joe Young on the guitar, and Junior Blackmon on drums. This was gonna be my first album, and I didn't want to record all other people's stuff. I did a couple of covers. I did a Jimmy Reed tune—"Goin' by the River"—and I did B. B. King's "Get Out of Here" and Junior Parker's "I'll Forget about You." A guy named Piney Brown wrote "Evaleena." That's a song I was gonna do with him, and he wrote that about some chick, you know. I wrote the other eight tunes on the album in one day. It was a rushed thing, but it was a good session. "You Don't Love Me No More" and "School Time" are great numbers. Sam put the album out as *Billy Boy Arnold: More Blues on the South Side.* It's a good record.

Lafayette Leake was an advanced musician. He was playin' with Willie Dixon on a regular basis, and he did a lot of recording with Chuck Berry and other Chess artists. There was a big gospel scene in Chicago, and Lafayette Leake used to play piano and organ on all the gospel records that came out of Chicago. He used to play with Mahalia Jackson. He could play classical stuff on the piano, too. A lot of people criticized him for playin' with Willie Dixon. People would ask him, "Man, why are you playin' with Dixon? You too good a piano player." And he would say, "Hell, it doesn't matter if you're playin' with Dixon or anybody else. 'Cause you gettin' paid for it." The way Lafayette Leake looked at it—and it's true—you got a twelve-tone music system, and all of music is played on those twelve tones. Whether you're playin' blues, jazz, classical, or whatever. And he didn't differentiate.

: : :

Paul Butterfield put his own band together in 1963. He started workin' with Elvin Bishop on guitar, and then he hired my brother Jerome on bass and Sam Lay on drums. Sam Lay was from Cleveland. Little Walter used to play in Cleveland a lot, and he met Sam Lay down there and brought him to Chicago to join his band. Sam and Jerome had been playin' with Howlin' Wolf. Wolf was real hard on musicians. It was like bein' in the Army. If you came in with mismatched socks or didn't have the right uniform on, he'd fire you. Everything had to be just so. I think Sam Lay and my brother left the Wolf 'cause they saw an opportunity. Butterfield and Musselwhite was the first two white guys who was really doin' the blues and was really accepted by the black audience and everybody. Butterfield paid better money than the Wolf. He was young and aggressive, and he could bring the blues to white audiences. And the music was good, too. Butterfield wasn't just out for the money. His main thing was to have a tight band that sounded good. So Sam Lay and Jerome felt that it was a better opportunity with Butterfield, and, as long as it lasted, it was.

Butterfield got a gig in Old Town, a white neighborhood on the North Side, at a place called Big John's. He became the house band there. The white people down there in Old Town, they didn't know nothin' about Muddy Waters and people like that, but Butterfield really went over. When my cousins, who didn't like blues, saw Jerome playin' with Paul Butterfield, they accepted what Paul Butterfield was doin', even though it was the same thing *I* was doin', 'cause they thought the white people must be right. And when all my black friends who was lookin' funny at me when I was playin' the harmonica and tryin' to sing like Sonny Boy saw Butterfield and Musselwhite, they kind of changed their attitude.

The first time I saw Paul with his own band was after he hired my brother and got the gig at Big John's. I'd go down there, and Paul would always ask me to do a couple of numbers. When Paul started doin' gigs out of town, he asked me and my band to play in his place at Big John's if we weren't giggin'. The club owner didn't know who we was, and our music was new to him, but he knew Paul and trusted him. He said, "Wow! Well, okay." I went over pretty good down there, and they gave me a Wednesday or Thursday night gig.

Buddy Guy and Junior Wells started playin' at Big John's, and then Paul got Muddy Waters in there. It was Paul who got the black blues bands their first gigs on the North Side, 'cause he knew the club owners. And the white audiences didn't know about Muddy or Wolf or Buddy Guy, either, until they started playin' at Big John's. But now *we* was bein' accepted by the white audiences. The blues scene at Big John's ended around 1966, when the owner got into trouble with the black union. He didn't respect them. He said that

The Paul Butterfield Blues Band, 1966. *Standing, left to right*: Jerome Arnold, Mike Bloomfield, Mark Naftalin, and Elvin Bishop; *seated, left to right*: Paul Butterfield and Billy Davenport
Michael Ochs Archives/Getty Images

they couldn't tell him what to do. He didn't know the power they had, and he tried to break a union contract.

Over time, more white people was listenin' to blues than blacks, who were sort of weanin' themselves away from traditional blues. The black bands started workin' up on the North Side and the suburbs. The Aces was playin' out in the suburbs. I was playin' at an Italian club way out on 63rd, way out of Chicago. There were no blacks comin' in there, 'cause there were no blacks livin' out there. But those clubs wanted black bands. They wanted black music.

Butterfield signed with Elektra, and my brother Jerome toured with him all over. Paul got Mike Bloomfield on lead guitar, and Elvin Bishop ended up playin' mostly rhythm, 'cause he couldn't play the kind of lead that Bloomfield could. They had a good thing. Sam Lay quit or got fired or got sick at some point, and Butterfield got Billy Davenport to play drums. Billy told Jerome, "I used to play with your brother Billy."

:::

Charlie Musselwhite is from Kosciusko, Mississippi, and my wife, Mary, was born in Kosciusko, too. Charlie was listenin' to the *real* blues when he was just a kid. He loved the blues *then*.

When I met Paul and Charlie, I was workin' a day job and I had to give up my band temporarily. So I got the guitar out again and bought a bass and started learnin' how to play 'em. I played bass with a couple of people—I played bass behind Buddy Guy at Theresa's one night—and then Johnny Young came to me and said, "Billy Boy, come play bass with me."

Then Johnny Young and I started playin' with Charlie Musselwhite. I played bass. Sometimes we would have Fred Below on the drums. I'd been knowin' Below since he was with the Aces, and he played on one of my record sessions. I played bass with Eddie C. Campbell, too, out in Waukegan. Eddie C. had a manager named Jay Banks, a big fat guy who tried to start his own musicians union 'cause he didn't want to pay the Chicago union.

I wasn't a good bass player. I wasn't like some of the other guys that was into it. I just tried it out. I was experimentin'. I wasn't near the quality of bass player like my brother Jerome. He was one of the top bass players around town.

Johnny Young and I played with Charlie at the Aragon Ballroom in Chicago and up in Wisconsin. Me and Charlie played the Cafe Au Go Go in New York City for two weeks in 1967. We had a young white kid on guitar who wasn't really up to snuff. Charlie found out that Magic Sam was goin' to New York at the same time to help with his father-in-law's business, so Charlie got Sam to play the first couple of nights at the Cafe Au Go Go with us. Magic Sam was a great singer and a great guitar player, but he didn't write songs and he wasn't comfortable outside of his main bag. He wasn't a guy who

Billy Boy Arnold playing bass, 1964
Photograph by Raeburn Flerlage; Chicago History Museum, ICHi-124881

could sing somebody else's style. When we got back from New York, we played the Trianon Ballroom and places on the North Side like Big John's.

Charlie Musselwhite is a great harmonica player and singer. He's made some outstandin' records. He's *still* makin' great records. Charlie studies a lot, and he knows a lot of stuff on the harp. He's dedicated. Me and Charlie played together at the Chicago Blues Festival in 2019.

::: :::

Sometime around 1964 or '65, Muddy Waters Junior needed a bass player, so he got me to come down to the Red Onion and play bass for him. Little Walter came in that night, and he asked me, "Billy, ain't you blowin' your harp no more?" I said, "Yeah, I'm still doin' that, but I'm doin' this, too," but Walter acted like he kind of felt that everybody was abandoning everything that he was about.

When Little Walter was ridin' high, he'd walk into a club and everybody would say, "Little Walter!" They'd try to get him on stage, but he'd wave his hand, you know, and shoo 'em off. When he started losin' popularity, he'd come down to Theresa's and jam. He'd tell Junior, "Let me play somethin'" and sit in, and he'd act real regular and friendly. When you're drinkin' and goin' downhill, you do that.

Walter had a white Cadillac, the last Cadillac he bought. And it sat out there for a couple of months on 48th near Theresa's, all beat-up and run-down. Walter had gotten to the place where Leonard Chess must have thought that Walter didn't have nothin' in him no more and stopped recording him. Walter's last few sessions wasn't great. It sounded like he had lost what he had. And he was playin' acoustic harp on "Mean Ole Frisco" and tunes like that, so he didn't have the punch that he once had.

Little Walter wasn't a fighter, and he wasn't a mean guy. I don't think Walter had a temper, but he'd get drunk and say things that offended people. Walter was down on 39th one time with some woman he had brought from St. Louis, and she was makin' a scene and cursin' Walter. The cops came over there, and Walter got smart with 'em. One of the cops—a black cop—hit him and knocked him out. And then he found out who Walter was. "Oh, man, that's Little Walter?" the cop said. "I got some of his records!"

Walter started drinkin' heavy. In my opinion, that's what brought him down. Walter never had much confidence in himself. Walter's driver told me that when Walter made "Juke" and he went to play at the Apollo Theater in New York City, the stagehands there laughed at him—"Here come them motherfuckers with that down-home bullshit"—and it made Walter feel bad. Here's a motherfucker swingin' a bucket and moppin' floors and shit, and here *you* are, a star at the Apollo Theater, drivin' a brand-new Cadillac with a hit record, and you gonna let *him* put *you* down? Walter was insecure. And it got to the point where he had to drink real heavy before he'd go on stage. The things that made him popular started fadin' out, but instead of keepin' on and improvin' himself, he let alcohol get the best of him. And I guess Leonard Chess was askin' him, "What you got, man?" Leonard must have figured that Walter had blowed out all his riffs. Alcohol and insecurity brought him down. Walter got to the place where he was a drunk and he just lost it.

When Walter had a good band he wouldn't pay 'em right, and they left him. Walter's musical thing was built around a band, especially a good, tight rhythm section that fit what he did. Fred Below fit right in with Little Walter. The Aces and Robert Jr. Lockwood were really the type of musicians that Walter needed.

I wish somebody could have gotten to Little Walter before he died and straightened him up. Walter thought all the harp players in Chicago was out to get him, but we couldn't touch him no kinda way. He was way ahead of us. Walter wasn't tight with many people. He thought that everybody was tryin' to take over and put him out of business, I guess. I think Walter liked me, 'cause he knew that I had started playin' harp before I even knew he existed. He knew that I was comin' out of the John Lee Williamson bag, just like he did, and that I had made "Hello Stranger." Walter knew that I didn't start out tryin' to copy him.

Little Walter at Theresa's Lounge, 1965
Photograph by Raeburn Flerlage; Chicago History Museum, ICHi-133579

The night Walter died—it was February 1968—he was hangin' out down on 51st Street with a lot of wineheads. They was drinkin' up in the alley, and Walter was drinkin' with 'em and partyin' with 'em. What I heard was that there was some kind of a drunken brawl, and somebody stripped the watch off the sister of a woman Walter was goin' with. Walter started shootin' off at the mouth and some guy hit him in the head. I don't know what he got hit with. Walter got back home to his old lady's place, and he called up Sam Lay and said, "Come up here with your gun and bring a couple of guys with you. I'm going to kick somebody's ass."

The next morning Sam Lay called up Walter's old lady, and she told him Walter had died in bed. They took him to Michael Reese Hospital, but he was dead on arrival. Walter died just like Sonny Boy, from bein' hit on the head. They died twenty years apart. Sonny Boy got killed in 1948, and Walter got killed in 1968.

Little Walter never reaped the benefits from his talent, so that is tragic. If Walter's health had held out and he had lived a few more years, he would have been a wealthy man, 'cause his royalties would have been in the millions. His records sold all over the world, and they're still sellin'. All these young white guys have come along and discovered Little Walter over and over. With the Rolling Stones and those other bands coverin' his tunes, his publishing royalties would be big. Walter would have been able to live comfortably, even if he didn't play at all. For a long time, his royalties was split up between his three sisters, but recently they found out that Walter had a daughter, and so now the money goes to her, as I understand.

: : :

After Little Walter started goin' down in popularity, the harmonica was losin' ground. A lot of the guys who specialized in harp, and singin' and playin' Little Walter and Muddy stuff, was losin' gigs in the clubs. I was still playin' harp in the clubs, but I didn't feature it all night. And I could sing all kinds of different material besides blues—Chuck Berry, Fats Domino, Ernie K-Doe, Allen Toussaint.

Pete Welding was friends with a guy named Norman Dayron. Dayron had a recording machine, and one day in 1963 he invited me, James Cotton, Paul Butterfield, and Elvin Bishop over to somebody's apartment and we started experimentin'—playin' stuff and recording some things. One of the things we recorded that day was a harmonica instrumental called "South Side Boogie." Elvin Bishop played guitar and the three of us jammed on harmonicas. Cotton was playin' one of those big Marine Bands that Rice Miller was into.[2] I never did like the sound of that big Marine Band. You can't choke it to get the real blues sound out of it. But since Rice Miller was a big star, other guys like Cotton jumped on it. Cotton experimented with a lot of different harmonica sounds and gimmicks. He was really *into* the harp, you know. "South Side Boogie" wasn't a professional recording. I don't know if it was actually ever

2. Hohner Marine Band model 365.

released, but it got out on some bootlegs or somethin', 'cause people sometimes ask me about it.[3] I remember all of us bein' together, but I never did hear the tape, and I don't remember the other things we recorded that day.

Later that same year, Pete Welding called me and told me, "Come on down to the Fickle Pickle tonight and sit in with Little Johnny Jones." The Fickle Pickle was a folk music club up on the North Side. I had met Johnny Jones when I was twelve years old at Sonny Boy's house, and then again at Sylvio's, and I had seen him playin' with Elmore James all through the 1950s, so you know I had a good feelin' about him. So I went down there—it was a small club in a basement—and sat in for a set with him.

I didn't know about it, but Pete and Norman Dayron had Dayron's recording machine set up that night, and they recorded the show. I don't drink at all now, but in my younger days I used to drink a bit, and I remember I had too much to drink that night. We just had fun on that show. We was just improvisin'. I'm sure I did some Sonny Boy stuff, 'cause Johnny Jones knew that material, 'cause he was a Big Maceo disciple. I remember we sang "Worried Life Blues" together that night. I'd sing one verse, and then Johnny would sing the next. Years later, Bruce Iglauer released the tape of that set on Alligator.[4]

I rented time in a studio over on the North Side in June 1966 to record some original tunes. I went in there with my brother Jerome on bass, Mighty Joe Young and Jody Williams on guitars, and Reynolds Howard on drums. Reynolds was my regular drummer, but he wasn't a real blues drummer. We recorded three tunes—"I Left My Happy Home," "Billy Boy's Jump," and "Crying and Pleading." I did another session that year in September and added Mickey Boss on tenor. I produced those sessions myself.

When Pete Welding got his Testament Records label goin', he

---

3. "South Side Boogie" and four other tunes recorded by Norman Dayron at this session appear on *3 Harp Boogie*, released in 1993 by Tomato Records.

4. *Johnny Jones with Billy Boy Arnold*, Alligator Records ALCD 4717, 1979.

wanted me to go in together on that as his business partner. But I wasn't interested in the business part, so I turned him down. At the time I thought that was the smart decision. I thought it would take away from the artistry or somethin'.

I played Pete the tapes from those 1966 sessions, and he asked me if I would lease them to him so he could release them on Testament. So I gave him the tapes, and he issued the three songs from the first 1966 session on an album called *Goin' to Chicago*. Years later, Pete released the tracks from both sessions on a Testament CD with the same title. Pete moved out to California, and he passed away out there in 1995. I was real sorry to hear that he had passed.

: : :

In 1966, I did a gig with Willie Dixon. Carey Bell, his harmonica player, couldn't make the gig, and I went to Colorado with Willie and Lafayette Leake and the Chicago Blues All Stars for about three or four weeks. Willie was a *very* nice guy, and a very interesting person. When you'd listen to him talk, you knew that he had a lot of wisdom and a lot of knowledge. Willie Dixon was a man to know. He knew which guys he wanted in the studio, and he helped a lot of musicians. I had known *of* Willie Dixon since 1947, 'cause he played bass on three or four sessions with Sonny Boy. And on the record labels they would have "Blind John Davis, piano. Sonny Boy Williamson, blues singer with harmonica. Willie Dixon, string bass. Charles Saunders, drums." That's when I first heard Willie Dixon's name. He wasn't writin' any songs for Lester Melrose at that time. See, Melrose was the middleman for RCA Victor, and he ran the publishing company. He wanted his artists to record their own songs, 'cause that way he would keep all the publishing money.

Willie Dixon was a smart man, and he learned a lot from the artists he worked with in the early days—people like Sonny Boy Williamson, Big Bill, and Tampa Red. Dixon figured out that the real money in the music business was in publishing. He started writin' songs when he was playin' bass with the Big Three Trio to get in there on the publishing. The Big Three Trio was on Bullet Records, and he was writin' stuff for them. Then Willie Dixon got with Chess Records and started writin' songs for their artists.

Willie Dixon had been around. He came from Mississippi. He came from down there where the blues was happenin', and he knew all those old blues tunes. "Little Red Rooster" was his biggest hit. That came from one of Memphis Minnie's songs. Sam Cooke covered that song. And Dixon wrote "My Babe" for Little Walter, which was Walter's second biggest hit. Willie Dixon wrote some tremendous songs for those Chess artists. He was one of the greatest songwriters out there. And then in the 1960s, the rock groups started coverin' his songs, and that's where the real *big* money started comin' from. Willie Dixon made big money in his lifetime, which was great. He must have been a multimillionaire when he died.

I asked him one time, "Did those artists appreciate your tunes?" And he said, "Man, them guys got an attitude." But Willie Dixon helped 'em a lot, and I guess their attitude probably changed. Muddy was writin' his own little songs, but he *needed* those Willie Dixon hits to pull him out of a rut. "Hoochie Coochie Man" and "I Just Want to Make Love to You"—those are some big records that made big money. Little Walter wrote some good stuff, too, you know, but I'm sure he was glad that he recorded "My Babe." Willie Dixon wrote "Diddy Wah Diddy" and "You Can't Judge a Book by the Cover" for Bo Diddley. And "Wang Dang Doodle" sold a million for Koko Taylor. Willie Dixon was a hell of a songwriter.

: : :

When white people started acceptin' the blues and investin' in it, they expanded it. You wasn't makin' no money on the South Side. The club owners didn't have the base and they didn't have no money. They wouldn't give you no more than they had to, and they would screw you if they could. That's why the union stepped in, but you couldn't hardly live off the union scale. You were just barely makin' a living. If you was playin' a gig on the South Side and you didn't have no contract and it was rainin', the club owner might let you play one set and then say, "You guys better knock off, 'cause there ain't nothin' happenin' tonight."

When black blues musicians started playin' the white clubs and gettin' white managers, things changed. The money got much, *much* better. Mighty Joe Young got a manager named Scott Cameron. Cameron got Joe a gig at the Wise Fools Pub on the North Side, playin' Friday, Saturday, and Sunday for good money. When Joe showed up to set up on Friday night, the owner came in. He had a bad cold, and he said, "Joe, I'll see you next week. I'm goin' home and stayin' in bed for a while." And he paid Joe for the whole week-end, right there on the spot. So that was the difference—Joe had Scott Cameron as his manager. Scott Cameron managed Muddy and Willie Dixon, too. He was a Chicago guy.

Blues musicians made more money and got more recognition playin' for white audiences than they did playin' locally and tourin' the chitlin' circuit, as we called it. A lot of the guys in Chicago was playin' at white clubs, playin' out in Cicero and places like that, 'cause the white clubs wanted to book that type of music. More blues clubs started openin' up on the North Side. I didn't get a chance to think about whether the blues was goin' to stay viable af-ter windin' down with black audiences, 'cause after Paul Butterfield and those guys got more white people to listen to it, the blues just got better and better, economically.

And then it got to the place where we was playin' more for whites than for blacks. But I never looked at it as a racial thing. I looked at it as people, and I was doin' what I do. I played the same way for anybody. I didn't feel intimidated. I could do my own songs, I could do Chuck Berry, I could do Fats Domino, I could do Little Richard. *And* Muddy Waters and the blues. I liked it all. In my expe-rience, the people want to hear what you do.

But some of the black blues players thought they had to change their act for a white audience. They thought they had to change their music or soup it up or rock it up. They wasn't used to playin' for white people, and they thought they had to do somethin' a little different, you know. When they was workin' for a white audience, they would come out and make a little statement, like "We got to love one another, we got to pull together." Stuff like that. They thought they had to give a little speech to the white audience about brotherly love, but I thought that the white kids wanted to hear me play and do what I do. I didn't feel like givin' no speeches about we got to come together.

And the guys started dressin' down when they played for white people—wearin' blue jeans and cowboy hats and all that. They were dressin' down for the hippies. But I never did follow that trend. I always dressed well. Back in the day, Muddy Waters always wore a shirt and tie and a suit, and Wolf's band wore uniforms. But when the hippie thing came in, the blues guys dropped the suits and ties and started dressin' casual. The white audiences was wearin' blue jeans with holes in the knees and in the back pocket, so the blues guys was just tryin' to get with the crowd, you know. That was the environment they were playin' in. James Cotton was a younger guy, and he wanted to be hip and everything. And so he got out there and the young white guys said, "Hey, man, you want to smoke some pot?" And Cotton started smokin' pot. And dressin' down and wearin' caps and jackets. Gettin' with the crowd. Gettin' with it.

Around 1967, Muddy Waters's manager started gettin' him work on the white college circuit. And then Junior Wells and Buddy Guy started workin' that circuit, too. Buddy and Junior was managed by a guy named Dick Waterman, who used to manage Bonnie Raitt. He got Junior Wells and Buddy Guy, and he started puttin' them on the college circuit.

At that time, I wasn't really active in the clubs and wasn't recording, so I didn't get into that college circuit scene right then. You had to have somebody like Dick Waterman in your corner. He was focused on Junior and Buddy, and he put 'em on that circuit and they started makin' money. James Cotton hooked up with the same agent that Paul Butterfield had, Albert Grossman. Grossman got James Cotton to leave Muddy and go out on his own. Cotton stayed out there for a long time and made some good money with that guy,

Louis Myers (*left*) and Billy Boy Arnold, 1972
Bill Greensmith

and he didn't even have no hit records. See, most of the time you had to have a hit record or some recognition, but if you had a guy like Grossman behind you with connections on the circuit, he could get you on there.

: : :

In 1970 I did another session that I produced myself. I got Louis Myers and Odell Campbell on guitars, Johnny "Big Moose" Walker on piano, and Big Moose's drummer, Chris Moss. Moose and Chris Moss was playin' at that time as a duo down in Old Town, up the street from Big John's. Chris Moss used to be a policeman. Later he moved to St Louis.

We just went into the studio one day and played some blues. I don't think we did any original material. I didn't feel like Louis played his best stuff on that session. Louis started out as a rhythm-type guitarist behind Little Walter, so he generally stayed in the background. I wanted somebody to play some lead guitar on this recording, so I went and got Sammy Lawhorn and took him down to the studio and had him overdub some wah-wah guitar. That session was released a few years later on the Red Lightnin' label in England.[5]

The guitar stuff that the blues guys did in the 1950s didn't go over in the '60s and '70s. Junior Wells was still tourin' with the Aces, but he decided he needed a guitar player with more flair, so he got Lefty Dizz. Lefty Dizz wasn't the guitar player that Louis Myers was, but what Junior needed was somebody more dynamic with more soul. Louis said, "You know what Junior did, that little motherfucker? He went out and got Lefty Dizz over me."

I didn't say nothin', but I knew why Junior did that. When Louis Myers and the Aces was playin' behind Little Walter, Little Walter had so much fire in his harmonica playin' that all they needed to do was to give him rhythm and fill in. Little Walter's harp stood by itself. Junior was a good singer and a great harmonica player, but over time he started playin' less harp and doin' more singin'. If you don't stay with the harp, you sort of lose your fire. And Junior was doin' the funky soul-music stuff, 'cause he wanted to get over. That's why Junior got Lefty Dizz. Lefty Dizz wasn't a great guitar player, but he had flair and personality, which audiences liked.

I had a similar experience playin' with the Aces up on the North Side around the same time. I told Louis and them, "Open up and play a couple of numbers, and then call me up." So Louis opened with some old-school stuff—"Honky Tonk" and stuff like that—and the club owner complained. The next night, I hired Bobby King to play guitar. He was a dynamite guitar player. He could take that guitar and play all that James Brown stuff like "There Was a Time" and play all the horn parts and everything. So I got Bobby King up there the next night, and he carried the show over.

Sometime in the 1970s, I produced some duo sessions with a guitar player named Ulysses Williams. We had played some gigs

5. *Sinner's Prayer*, Red Lightnin' RL 0014, 1976.

together, and we did some recording at my house. I had a recorder that could record in stereo. We was just playin' blues. Ulysses Williams played electric guitar. I played the tapes for Willie Dixon, 'cause I was singin' "Little Red Rooster" and some of his songs on there, but he wasn't interested. Those tapes were never released. I haven't heard 'em in a long time.

:::

Havin' a family didn't stop me from pursuin' music. I respected myself and my family. Just 'cause I had a day job didn't mean I didn't play music. But if you're not makin' records and you're not with a big-time agent and you're just playin' locally, you're not gonna make much money. You gotta have a lot of interests nowadays if you want to make a dollar or live a certain way.

I bought the house I'm livin' in now in 1970. We lived in apartments before that. I had a wife and two sons. I had a family to take care of. It's always best to own your own home. And, after all, I am "a man of considerable taste."[6]

I knew a woman who was a truant officer, and in the early '60s I got a job as a truant officer through her. That didn't last long. Then I started drivin' a bus for the Chicago Transit Authority, the CTA. I did that for about four years. It paid the bills. I wasn't too proud to take care of my family. I never stopped playin' music. I was still giggin' on the weekends, and I was learnin' the bass and the guitar.

Vee-Jay gave me some advance money for the sessions I did for them, but I never saw any songwriting royalties from them. Vee-Jay never told me or Jimmy Reed or any of their other artists about the publishing. They didn't give me no money, and they didn't give Jimmy Reed no money. Every time Vee-Jay would send me a royalty accounting, it said that there was a "balance outstanding." Which meant, "We didn't make any money on it." You knew damn well that

6. Arnold is quoting a song title from *Eldorado Cadillac*, his 1995 CD on Alligator Records.

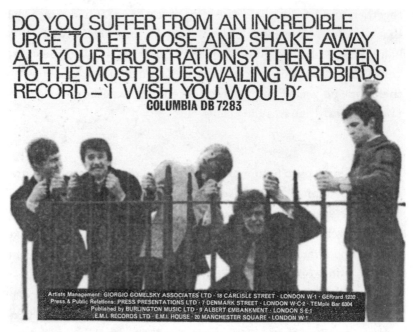

DO YOU SUFFER FROM AN INCREDIBLE URGE TO LET LOOSE AND SHAKE AWAY ALL YOUR FRUSTRATIONS? THEN LISTEN TO THE MOST BLUESWAILING YARDBIRDS RECORD – 'I WISH YOU WOULD'
COLUMBIA DB 7283

Advertisement for Columbia Records' release of "I Wish You Would" by Eric Clapton and the Yardbirds, 1964
Kim Field

they was makin' money on it. "I Wish You Would" sold somethin' like fifteen thousand copies in the first month in Detroit or somethin', but I didn't get one dollar in royalties from Vee-Jay.

Vee-Jay owned Conrad Publishing, so all the publishing money went to Vee-Jay through Conrad. Vee-Jay went bankrupt in 1966 'cause they defrauded the government on their taxes. They didn't even tell us they was closin', and after they declared bankruptcy, they were gone, and you couldn't sue 'em. Conrad Publishing was sold to the Goodman brothers—Benny Goodman's brothers Gene and Harry. The Goodman brothers had a huge music publishing business. Leonard Chess was their partner.[7] When he got into the

7. In 1953, Leonard Chess and Gene Goodman became equal partners in Arc Music BMI, a publishing company focused on rhythm and blues tunes. Arc Music was acquired by Bertelsmann Music Group (BMG) in 2015.

record business, Leonard didn't know nothin' about publishing, which is where the real money is, but later he went into the publishing business with the Goodman brothers.

In 1967 I was takin' my wife and son to Detroit on vacation, and I talked with Willie Dixon about my Vee-Jay publishing royalties. He said that I should call Gene Goodman in New York. So I called him up. Goodman had somebody in his office, and I heard him say, "Ooh, this is Billy Boy Arnold, the guy who wrote 'I Wish You Would.'" I told him that I had never gotten any publishing royalties for it. He told me that Conrad had never kept good records and that their royalty accounts only went as far back as a couple of years. He sent me a check for seven hundred and fifty dollars, even though "I Wish You Would" had been a good-sellin' record.

What I didn't know—and what Gene Goodman didn't tell me— was that "I Wish You Would" had been a hit record in England two years before. But not by me.

Billy Boy Arnold, Chicago Blues Festival, 1992
Photograph by Robert Barclay

8

All around the World

When I made "I Wish You Would," it went all around the world. Eric Clapton and the Yardbirds was young guys in England at the time, and they loved my music. They covered "I Wish You Would" and "I Ain't Got You" and released 'em as singles. And they was hits. And then the Animals and several other people covered those tunes, too.

When this was happenin', I had no idea about it. I never got any money from the Yardbirds' covers of my songs. The Yardbirds didn't rip nobody off, 'cause they made the payments to Conrad Publishing, Vee-Jay's publishing company, and they must have assumed that that money got to me. But Vee-Jay took that money.

I got my first offer to tour Europe in 1963 from a promoter from Switzerland named Kurt Mohr. He had issued a lot of Vee-Jay material by me, Jimmy Reed, Eddie Taylor, and Snooky Pryor on an LP called *Bluesville Chicago* for a French label in Europe, and he sent me a copy and asked if me and Snooky would tour over there.

Right after I got that offer, I ran into Snooky in a Sears store. Snooky was a carpenter, and he was in there buyin' some stuff. We talked about the Kurt Mohr deal, and Snooky said, "Naw, I ain't goin'. They didn't offer me enough money." I was thinkin' about goin' just for the excitement of doin' it, but I didn't want to go over there alone, so we ended up backin' out.

:::

The first time I played over in Europe was in the spring of 1975. I wasn't doin' much in Chicago, 'cause things was dryin' up. Muddy wasn't workin' around there. The only people workin' were Wolf and Junior Wells and people like that. I got an offer to tour Europe with the American Blues Legends. The other guys on that tour were Tommy Tucker (the guy that made "Hi Heel Sneakers"), Little Joe Blue, Homesick James, Eddie Burns, and Jimmie Lee Robinson. That was the first time I had been out of the United States.

The promoter for that trip was Jim Simpson out of London. He had been bookin' American acts over there on shows and tours and everything for several years. That 1975 tour started in London and then played on the continent for about a month. Germany, Switzerland, Spain, Holland—we played in all those countries over there. We played in London, and we played in Paris. We played in big auditoriums and coliseums for 100 percent white audiences. There wasn't much money in it, I'll tell you that. They paid us peanuts, and we didn't have the best supporting band, so most of us headliners had to back each other up, too.

I found out that the European audiences knew about "I Wish You Would" and about Bo Diddley and Howlin' Wolf and Muddy Waters, 'cause Chess and Vee-Jay had been sendin' all their records over there as early as 1954 or '55. That's how Eric Clapton and the Yardbirds and all those young British musicians heard "I Wish You Would," "I'm a Man," "Hoochie Coochie Man," and all that. The people in England was more into the blues than the audiences in the other countries, 'cause they spoke the same language.

Kurt Mohr was the one who first told me about the Yardbirds coverin' "I Wish You Would" and "I Ain't Got You." I got a lawyer, but I still didn't get nothin' out of it. I've re-recorded "I Wish You Would" several times, and I get royalties from those recordings, but not from the original Vee-Jay record or the Yardbirds' records. I never got the type of money I should have gotten, when you figure that a superstar like Eric Clapton recorded it. Junior Wells once

The stars of the American Blues Legends tour in front of the Village Bookshop in London, 1975. *Left to right*: Eddie Burns, Billy Boy Arnold, Jimmie Lee Robinson, Tommy Tucker, Homesick James, and Little Joe Blue
Bill Greensmith

showed me a check for eighty thousand dollars for a writer's credit for "My Baby Left Me a Mule to Ride," an old Sonny Boy Williamson tune that he and Buddy Guy recorded with Eric Clapton. Sonny Boy didn't capitalize on none of that.

I was proud and grateful, though, that those British bands thought enough of my music to cover it. That was a great compliment. And they wasn't responsible for the publishing royalties. I've toured Europe many times, but unfortunately I've never met Eric Clapton in person.

I made a second trip to Europe in December of 1975. I did a tour for about a week with Bo Diddley, Screamin' Jay Hawkins, Johnny "Guitar" Watson, James Booker, Jimmie Lee Robinson, and Margie Evans, a blues singer from Los Angeles. I hadn't had much contact with Bo Diddley after 1955, and I didn't perform with him on stage on that tour, but everything was cool between us. We each had our slot—three numbers. We played all the big cities—Paris, London, Berlin.

Screamin' Jay Hawkins was famous for comin' out of a coffin in his live shows, but he didn't do that on that tour. He just sang and played some piano. He was with his wife. I think she was Spanish or somethin'. I got to know him pretty well during that tour. We talked and rode together and all that. Jay was an interesting guy, and he put on a great show.

I had toured the South with Johnny "Guitar" Watson back in 1957. Johnny was a nice guy. He was a great writer. He was a show-stopper and very professional, and he had a lot of experience in the entertainment business. Johnny came out of Texas and started out as a piano player doin' Charles Brown–type stuff. A lot of guys was doin' a Charles Brown thing in those days. I had been tight with Jimmie Lee Robinson since 1954, when I used to see him on Madison Street with Freddy King.

James Booker was a genius on the piano. Oh, man, he was a good player. He could play all kinds of classical stuff on the piano. But he was a drug addict. He'd been in prison for drugs. Every day, the promoter had to take Booker to the hospital to see a doctor and get him a shot of heroin or whatever he needed so he could go out there and perform.

In 1977 I went back to England to do some shows with Tony McPhee's band. Tony is a British guy and a good guitarist. I recorded an album with Tony and his band while I was over there. We did a version of "Catfish Blues." I've always liked the version of that song that is on the flip side of Elmore James's original "Dust My Broom."

Billy Boy Arnold on stage at the 100 Club, London, 1975
Bill Greensmith

Rice Miller blows some beautiful harp on that record. I never did find out who that was on there singin' and playin' the guitar. Elmore told me it was Guitar Slim, but it's not.[1]

They wasn't payin' us American guys too much money on a lot of those tours, even though we was playin' for big crowds in these great big auditoriums and theaters and concert halls. The Europeans really like the blues. That didn't really surprise me. They embrace it, they're enthusiastic, and they want you to play the authentic blues. They appreciate the blues more than American audiences. They know all your history and they have all your records. It was interesting. They knew everything about me and about my career, and about the careers of the other artists, too. All the shows went over well, and I got a lot of good reviews and recognition.

It was a great experience to go to Europe. I really enjoyed seeing all those different countries and all those different places. My favorite European countries are Holland and Spain. Spain is a beautiful place. I love Paris, and London is a great city, too.

::::

I went over to Germany in 1982 to play some shows over there. I got hooked up with a piano player named Christian Rannenberg, who had connections with a German promoter named Rolf Schubert. Blind John Davis did tours with him. Those shows did well, so after that I started goin' over to Germany for about a month every year to tour with Christian Rannenberg's band all over Germany, Holland, and Belgium. In 1984 I recorded a live album in France. It came out a few years later on an Evidence CD called *Ten Million Dollars*.

There is an agent who has been tryin' for ten or fifteen years to get me to tour Brazil and other places in South America. He told me, "Eddie C. Campbell came down here." I knew Eddie C. for years before he passed, so I asked him about it. Eddie C. said, "Yeah, I

1. Andrew "Bobo" Thomas is the uncredited performer on "Catfish Blues," the flip side of Elmore James's original recording of "Dust My Broom," Trumpet 146, 1951.

slept on a couch in his office." That was a turnoff for me. Even if I was a young guy, I wouldn't do that. No, you gotta get me a hotel!

: : :

I was still playin' around Chicago, but I was also workin' on advancin' myself. I went back to school in 1987. I took day and night classes at Roosevelt University and at National Louis University, where I got a BA degree. That helped me get a job as a parole officer for women who had gotten out of prison. I didn't have that job very long. The work was all right, but I'm not the policeman type. I'm not the type of person that likes to punish people. If I'd catch 'em smokin' marijuana or doin' somethin' they wasn't supposed to be doin', I didn't say nothin'. I thought those women was under enough stress without me addin' to it.

As the 1990s started, I still had a name and I was tourin' out in California. I did a record out there with Mark Hummel—Rusty Zinn played some nice guitar on that—but I had a bad cold and my voice was not in shape.[2] Randy Chortkoff, a harmonica player and bandleader, booked me, Jimmy Rogers, Luther Tucker, and Dave Myers on a show out there. We talked afterwards, and Randy said, "I want to get you with a good band and do a good record on you." I said, "Well, I don't really have any material together right now," but in the end I said okay. I went back out to California, and Randy got these musicians together and produced the session. Rob Rio wrote a song, and I wrote three or four tunes.

Bruce Iglauer, the owner of Alligator Records, had told me a couple of years before this that he would like Randy to do an album on me, and I said, "Yeah, maybe so," but I didn't pay much attention to it then. But then Randy leased the session he produced to Alligator, and they put it out in 1993 on a CD called *Back Where I Belong*.

Randy was kind of footloose with the money, and me and him kind of parted company. But the CD was well received, and Alligator

2. *Consolidated Mojo*, Electro-Fi Records 3392, 2005.

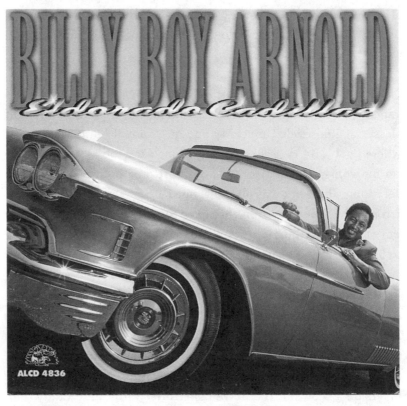

The cover of *Eldorado Cadillac*, one of Billy Boy Arnold's two comeback albums released by Alligator Records in the 1990s
Designed by Matt Minde; photograph by Paul Natkin, courtesy of Alligator Records

told me they wanted to do another one, so I started writin' songs for that. In 1995 I did another session, and Alligator put those tunes out on a CD called *Eldorado Cadillac*.

I thought that both of those Alligator records was great—especially *Eldorado Cadillac*. I had been playin' all the time, but I hadn't recorded in a while, so those records could be considered my comeback, in terms of recording. They earned me awards from *Living Blues* magazine in 1994 for Comeback Artist of the Year and for Best Harmonica. If you ain't makin' records, you ain't really doin' it, as far as the world is concerned.

Left to right: Marty Ballou, Billy Boy Arnold, Duke Robillard, and Jeff McAllister, East Coast Blues Festival, Byron Bay, New South Wales, Australia, 1993
Duke Robillard

I got invited to be part of a tour of Australia in 1993. Forty-somethin' musicians was goin' from the United States. William Clarke was on that show. Duke Robillard was on that show. There was the Gospel Hummingbirds, a black gospel group from Oakland, and Joe Louis Walker and his band. There was a lot of people on that tour. I was just singin', mostly, on that tour. Duke and his band backed me up on the shows, and I just thought that Duke was one of the greatest guitar players I had ran into in a long time.

Bo Diddley came into town in 1996 to record an album called *A Man amongst Men*.[3] Bo always did have a way with song titles! They wanted me on the session 'cause of my history with Bo. He

3. *A Man amongst Men*, Atlantic 82896-2, 1996.

wanted me to play some harp on two or three tunes. We hadn't seen each other in years, but everything went fine between us. I never fell out with Bo Diddley. It was good to play with him again.

Big Bill Broonzy used to do shows at the Old Town School of Folk Music in Chicago, and in 1996 Eric Noden produced a tribute to him there. They had a lot of people playin' Big Bill's stuff. Buddy Guy was part of it. I told Eric that I knew Big Bill and knew about his music, so he asked me if I would do some of Big Bill's songs on the show.

Around 2000 I went to see Kim Wilson play a show in Chicago. This wasn't with the Fabulous Thunderbirds, this was with Kim's blues band. He had Duke Robillard on guitar. Duke had just broke his leg, I remember. I had never met or seen Kim, and I thought that he was the greatest harmonica player around.

Then in 2001 I met Holger Petersen up in Canada, and he asked me to do a record for his Stony Plain label. He knew Duke, and we got Duke to produce it, with Duke's band backin' me up. I went to Massachusetts, and that's how we did that *Boogie 'n' Shuffle* album. When I record, I like to do cover songs that I like, but I always want to have some original material in there written particularly for that record. So I wrote seven or eight songs for that album. The session went very smooth, and that record went over so well that I asked Duke to do another record with me a few years later. I sent him the material, and he put a band together. That ended up coming out on Stony Plain in 2014 as *The Blues Soul of Billy Boy Arnold*.

I played harmonica in third position on a couple of tunes on that record—"99 Lbs." and "You Give Me Nothing to Go On." The song "99 Lbs." is by Ann Peebles. Her husband wrote that tune 'cause Ann Peebles actually weighed ninety-nine pounds. When she made her big hit, "I Can't Stand the Rain," she was my favorite singer. I really love her voice, and I liked that original album she did, *Breakin' Up Somebody's Home*. I liked her style and everything, so that's why I did "99 Lbs."

It was great working with Duke on both of those Stony Plain CDs. I think they are some of the best recordings I've made.

I played a great big international music festival up in Canada a few years ago. They had a lot of groups from all over the world. This guy from Mali, Boubacar Traoré, was on the bill, and I was lucky enough to catch his show. He was playin' the guitar, and he had another guy playin' some other instrument. Just the two of 'em. And what they was playin' was *so* bluesy! It was kinda like John Lee Hooker. Oh, man! I'm tellin' you, I flipped over his music. I was really impressed. I tried to talk to him after the show, 'cause I was so taken by his music. I bought his records right on the spot. He was a nice guy. He didn't really speak English, but I was tellin' him, "What you was playin', that's where the blues come from."

I did another European tour in 2007. Instead of comin' back home after it was over, I went to Germany to work with Christian Rannenberg on a recording he called *The Walter Davis Project*.[4] This was a tribute to one of my all-time favorite blues musicians. When I was just a kid, my aunts and all the black people *loved* Walter Davis. That's why he had such a long career. He recorded from 1930 to 1952. I love his singin' and piano playin'. *The Walter Davis Project* was a real enjoyable session. I did eight or nine tunes on it. Charlie Musselwhite, Jimmy McCracklin, Henry Townsend, and some other people have songs on there, too. If you're interested in Walter Davis, Document Records released all of his recordings on a bunch of CDs.[5]

The Walter Davis Project came out on Electro-Fi Records. They had me do a couple of other albums for them. In 2008 I did a CD of Sonny Boy Williamson songs.[6] If it wasn't for Sonny Boy, I never would have tried to play the harmonica. A few years later, I did a tribute to Big Bill Broonzy with Eric Noden.[7] Eric Noden can really play the guitar. He's studied Big Bill's style, and he can really do it justice.

In 2011 producer Larry Skoller hired me to be part of a show of

4. Various artists, *The Walter Davis Project*, Electro-Fi 3435, 2013.
5. *Walter Davis: The Complete Recorded Works, 1933–1952*, vols. 1–7, Document DOCD-5281 to DOCD-5287, 2017.
6. *Billy Boy Arnold Sings Sonny Boy*, Electro-Fi 3405, 2008.
7. *Billy Boy Arnold Sings Big Bill Broonzy*, Electro-Fi 3430, 2012.

his called "Chicago Blues: A Living History." The idea of the show was to play music from the whole history of Chicago blues, from the 1940s up until the current time. I did some of Sonny Boy's tunes, John Primer specialized in the Muddy Waters stuff, and Billy Branch covered the harmonica players. We did quite a few shows overseas with that concept, and Larry put out two albums of it.[8]

Later that same year Bob Riesman came out with his book on Big Bill Broonzy.[9] Bob put together a show with me and Eric Noden to promote the book and do a tribute to Big Bill. We did that show in New Orleans, Memphis, New York, and Boston.

James Wheeler passed away in 2014. He had just come by my house, 'cause I asked him to show me some stuff on the guitar. He was doin' real well and lookin' good. He ran the Thursday night jam at Rosa's Lounge over on the North Side for two or three years. The owner of Rosa's, Tony Mangiullo, really liked James, and he was always throwin' stuff Wheeler's way. Wheeler would play behind all the different guys who played at Rosa's. Tony is from Italy, and he would take a band over there every year. One year he took me, Wheeler, Bob Stroger, Detroit Junior, and Willie Smith over there. That was a hell of a band, and we all had a great time over there.

James Wheeler was real laid back. A lot of people thought he was kinda stuck up and arrogant, but he was just a shy person. James was real quiet and conservative, and he didn't take up with everybody. He had this clique of musicians that he liked and enjoyed playin' with. He was a genius on the guitar.

In 2012 I was really honored when the Blues Foundation inducted me into their Hall of Fame. They put my song "I Wish You Would" in there, too. A few years later, I was inducted into the Chicago Blues Hall of Fame. It's great to be recognized like that, and to be included along with so many great blues musicians and singers.

8. Various artists, *Chicago Blues: A Living History*, Raisin' Music RM1001, 2009; Various artists, *Chicago Blues: A Living History—The (R)evolution Continues*, Raisin' Music RM1004, 2011.

9. Bob Riesman, *I Feel So Good: The Life and Times of Big Bill Broonzy* (University of Chicago Press, 2011).

Billy Boy Arnold and Charlie Musselwhite relaxing backstage at the Chicago Blues Festival, 2019
Photograph by Kim Field

A few months ago, I did a tune for a Rolling Stones blues album.[10] It was a bunch of us Chicago musicians playin' songs that the Rolling Stones wrote. I did "Play with Fire." The Stones own all the rights, 'cause it was their songs, but we got our session money. It was cool.

: : :

I turned eighty-five this September, but I'm still out there performin'. I played a big show in England maybe seven or eight years ago. Duke Robillard was on that show, and the Animals was on the bill, too. They covered "I Ain't Got You" back in 1965 when they was just startin' out.

I played the Chicago Blues Festival in 2019. Charlie Musselwhite invited me to do two or three numbers with him on his set, and I also did a set of my own the next day with guitarist Billy Flynn's band. I played some gigs in Spain later that year. I tour occasionally

---

10. Various artists, *Chicago Plays the Stones*, Raisin Music CBE1701, 2017.

with Mark Hummel on his Harmonica Blowout shows, and I still play around the country in clubs like Antone's down in Austin.

When I perform, I mostly do songs that I wrote myself and recorded. The good thing about makin' records is that it forces you come up with original material, and then you can do a full live show with just your own material and keep that material alive. That material is still viable 'cause everybody knows me by those songs.

My songs have different twists to 'em, and if the backup band isn't familiar with 'em, they won't start 'em off right. I had guitar players tellin' me, "Man, I ain't got time to learn all your material. Let's just play some blues." So I started playin' guitar on stage, especially on the intros, to make sure I get the right feel on my songs when I do 'em live.

I try to keep that blues feeling in my shows. I only do songs that are effective and that have the blues feel, and I try to do a good job on 'em. I usually write down a set list. I usually have songs in mind. When I did my own set at the Chicago Blues Festival, I put in some songs that most performers around Chicago wouldn't do 'cause they couldn't do them effectively. I did Big Maceo's "Texas Blues"—that was one of his big hits—and Sonny Boy Williamson's "War Time Blues." When I play with Mark Hummel on one of his Harmonica Blowouts, I have three or four songs on the show, so I'll have 'em all ready for the band and we'll rehearse 'em beforehand. When I play a club out of town, like Antone's down in Austin, I'll send the backup band a list of most of the songs so they can listen to my records and learn the licks. And then when I get down there, we get together and do a little rehearsal, and we have the list of the songs and I just call 'em off in the keys so the band will know what to play. That's the way I usually do it. I could just go down there and just do this and do that, but sometimes you get on the stage and you can't think of somethin' you'd like to do. So if you have a set list, and the band has the set list, they know what you gonna do. It's easier, you know. You might be feelin' good, and then you can be more spontaneous. If Kim Wilson is in town and you go by the show and Kim says to come on up and do a couple of numbers, then you can do whatever comes to mind that you would like to do.

Even after all these years, I haven't forgotten my original inspiration. I still play Sonny Boy Williamson's songs, and I can do justice to 'em.

Crowd at the Chicago Blues Festival, 1999
Chicago History Museum, *Chicago Sun-Times* collection, ST-11003352-0014

9

My Blues Dream

As I said before, when I was a kid I would daydream about my blues idols becomin' rich and how people all over the world would love the blues as much as I loved it, if they could only hear it.

When I first saw Paul Butterfield at Pepper's, I wasn't surprised. I was *expectin'* it, 'cause it was part of my dream. Paul Butterfield was stung by the same thing that I got stung by—that boogie blues feeling that gets down into your soul. When Little Milton made his record "The Blues Is Alright," well, I didn't need no record to tell me that. The blues has always been all right to *me*. I always thought it was the greatest music in the world. I like other kinds of music, but what inspired me to be a singer and be in the business was the country blues—the blues from the South, from the original blues singers.

My friend Dick Shurman told me one time, he said, "You're playin' the older styles of blues." Now, who came up with a *new* style of blues? I ain't heard a new style of blues. Where is this new style at?

One thing I found out about the music business: if you make a record, the artist has to be in total control. When an artist like Sonny Boy Williamson makes a record, it isn't the piano player, it isn't the guitar player, it isn't the drummer or the horn man. That's insignificant.

Take B. B. King. It didn't make no difference who the rhythm section was on his records. B. B. King *was* the show. If you rely on the other guy, like I relied on Jody Williams, it causes problems, 'cause when you remove a guy like that from your band, it leaves a hole. You are the artist, and you gotta be in control. The artists who inspired me—people like Sonny Boy and Big Bill—they controlled the show. I tried to be in control of my songs and my thing, 'cause if you depend on somebody else, and they don't show up or they leave, then it weakens your show.

When I first started out, I never had anybody in my band that could really outdo me, so to speak. I had players in my band who wanted to overthrow me and make their own records, but they couldn't sing different styles of blues songs or do any rockish material. I was out there singin' the rock and roll. Chuck Berry, Fats Domino, Lloyd Price—my main thing was singin' those songs. Those guys in my band couldn't outsing me, and they didn't have the charisma or personality. Mighty Joe Young and Jody Williams and Syl Johnson and Odell Campbell, they could all play B. B. King-style guitar. They all would have replaced me if they could have, but I had a name 'cause of my records. I've had several black club owners tell me that the other musicians didn't have the class that I had. And the black audiences liked me. I was young, and I dressed real nice. The club owners liked me, the people liked me, and I had the records. "I Wish You Would" wasn't a smash, but it was a hit and it was different.

Another thing I learned is that you have to write your own songs. There was always a lot of good players around, but in order to get recognition you had to make a record, and to get the chance to make a record you had to have your own material. Take Junior Wells, for instance. He was a good musician. Junior was a great harp player and a great singer and everything. But Mel London and Willie Dixon wrote all or most of the material that he did. Junior wasn't a songwriter. He didn't try to write. I knew from when I was eleven or twelve years old that you had to write your own material. I started out tryin' to write from the very beginning, 'cause I knew you had to write your own songs and present 'em to the record company.

You have to have your own sound, too. Look at John Lee Hooker. His voice and guitar *is* John Lee Hooker. He didn't need no band. That's why he recorded for hundreds of record companies, 'cause he was John Lee Hooker wherever he went. It didn't make no difference what kind of background they put behind him. Most of his records didn't have nothin' but a guitar. Maybe a second guitar— Eddie Burns or somebody. Lightnin' Hopkins or Little Son Jackson didn't need nobody. All of those guys could just show up with their guitar. They didn't need no band, 'cause their voice and their guitar *was* their sound.

Again, you take B. B. King. He could go anywhere and get a piano player or a drummer or what have you. Nobody in the background or no horn player made B. B. King. B. B.'s voice and the guitar playin' *was* the B. B. King sound. So B. B. could go anywhere in the United States or anywhere in the world and work the B. B. King sound.

Now you take the two Sonny Boys—John Lee Williamson and Rice Miller. They each had their own sound. Whoever was playin' the piano or the guitar didn't really enhance their records. Their reputation was built on their voices and their instruments and their personalities that came through the record.

Jimmy Reed was another guy who had his own sound. All he needed was a second guitar player and a drummer and a bass, and he could be Jimmy Reed anywhere. He could record for anybody, and he would always have that Jimmy Reed sound.

Muddy Waters made some pretty good records before he got Little Walter and Jimmy Rogers and Otis Spann, and he wrote some good songs, but what put Muddy on the charts was the sound of his great band and the songs that Willie Dixon wrote for him. Puttin' that band together made Muddy a star, but in the long run it ain't good to be so dependent on musicians that you don't sound like your records when they ain't with you. You see, if you get a guy who can outdo you, a lotta people will tell you, "Hold on to that guy." But you don't want to hold on to that guy, 'cause he ain't *you*. If that guy decides that he wants to go his own way, then you're lost, and you gotta go get somebody else. So you can't really lean on nobody.

Little Walter really put Jimmy Rogers in a trick bag. His harp playin' on Jimmy's records was so dynamic that Jimmy couldn't perform those tunes without a top harp player. If he did tunes like "That's All Right" or "Ludella," they wouldn't have been effective, 'cause without Walter and that dynamic harp, they would have just been another song.

A lot of the guitar players in Chicago that came out of Mississippi was snobs. They came to Chicago to better themselves. And if they played guitar, the first thing they'd want to do is get away from the blues. But most of 'em, they *couldn't* get away from the blues, 'cause they ain't never *had* the blues in the first place. They didn't have what it takes to be a blues musician. They thought all you had do was bend a string like B. B. King. Now, don't get me wrong. B. B. King is one of my favorite artists. I love B. B.'s music and he was the friendliest, nicest guy you'd ever want to meet.

These guitar players didn't like Muddy Waters at all. As far as they was concerned, he couldn't play no guitar, and they didn't like his singin', either. Most of 'em didn't want to play like Muddy, 'cause they didn't like the country blues like I did. But Muddy Waters was a star. He was a hit.

And don't mention John Lee Hooker. They *hated* John Lee Hooker. I thought he was the *greatest*. "Hobo Blues," "Boogie Chillun," "I'm in the Mood"—all those great records was really moving, 'cause Hooker's guitar and his voice were his personal expression. That's what made John Lee Hooker so significant. Some of the musicians wrote him off 'cause he wasn't playin' the kind of guitar they wanted to try to play. But when John Lee was singin', his heart was in it. Muddy made some records that were significant in that way, too. And most of 'em didn't like Bo Diddley. Or Chuck Berry. I heard a lot of the guys say that Chuck Berry wasn't shit, John Lee Hooker wasn't shit, Bo Diddley wasn't shit. That's the way they looked at it, you know.

But all those guys that these snobs say wasn't shit, they was all *great*. I think Chuck Berry is great. John Lee Hooker is one of the greatest blues singers who ever came in the picture. Muddy Waters was my favorite. Howlin' Wolf, Lightnin' Hopkins—I liked all those guys. And when Freddy King made his record "Hideaway," a lot of people said, "He ain't playin' shit." But he got a hit record. What more do you want? I thought Freddy was the greatest.

I didn't come from down South, but I was black and I was singin' the blues. A lot of people that knew me from the city didn't understand why I loved the blues. It was black music—those black-bottom goodies. That's what I liked and that's what I wanted to do. The other people my age was listenin' to bebop and those doo-wop groups. They wasn't listenin' to blues. I was the only young guy in my crowd that liked blues.

There were black people that wanted to be blues singers, but they wanted to dress it up and try to make it what they thought was more appealing. The black audience always strived to get away from the roots of the blues, 'cause of the way they was depicted in America. Everything black people did was to be played down.

But I wasn't tryin' to escape the blues like most black people who was ashamed of themselves and had no confidence. Anything that blacks did, they thought, would not be accepted. We were taught to be ashamed of ourselves and abandon anything that we created, but I wasn't ashamed of it. I *liked* what we created. Even as a kid, I knew that if other races could hear this music, they would love it. I didn't realize a lot of things then that adults realized, but now, as an adult, I still *love* that music.

But most black people—even some musicians, like Blind John Davis—thought it was hip to put the blues down. Blind John was a good friend of mine, and I thought he was a real bluesman 'cause he played on Sonny Boy's records, but when I asked him about it, he said, "I don't remember none of that stuff." He was just makin' a profession. And one time he told me, "I went into a club and they was playin' that junk that you play." Now see, he thought he was bein' uppity and that made him rise above. Ransom Knowling played on all those records with Tampa Red and all of them, but he was a snob who thought he was above the blues singers. He worked at the juvenile detention home, and I guess he thought he had more education than Arthur "Big Boy" Crudup or Big Joe Williams or Tampa Red, so he looked down on 'em. Somebody told me that Ransom Knowling once said, "Who in the world is buyin' that shit?"

Leonard Chess wasn't recording those guys to sing "Danny Boy." He wanted 'em to sing the blues, 'cause that's what he was sellin'. Gospel singers like Sam Cooke and Aretha and people like that, they turned to secular music to make money. That didn't take anything away from their talent, but some of the black public criticized them. They said, "Oh, you went away from your roots. Now you singin' blues." When you mentioned blues, a lot of black people would say, "Aww, man, I don't like that shit." They thought it was hip to put the blues down. But I didn't. Those first John Lee Hooker records with just him and his foot—there's so much tone and so much feeling. Muddy Waters, Lightnin' Hopkins, Little Son Jackson— I loved those guys. They couldn't get too bluesy for *me*. The deeper they get, the better I like it. They could express themselves on their instruments and with their voice, and they was sayin' somethin'. It was the real blues. And I *loved* it. And that's the story of the blues for me. It's a people music.

There's a difference between playin' the blues and playin' *at* the blues. A lot of young players, they start out and they hear the blues and, like me, they like it. But then, when they get into it and start tryin' to put their own feelin' and their own expression into it—and there ain't nothin' wrong with that—some of 'em lose the groove of what the blues is all about. A lot of the young players today can't play the blues with any significant feelin' to it, so they have to play *at* the blues. Those rock stars make all that goddamn noise 'cause they can't really play the blues the way it's supposed to be played. Now they might think it's the blues the way they hear it, but it ain't the blues the way *I* hear it. They hear the expression in the real blues, but they just play it the way they play it and then they talk about it as if it's a new style. Ain't no goddamn new style. They ain't created or invented nothin'.

Some people think, "Aww, the blues ain't shit. Anybody can sing the blues." No, just anybody *can't* sing the blues. Not effectively. Yeah, you can get up there and sing, but if you ain't born with the gift to sing the blues, you won't make it. That's how Sonny Boy Williamson's voice captured me, 'cause his voice had that blues appeal in it.

I like to sing the blues the way I feel the blues. I feel the blues the way the originators—Judge Riley called 'em "the original blues singers"—felt 'em. I'm not saying that I'm as good as them, but that's the way I try to sing the blues. I can sing different styles of music, but whatever I do, I'm gonna make it bluesy.

Classical music is instrumental music. Jazz is instrumental music. Blues is about singin'. Blues is about tellin' a story. Country and western music is the same way. You play the guitar or whatever and you sing the song. If you make a record, you got to tell a story. And if the band is playin' too loud and the people can't hear what you're singin', then they don't get the *message*. The blues is vocal music, really. I know about "Juke" and all that, but you don't hear many blues records with no vocals, 'cause where's the story?

This is just my opinion, but I think that the harmonica and guitar are the two main instruments of blues music. From the 1920s all the way up to the 1950s, the piano dominated the blues. I'm a big lover of blues piano and boogie. Boogie-woogie ain't nothin' but blues played up tempo, and the boogie-woogie beat is what the blues is all about, whether it's on the harmonica, guitar, or piano. Art Tatum didn't play a lot of blues, but his piano intro behind Big Joe Turner on "Wee Baby Blues" is dynamite. My top piano players are Josh Altheimer, Otis Spann, Dave Maxwell—I did some shows with Dave in Boston—and this guy here in Chicago, Johnny Iguana.

Startin' in the 1950s, the piano kind of lost ground to the guitar. Most people used to have pianos, but they became sort of obsolete. Most of the clubs used to have those big, old upright pianos, but when the newer clubs started comin' in, they didn't have no pianos. So Sunnyland and those guys started gettin' those electric pianos so they could carry their own piano with them. But a lot of the club owners, they didn't want no piano. They wanted a harmonica player or a guitar player. Those instruments was easy to carry, and there was so much you could do with 'em.

I'm not sayin' that I'm an authority or anything, but, in my opinion, there are four men who set the patterns for blues harp and guitar. They're the guys who are responsible for the way the blues is played in the world today.

On the harmonica, it's Sonny Boy and Little Walter. Sonny Boy recorded from 1937 until 1947. He was the first harmonica player to play solos with a band. He made the harmonica a lead instrument. Little Walter started recording with Muddy in 1946 and kept it up until he died in 1968.

On the guitar, it's T-Bone Walker and B. B. King. The guitar was played acoustically until T-Bone Walker played it electric style, and he played that style of guitar from 1938 up until his death. And then along came B. B. King, who took it a step further than T-Bone on the guitar.

The way the twelve-bar blues is played today is coming from the perspective of those four guys and is based on the structure that they laid down. All this rock-and-roll stuff comes from them.

I'm a harmonica freak, and there are a lot of fantastic harmonica players on the scene today. Rod Piazza is a dynamite harp player. Mark Hummel is a great harp player. So are Hook Herrera and Jerry Portnoy. Magic Dick is a great harp player and a great singer. I first met him out in Boston years ago.

Steve Guyger is one of the few guys who can really sing and play like Sonny Boy Williamson. Steve can sing better than anybody I've heard around.

Gary Primich used to live in Austin for a while. He was a great harp player and a great singer. He added his own thing to it. Gary was a hell of a musician.

Lee Oskar is bad on that harmonica. He and I did some tours together with Mark Hummel, and I was really impressed by his playin'. He can play the shit out of that harp and make it sound like different instruments. Lee gave me some good compliments when we was on the road with Mark. He told me, "I really like your stories. You have some good stories." I never thought of 'em as stories. Just songs.

Lee makes his own harmonicas, too. Junior Wells played 'em. I still play the Hohner Marine Band. That's what Sonny Boy played, and that's the harp I started out on. Little Walter played the Marine Band. It's got a wooden comb. I just don't care for the plastic harps.

There are still a lot of dynamite harmonica players here in Chicago. Joe Filisko is a hell of a harp player. He can play all different styles. He has classes at the Old Town School of Folk Music where he teaches kids how to play different styles, and he has 'em playin' Sonny Boy Williamson stuff real good. Billy Branch is a good harmonica player. Dave Waldman can really play the harp. Billy Flynn is best known as a guitarist and mandolin player, but he is also a *great* harp player. Billy is a good man to play with. Some guys, when you play with 'em, they'll go off into their own thing. Billy really works with you to make you sound good. He's right up there with Lacy Gibson and James Wheeler as one of the top guitar players in Chicago.

Paul Oscher is a creative genius in every sense of the word.[1] I have the highest regard for him. Paul could already play good when he got the harmonica job with Muddy. He's livin' in Austin now. He can play guitar, piano, harp—everything—and he can get down on all of 'em. He can put you in the mood. Take you right to it. He can play the blues. I told him, "When I do a show with you, you put me in the mood to *play*."

If I've got a gig comin' up, I'll listen to some of the great artists

---

1. Paul Oscher (1947–2021) grew up in Brooklyn and picked up his first harmonica at age twelve. Within three years he was performing in clubs, and at the age of seventeen he became the first white musician to join Muddy Waters's band. Oscher worked with Muddy from 1967 to 1972, appearing on three of Muddy's albums, and went on to record with Hubert Sumlin, Keith Richards, Levon Helm, Eric Clapton, Keb' Mo', and Mos Def, among others. In 2006 Oscher received two Blues Music Awards, Acoustic Artist of the Year and Acoustic Album of the Year, from the Blues Foundation.

that move me. I'll put on some of my deep Muddy stuff, or Walter Davis, or Sonny Boy stuff the day before and listen to 'em to get me in that blues groove. That's why I love to do shows with Paul, 'cause all I have to do is hear him play and I'm inspired. He gets right to the core of it. Paul gets in that groove. And it inspires me to think about what I'm going to do on the show, and it gives me that feelin' and inspiration to get really down in it. Paul Oscher is really a unique person. He has so much feelin'. He's multiple talented. I really love his music. One year we did Deak Harp's Harmonica Block Party in Clarksdale together, and Paul did a hell of a show, playin' guitar and harp. He sounded great. It was a good crowd down there in Clarksdale. Deak puts on a damn good show. Billy Flynn, Kenny Smith, and Bob Stroger backed me up. I really enjoyed it.

Sugar Blue was a younger guy who came on the scene in the 1980s and was playin' with Willie Dixon. He had recorded with the Rolling Stones, too. To me, he was an awesome harmonica player. See, we was all followin' Sonny Boy or Little Walter. We was tryin' to play the country blues. At least I was. I have the utmost respect for Sugar Blue. He's the Charlie Parker of the harmonica. He's in a world of his own. I've never seen a guy perform with a harmonica and just blast the whole joint out with it. He wasn't tryin' to sound like Little Walter or Muddy Waters or nobody. But he knew so much about the harmonica that he could give you those notes and riffs when he was feelin' it. I saw his band do a thing on the West Side and afterwards I told him, "Man, this is the first time I seen a band with three virtuosos in it." I'm talkin' about Sugar Blue; Rico McFarland, the guitar player; and Sugar Blue's wife, Ilaria, who plays bass. They're all dynamite. Sugar Blue has a lot of energy and a dynamite band, and it's inspiring to hear them play. He calls me sometimes when he's travelin'.

To me, the man that can fit in Little Walter's shoes today is Kim Wilson. He has all the nuances, all the right vibrato. And there's another thing about Kim that's like Little Walter. Walter could play behind anyone. In 1959, when Walter and Junior Wells was playin' at McKie's Disc Jockey Show Lounge, this girl singer named Tiny

Topsy was on the show, and Walter played some very different and innovative accompaniment harp behind her that was nothin' like how he played behind Muddy Waters. Kim and I were both on the "Lightning in a Bottle" show in New York City in 2003—they filmed me and Kim and Lazy Lester playin' "Juke" with Jimmie Vaughan on guitar—and I saw Kim back up several singers on that show. He could back 'em up on any kind of stuff they was doin'. Some harp players would just be in the way, but Kim is a master at how to phrase it and how to add somethin' to it. Walter could do that, too.

Louis Myers and Kim Wilson are the two guys that had the qualities of Walter. Louis was more like an imitation of Walter, but Kim's got all the qualities that Walter had *and* his own thing. That's what makes Kim the top man, 'cause he ain't blowin' Walter's solos note for note. Kim can solo all night without repeating himself. If you play harp, he'll blow your mind. He's an artist, like Little Walter was.

There are a lot of black musicians around Chicago who play the blues 'cause they hear that the blues stars are makin' a lot of money. When they hear that B. B. King and John Lee Hooker became millionaires, they jump on the blues wagon. But it's not really in 'em to want to keep the tradition goin'. And I guess maybe you *can't* keep the tradition goin'—you gotta move on. They say, "Well, the blues is okay," but they ain't really into it from their heart. They're into it 'cause they think that the blues could be a way to make it. But if they don't have it in 'em, then they can't put it on record and express it. And there you go.

Most of the white guys that are playin' blues is doin' it 'cause they like the music. One white guy told me, "If I wanted to really make money, I'd sell dope. I wouldn't get into music." But he loved the music.

I don't see many black musicians that are tryin' to do anything with the blues. Black people come to the Chicago Blues Festival 'cause it's free. Some of the white kids go for the same reason— 'cause it's a thing—but some of 'em are there 'cause they've listened to artists like James Cotton, Billy Boy Arnold, or Little Walter. But the black people who go to the festival don't even know who Little Walter is. They could care less, you know, and they ain't gonna buy no blues records.

Ray Charles is one of my favorite artists. Ray Charles wasn't ashamed to sing the blues. He said he *liked* the blues, but he wasn't steeped in the blues like John Lee Hooker. Ray Charles could play and sing in different styles, and he went to the top. That's why black people liked artists like Ray Charles—'cause he would sing some blues, but he could play all these other styles, too.

If you're talkin' about the traditional blues that Muddy Waters and Sonny Boy Williamson and Little Walter played, I don't see that goin' any further, as far as black people are concerned. The black audience is just not that interested in the blues. Some black people will say, "I like jazz," but most of 'em don't know what jazz is. They come from a black culture that loved jazz and was really into it, but today they don't even realize that jazz was derived from the blues. And where is jazz goin' today? I think that blues and jazz have run their course. I'm not sayin' that they are through, 'cause they still like the blues all over the world, but I don't see any pioneers comin' up that are revivin' those styles. All the guys in Chicago who are playin' the guitar, they're playin' off what those older guys laid down. They don't really have no true identity or creativity.

Most of the people who appreciate the blues are the older set. The people who like the old, traditional blues are the older people. Where is the blues goin' from here? Where are the blues heroes now? I don't know if there are any left. The original blues heroes just had that blues feelin', and they went into a studio and made a record. Some of 'em clicked and made a name, and now we have to go buy what they left for us to listen to. Even the black performers who got into what they called "the chitlin' circuit," they can't make any money at all now, 'cause that ain't happenin' now. So you wonder where the music business is going. I guess rock and roll is playin' out, too. It's a different scene now. There really is no music business anymore.

I don't know if I had to do it all over again whether I'd go a different route. I probably would have got more experience playin' with different people before I went out on my own. I would rather have recorded for Leonard Chess in Chicago. When you recorded with Leonard Chess, you was on your way somewhere. But it didn't come out too bad, 'cause I had "I Wish You Would." That song put my name on the map, all around the world. I took advantage of the things that came my way. I'm more seasoned now. I still write songs, and I want to record them on another album. And there are a lot of songs by other artists that I'd like to do.

I'm eighty-five now, but I'm battin' a thousand. It just depends on how you think and what you do with yourself. You got to keep your mind active and positive. There's no other way to go. When I was comin' along, everybody was into the drinkin' thing. Back in those days, everybody drank that hard whiskey, and I saw what it did to them. Blind John Davis told me that Big Bill's whiskey of choice at the clubs would be 100 proof. Big Bill drank up all his profits. One time I ran into Lefty Dizz at the Checkerboard, and I said, "Hey, Dizz, come on. I'll buy you a drink." He said, "I don't drink nothin' but 100-proof Wild Turkey." And he'd be drinkin' that all night. One time when I was with Buddy Guy, he poured some whiskey in a glass and he said, "You drink? You want some of this?" And I said, "No," and he said, "Man, I don't blame you. This'll make you mistreat your wife and kids." And he took that whiskey and drank it straight.

I remember when Junior Wells didn't drink *nothin'*. He used to criticize me and Luther Tucker and James Cotton and Little Walter about drinkin'. But when he and Buddy got big, he started drinkin'. A lot of times people feel that they have to drink when they're successful. But that hard drinkin', it takes a toll on you. That drinkin' will do you in.

I used to drink when I was younger, but I don't drink now. At Christmas time I might drink a little glass of wine or somethin' like that. I never did smoke. I smoked a reefer once. I ain't got nothin' against it, but it's not my thing. You know, Bo Diddley and Chuck Berry didn't smoke or drink, either.

I was on a three-week tour with Buddy Guy and his band a while back. Buddy is a nice guy. He's a superstar now, and he's earned it. Buddy Guy is a house rocker, man. He can tear a house up. One night, after I played "I Wish You Would," Buddy came up to me and told me, "Billy Boy, you made some good stuff, and you're still doin' it." I thought that was a great compliment.

Seventy years ago, as a kid, it was my dream that the blues would become loved all over the world and that blues musicians would get the success they deserved. People thought I was crazy. All the adults thought, "What's wrong with him?" But it came to pass, *exactly* as I thought it would, and it was my calling to play a part in makin' my dream come true. I had a burnin' desire to find the blues and to be a part of it. That's the only way I can describe it. That's what my whole life has been about. I love the blues just as much now as I did then. I believe more than ever that the blues is the greatest music in the world. That's what the black people in America gave to the world: the blues and soul.

Acknowledgments

First of all, I want to thank Kim Field for suggestin' the book in the first place and for doin' all the hard work to make it real. I also want to express my appreciation to Dick Shurman for his friendship and support over the years, and to Scott Dirks for everything he's done to tell the story of the blues. I want to especially let all my fans around the world know how grateful I am for their support. And, as always, I want to thank my lovely wife, Mary, for her love and encouragement.

—Billy Boy Arnold

I can personally attest that Billy Boy Arnold's total recall of past events is exceeded only by his patience. He endured many hours of interviews, answered my many half-baked questions without complaint, and tolerantly set me straight on what the glory days of the Chicago blues scene were really like. Thank you for trusting me with your incredible story, Billy Boy.

I want to thank my longtime friend Mark Hummel, who played a key role in getting this project off the ground by enthusiastically introducing me as a person of some kind of credibility to Billy Boy backstage at the Alberta Rose Theatre in Portland, Oregon.

Dick Shurman's endorsement was critical in getting Billy Boy to agree to participate in this project, but Dick's assistance didn't end there. He read early drafts of the manuscript, gave me predictably sage advice about organization, corrected a multitude of errors, and suggested important areas to discuss with Billy Boy about which I didn't know enough to ask. When the coronavirus made it problematic for me to travel from Portland to Chicago, Dick stepped in and helped Billy Boy comb through his photo collection. Dick is a legend in the music business not only because of his brilliance as a producer but because of his generosity and integrity. Dick is one of the best friends the blues has ever had, and thanks to this project I have become just another of the many people who owe him one (or two or three).

David Dunton, who in another lifetime edited my first book, provided the first outside validation that this was a commercially viable project. David shared with me not only his wise counsel about how to find the right publisher for this book but his extensive industry contacts as well. Peter Guralnick, who showed me what music writing could be when I read his classic *Feel Like Going Home* in 1971, was also enthusiastic and encouraging about the importance of getting Billy Boy's story in print and helpful in making that happen.

It's not an exaggeration to say that this book might never have been published without the help of Bruce Iglauer, the passionate and hardworking mastermind behind Alligator Records, one of the most successful blues labels ever. Bruce and Alligator were responsible for rejuvenating Billy Boy's musical career by issuing two outstanding Billy Boy Arnold CDs in the 1990s. Bruce introduced me and this project to the University of Chicago Press (publisher of Bruce's highly recommended memoir, *Bitten by the Blues: The Alligator Records Story*), thereby launching the association that produced this book. Bruce also contributed several photographs for the book. I can't thank him enough.

Billy Boy Arnold and I are very proud to be associated with the University of Chicago Press, one of the world's finest publishers. Executive editor Tim Mennel and series editor Carlo Rotella were champions of this project from the beginning, and their thoughtful insights and suggestions have made this a much better book. I also want to give a well-deserved shout out to Susannah Engstrom, who patiently shepherded me through the manuscript submission process. Leslie Keros proved to be the ideal copy editor for this book, given her mastery of language and her deep knowledge of the music. Her diligence and expertise are reflected on every page. Tamara Ghattas supervised editing and production and helped build a very handsome book, and Siobhan Drummond did a marvelous job on the index.

The Blues Dream of Billy Boy Arnold builds on the outstanding work of writers and blues researchers who recognized the importance of Billy Boy's unique story and music decades before I began documenting it. Mike Rowe's fascinating interviews with Billy Boy, published in *Blues Unlimited* magazine over three issues during the winter of 1977–78, provided the first in-depth coverage of Billy Boy's recordings and career. Mary Katherine Aldin's excellent 1994 interview with Billy Boy in *Living Blues* magazine added another layer to his story. These rich and fascinating profiles gave me a road map that guided my own efforts and challenged me to meet their very high bar for journalistic quality.

Billy Boy and I wanted this book to be richly illustrated, and the University of Chicago Press was very supportive of that goal. Billy Boy volunteered many stunning images from his personal collection, and Bruce Iglauer, Duke Robillard, Robert Barclay, and Scott Dirks all provided photographs as well. A very special thanks is due to Bill Greensmith, who contributed several of his own outstanding photos and combed through the vaults of the *Blues Unlimited* archives to find other historically important and visually striking images for this book. Blues fans the world over owe a huge debt to the passion, scholarship, and boosterism of British blues researchers like Bill, who played such a big role in teaching us Americans about our own best music.

Scott Dirks, coauthor of *Blues with a Feeling*, the remarkable biography of harmonica genius Little Walter Jacobs, offered a host of suggestions on areas about which to question his good friend Billy Boy Arnold and helped with visual material as well. Scott's exceptional published research on the history of the Chicago blues scene led to me ask him to create maps of the South and West Sides for this book to help make more real the neighborhoods that produced both Billy Boy and the Chicago blues sound, and he did a wonderful job.

Fred Ingram beautifully rendered those maps and did a masterful job of retouching some of the vintage photographs that appear in these pages. Thanks so much for your stellar contribution, Fred.

Another person who added immeasurably to this book is the renowned blues researcher and historian Stefan Wirz, who kindly allowed me to include his extensive Billy Boy Arnold discography in this book. Anyone interested in the history and the details of blues recordings should do themselves a favor and visit his American Music website at https://www.wirz.de/music/american.htm.

Jeff Fereday never flagged in encouraging me to launch this project and bring it to completion. Jeff read several drafts of the manuscript, caught a slew of errors, championed clarity, and offered up several insights that helped me decide how to structure Billy Boy's narrative. Thank you, Jeff.

All my love and deepest gratitude to my wife, Megan, who makes me a better—and much happier—person and brings her own special music to our partnership.

—Kim Field

Discography

Billy Boy Arnold's recording sessions are presented below in chronological order. Each session entry begins with the artist's name as it appears on the released recording and lists the personnel, location, and date of the session. Song titles are listed in the left column with corresponding catalog numbers on the right; dashes indicate identical catalog numbers. Each session entry concludes with the albums on which those recordings appear. This discography is drawn from the extensive Billy Boy Arnold discography compiled by Stefan Wirz, available at https://www.wirz.de/music/arnoldbb.htm. Copyright Stefan Wirz.

BILLY BOY ARNOLD WITH BOB CARTER'S ORCHESTRA

Billy Boy Arnold, vocals, harmonica; unknown tenor sax, piano, guitar; Curtis Ferguson, bass; unknown drums

Chicago, ca. April 1953
- I Ain't Got No Money   Cool 103, Red Lightnin' RL 0012, Wienerworld 5100
- Hello Stranger   —
    Billy Boy Arnold, *Blow the Back off It* (Red Lightnin'); *Down Home Blues Chicago: Fine Boogie* (Wienerworld)

BO DIDDLEY

Bo Diddley, vocals, guitar; Billy Boy Arnold, harmonica; Otis Spann, piano; James Bradford, bass; Clifton James, drums; Jerome Green, maracas

Chicago, March 2/3, 1955
- I'm a Man   Checker 814, Checker 997, Jasmine JASMCD3165
    Bo Diddley (Chess); Billy "Boy" Arnold, *Come Back Baby, I Wish You Would* (Jasmine)

Omit Arnold:
- Bo Diddley   Checker 814, Checker 997, Jasmine JASMCD3165
    Bo Diddley (Chess); Billy "Boy" Arnold, *Come Back Baby, I Wish You Would* (Jasmine)

Originally unissued tracks:
- I'm a Man (alt. tk.)   Chess 9331
- Little Girl (alt. tk.)   —
    Bo Diddley, *Rare and Well Done* (Chess)
- Little Girl (Can I Go Home with You)   Checker 1436, Jasmine JASMCD3165
- You Don't Love Me (You Don't Care)   —
    Go Bo Diddley (Checker); Billy "Boy" Arnold, *Come Back Baby, I Wish You Would* (Jasmine)
- Sweet on You Baby   Red Lightnin' RL 0012, Ace 610, Jasmine
                                               JASMCD3165
    Billy Boy Arnold, *Blow the Back off It* (Red Lightnin'); *House Rockin' Blues* (Ace); Billy "Boy" Arnold, *Come Back Baby, I Wish You Would* (Jasmine)
- You Got to Love Me Baby   Red Lightnin' RL 0012, Ace 610, Chess 4-9340
    Billy Boy Arnold, *Blow the Back off It* (Red Lightnin'); *House Rockin' Blues* (Ace); *Chess Blues* (Chess); Billy "Boy" Arnold, *Come Back Baby, I Wish You Would* (Jasmine)
- Rhumba (unissued)

JEAN DINNING

Jean Dinning, vocals; Billy Boy Arnold, harmonica; unknown guitar; unknown saxophone; Willie Dixon, bass; Clifton James, drums

Chicago, ca. May 1955

- Bo Diddley   Essex Records 395, Quality K1379, Bear Family BCD 17417

  The Popsters: They Tried to Rock, Vol. 4 (Bear Family)

BILLY BOY

Billy Boy Arnold, vocals, harmonica; Henry Gray, piano; Jody Williams, guitar; Milton Rector, bass; Earl Phillips, drums

Chicago, ca. May 1955

- I Was Fooled   Vee-Jay 146, Red Lightnin' RL 0012, Charly CRB 1016, Jasmine JASMCD3165

  Billy Boy Arnold, *Blow the Back off It* (Red Lightnin'); Billy Boy Arnold, *Crying and Pleading* (Charly); Billy "Boy" Arnold, *Come Back Baby, I Wish You Would* (Jasmine)

Omit Gray:

- I Wish You Would   Vee-Jay 146, Vivid 109, Red Lightnin' RL 0012, Charly CRB 1016, Jasmine JASMCD3165

  Billy Boy Arnold, *Blow the Back off It* (Red Lightnin'); Billy Boy Arnold, *Crying and Pleading* (Charly); Billy "Boy" Arnold, *Come Back Baby, I Wish You Would* (Jasmine)

Billy Boy Arnold, vocals, harmonica; Henry Gray, piano; Jody Williams, guitar; Quinn Wilson, bass; Earl Phillips, drums

Chicago, ca. October 1955

- Don't Stay Out All Night   Vee-Jay 171, Red Lightnin' RL 0012, Charly CRB 1016, Jasmine JASMCD3165

- I Ain't Got You   —
- Here's My Picture   —
- You've Got Me Wrong   —

  Billy Boy Arnold, *Blow the Back off It* (Red Lightnin'); Billy Boy Arnold, *Crying and Pleading* (Charly); Billy "Boy" Arnold, *Come Back Baby, I Wish You Would* (Jasmine)

Billy Boy Arnold, vocals, harmonica; Henry Gray, piano; Syl Johnson, Odell Campbell, guitar; Fred Below, drums

Chicago, ca. November 1956

- My Heart Is Crying   Vee-Jay 238, Red Lightnin' RL 0012, Charly CRB 1016, Jasmine JASMCD3165

- Kissing at Midnight   —

  Billy Boy Arnold, *Blow the Back off It* (Red Lightnin'); Billy Boy Arnold, *Crying and Pleading* (Charly); Billy "Boy" Arnold, *Come Back Baby, I Wish You Would* (Jasmine)

Billy Boy Arnold, vocals, harmonica; Sunnyland Slim, piano; Syl Johnson, guitar; Mack Thompson, bass; Reynolds Howard, drums

Chicago, ca. September 1957

- Rockin' Itis   Vee-Jay 260, Red Lightnin' RL 0012, Jasmine JASMCD3165

- Prisoner's Plea   Vee-Jay 260, Vivid 109, Red Lightnin' RL1002,
                                                     Jasmine JASMCD3165
     Billy Boy Arnold, *Blow the Back off It* (Red Lightnin'); Billy "Boy" Arnold, *Come Back Baby, I Wish You Would*
     (Jasmine)

Originally unissued tracks from the same session:
- No, No, No, No   Charly CRB 1016, Jasmine JASMCD3165
- Every Day, Every Night   —
     Billy Boy Arnold, *Crying and Pleading* (Charly); Billy "Boy" Arnold, *Come Back Baby, I Wish You Would*
     (Jasmine)

BILLY BOY ARNOLD

Billy Boy Arnold, vocals, harmonica; Blind John Davis, piano

Chicago, April 15, 1962

Originally unissued:
- We All Got to Go   Testament TCD 6011
- Mattie Mae   —
     Down Home Harp, Testament

Billy Boy Arnold, harmonica; James Cotton, harmonica, vocals; Paul Butterfield, harmonica; Elvin
Bishop, guitar

Chicago, ca. 1963
- Three Harp Boogie (a.k.a. South Side   Roots TR 1005, CBS S2BP 22025, Bullseye
  Boogie)   Blues 9530
     Rare Gems (Roots, CBS); *Rare Chicago Blues, 1962–1968* (Bullseye Blues)

JOHNNY JONES WITH BILLY BOY ARNOLD

Billy Boy Arnold, harmonica, vocals; Johnny Jones, piano, vocals

Fickle Pickle, Chicago, June 25, 1963 (live)
- Sloppy Drunk Blues   Alligator AL 4717, Sonet SNTF 821, Flyright LP549
- Early in the Morning   —
- I Hear My Black Name Ringing   Alligator AL 4717, Sonet SNTF 821, Roots TR 1005,
                                                     CBS S2BP 22025
- I Have Got to Go   Alligator AL 4717, Sonet SNTF 821
- My Little Machine   Flyright LP549
- Goin' to the River   —
     Johnny Jones with Billy Boy Arnold (Alligator, Sonet); *Chicago Blues: Live at the Fickle Pickle* (Flyright); *Rare
     Gems* (Roots, CBS)l

BILLY BOY ARNOLD

Billy Boy Arnold, vocals, harmonica; Mighty Joe Young, guitar; Lafayette Leake, piano; Jerome
Arnold, bass; Junior Blackmon, drums

Chicago, December 30, 1963
- School Time   Prestige 7389, Bluesville 45-827-B, Original Blues
                                                     Classics 562-2, Ace CH 253/CH 250
- Goin' by the River   Prestige 7389, Original Blues Classics 562-2,
                                                     Ace CH253

• You Don't Love Me No More	Prestige 7389, Original Blues Classics 562-2, Ace CH253
• You're My Girl	Prestige 7389, Bluesville 45-827-A, Original Blues Classics 562-2, Ace CH253
• Oh Baby	Prestige 7389, Original Blues Classics 562-2, Ace CH253
• Evaleena	—
• I Love Only You	—
• Two Drinks of Wine	—
• I'll Forget about You	—
• Billy Boy's Blues	—
• You Better Cut That Out	—
• Get Out of Here	—
• Playin' with the Blues	Original Blues Classics 562-2

Billy Boy Arnold, *More Blues on the South Side* (Prestige, Original Blues Classics, Ace)

Billy Boy Arnold, vocals, harmonica; Mighty Joe Young, Ted Mosley, or Jody Williams, guitar; Jerome Arnold, bass; Clifton James or Reynolds Howard, drums

Chicago, ca. June 1966
• I Left My Happy Home	Testament T-2218
• I Left My Happy Home (alt. tk.)	Testament TCD 5018
• Billy Boy's Jump	Testament T-2218
• Crying and Pleading	Testament T-2218
• Baby Jane	Testament TCD 5018
• Rock and Roll	—

Goin' to Chicago (Testament T-2218); Billy Boy Arnold, *Goin' to Chicago* (Testament TCD 5018)

Billy Boy Arnold, vocals, harmonica; Mickey Boss, tenor sax; Mighty Joe Young, guitar; Jerome Arnold, bass

Chicago, September 8, 1966
• Baby Left Me a Mule to Ride	Testament TCD 5018
• Hello Baby	—
• I Love Only You	—
• Evalina	—
• Come See Me Early in the Morning (tk. 1)	—
• Come See Me Early in the Morning (tk. 2)	—
• Why Is Everybody Down on Me	—

Billy Boy Arnold, *Goin' to Chicago* (Testament)

Billy Boy Arnold, vocals, harmonica; Johnny "Big Moose" Walker, piano; Louis Myers, guitar (except "Sinner's Prayer"); Odell Campbell, bass, Chris Moss, drums (Sam Lawhorn, guitar, overdubbed on Red Lightnin' RL 0014)

Chicago, March 7, 1970
• Hi Heel Sneakers	Vogue 30285, Red Lightnin' RL 0014
• Back Door Friend	—
• I Was Fooled	—
• Annie Lee	Vogue 30285, Red Lightnin' RL 0014, Catfish KATCD 130
• Blues on Blues	Vogue 30285, Red Lightnin' RL 0014
• Ooh Wee	—

- I'm Gonna Move   —
- Tomorrow Night   Vogue 30285, Red Lightnin' RL 0014, Catfish KATCD 130
- Troubles   Vogue 30285, Red Lightnin' RL 0014
- Sinner's Prayer   Vogue 30285, Red Lightnin' RL 0014, Catfish KATCD 130

    Billy Boy Arnold Session, *Kings of Chicago Blues, Vol. 3* (Vogue); Billy Boy Arnold, *Sinner's Prayer* (Red Lightnin'); Billy Boy Arnold, *Catfish* (Catfish)

HUBERT SUMLIN AND HIS FRIENDS

Billy Boy Arnold, harmonica, vocals; Hubert Sumlin, Jimmy Dawkins, guitar; James Green, bass; Fred Below, drums

Chicago, January 20, 1971
- I Can't Loose [*sic*]   Vogue 30175, Blues Legacy 12503
- Everyday I Have the Blues   —

    Hubert Sumlin and Friends, *Kings of Chicago Blues Vol. 2* (Vogue); Hubert Sumlin, *Funky Roots* (Blues Legacy)

BILLY BOY ARNOLD

Billy Boy Arnold, vocals, harmonica; Bob Hall, piano; Martin Stone, guitar; Jimmie Lee Robinson, bass; Pete York, drums

Club 100, London, May 5/6, 1975 (live)
- I Wish You Would   Big Bear BEAR 8
- Sugar Mama   —

    American Blues Legends '75 (Big Bear)

Billy Boy Arnold, vocals, harmonica; Louis Myers, guitar; David Myers, bass; Fred Below, drums

Chicago, January 28, 1976
- Somebody Help Me   Indigo IGOTCD 2537, Red Lightnin' RL 0033
- She Fooled Me   —

    The Devil's Music: The Soundtrack to the 1976 BBC TV Documentary Series (Indigo, Red Lightnin')

Billy Boy Arnold, vocals, harmonica; Mickey Boss, tenor sax; Johnny Turner, guitar; Robert Wilson, bass; Mickey Conway, drums

The Raven & the Rose, Sierra Madre, CA, July 8, 1977 (live)
- Somebody Help Me with These Blues   Testament TCD 5018

    Billy Boy Arnold, *Goin' to Chicago* (Testament)

BILLY BOY ARNOLD WITH T. S. MCPHEE AND THE GROUNDHOGS

Billy Boy Arnold, vocals, harmonica; Tony S. McPhee, guitar; Alan Fish, bass; Wilgur [Wilgar] Campbell, drums

London, October 6 and 7, 1977
- Dirty Mother Fucker   Red Lightnin' RL 0024, Rockhouse 8008/67462, Smokestack Lightning SLS 0174, Sequel NEB CD 850, Music Avenue 250167/250288, Angel Air SJPCD415, Catfish KATCD 130
- Don't Stay Out All Night   —

- 1-2-99   —
- Riding the El   —
- Just Got to Know   —
- Christmas Time   —
- I Wish You Would   —
- Ah'w Baby   —
- Sweet Miss Bea   —
- Blue and Lonesome   —
- Eldorado Cadillac   —
- Mary Bernice   —
- It's Great to Be Rich   Red Lightnin' RLEP 0045, Catfish KATCD 130
- Just a Dream   —
- Catfish   —

    Billy Boy Arnold, *Checkin' It Out* (Red Lightnin', Rockhouse, Smokestack Lightning, Sequel); Billy Boy Arnold, *Dirty Mother* (Music Avenue 250167); Billy Boy Arnold with T. S. McPhee and the Groundhogs, *Blue and Lonesome* (Music Avenue 250288); Billy Boy Arnold, *Chicago Blues from Islington Mews 1977* (Angel Air); Billy Boy Arnold, *Catfish* (Catfish)

BILLY BOY ARNOLD

Billy Boy Arnold, vocals, harmonica; Saint James Bryant, piano; Jimmy Johnson, John Watkins, guitar; Larry Exum, bass; Fred Grady, drums

Paris, December 15, 1984
- Ten Million Dollars   Blue Phoenix 33.726, Evidence ECD 26061-2
- I Wish You Would   —
- Trust My Baby   —
- My Babe   —
- Just a Little Bit   —
- Going Home   —
- Yellow Roses from Texas (Just Love Won't Do)   Blue Phoenix 33.726, Evidence ECD 26061-2
- Last Night   Blue Phoenix 33.726, Evidence ECD 26061-2
- I Done Got Over It   —
- Sugar Mama   —

    Billy Boy Arnold, *Ten Million Dollars* (Blue Phoenix, Evidence)

Billy Boy Arnold, vocals, harmonica; Steve Darrington, electric piano; Martin Stone, guitar; Alan Fish, bass; Wilgar Campbell, drums

The Venue, London, ca. 1990 (live)
- Night Before Last   Catfish KATCD 141
- It Ain't Right   Catfish KATCD 141
- Catfish   Catfish KATCD 141
- I Ain't Got You   —
- Dirty Motherfuyer   —
- Prisoner's Plea   —
- Mary Bernice   —
- Trust My Baby   —
- Ooh Wee   —
- Riding the El   —
- Me and Piney Brown   —
- Shake Your Boogie   —

- I Wish You Would   —
- Blues Before Sunrise   —
    Billy Boy Arnold, *Live at the Venue* (Catfish)

Billy Boy Arnold, vocals, harmonica; Tom Mahon, piano; Rusty Zinn, guitar; Ronnie James Webber, bass; Mark Bohn, drums

San Francisco, October 1, 1992
- I'm a Man   Electro-Fi 3392
- Me and Piney Brown   —
- Here's My Picture   —
- Sonny Boy's Jump   —
- I Ain't Got You   —
- If You Would Just Let Me Love You   —
- I Hear My Name Ringing   —
- I Wish You Would   —
- She Fooled Me   —
- You Got Me Wrong   —
- My Heart Is Crying   —
- Prisoner's Plea   —
- Low Down Blues   —
- Dirty Muther Fuyer   —
    Billy Boy Arnold, *Consolidated Mojo* (Electro-Fi)

Billy Boy Arnold, harmonica, vocals; Lester Butler, Hook Herrera, or Randy Chortkoff, harmonica; Andy Kaulkin or Rob Rio, piano; Zach Zunis, Rick Holmstrom, Chris Faulk, or Mike Flanagan, guitar; Tom Leavy or Willie Brinlee, bass; Lee Smith or Jimi Bott, drums

Culver City, California, ca. 1993
- I Wish You Would   Alligator ALCD 4815
- Move On down the Road   —
- Fine Young Girl   —
- You Got Me Wrong   —
- Fool for You   —
- Wandering Eye   —
- Shake Your Hips   —
- Whiskey, Beer, and Reefer   —
- Prisoner's Plea   —
- High Fashion Woman   —
- Young and Evil   —
- Shake the Boogie   —
- Worried Life Blues   —
- Streetwise Advisors   —
    Billy Boy Arnold, *Back Where I Belong* (Alligator)

Billy Boy Arnold, vocals, harmonica; Carl "Sonny" Leyland, piano; Bob Margolin, James Wheeler, guitar; Steve Hunt, bass; Chuck Cotton, drums

Chicago, ca. 1995
- I Ain't Got You   Alligator ALCD 4836
- Sunday Morning Blues   —
- Don't Stay Out All Night   —
- Lowdown Thing or Two   —

- Been Gone Too Long   —
- Mama's Bitter Seed   —
- Man of Considerable Taste   —
- How Long Can This Go On?   —
- Too Many Old Flames   —
- Slick Chick   —
- It Should Have Been Me   —
- Sunny Road   —
- Loving Mother for You   —
    Billy Boy Arnold, *Eldorado Cadillac* (Alligator)

Billy Boy Arnold, vocals, harmonica; Johnny Burgin, Herman Costa, guitar; Sho Komiya, bass; Kelly Littleton, drums

B.L.U.E.S., Chicago, October 20, 1996 (live)
- Streetwise Advisor   Delmark DE-699, Delmark DE-746
- Billy Boy Medley   Delmark DE-699
    Blues Before Sunrise: Live, Volume One (Delmark DE-699); *This Is the Blues Harmonica* (Delmark DE-746)

MISSISSIPPI HEAT WITH BILLY BOY ARNOLD, CARL WEATHERSBY, AND ZORA YOUNG

Pierre Lacocque, harmonica; Barrelhouse Chuck Goering, piano, organ; George Baze, Carl Weathersby, guitar; Ike Anderson, bass; Kenneth Smith, drums; Billy Boy Arnold, vocals, harmonica

Chicago, April 5–7, 1998
- One More Chance   Van der Linden VDL103; CrossCut 11064, Les Disques Bros 9002-2
- Ghost Daddy   —
- It Hurts to Be Lonesome   —
    Mississippi Heat, *Handyman* (Van der Linden, CrossCut, Les Disques Bros)

BILLY BOY ARNOLD

Billy Boy Arnold, vocals, harmonica; Doug James, Gordon Beadle, sax; Matt McCabe, piano; Duke Robillard, guitar; John Packer, bass; Jeffery McAllister, drums

West Greenwich, Rhode Island, 2001
- Bad Luck Blues   Stony Plain SPCD 1266
- Let's Work It Out   —
- Just Got to Know   —
- Greenville   —
- Hello Stranger   —
- Home in Your Heart   —
- Blackjack   —
- Boogie & Shuffle   —
- Every Night, Every Day   —
- Come Here Baby   —
- Just Your Fool   —
- Greenback   —
- Interview with Billy Boy Arnold   —
    Billy Boy Arnold, *Boogie 'n' Shuffle* (Stony Plain)

Billy Boy Arnold, vocals, harmonica, guitar; Mel Brown, piano, guitar; Billy Flynn, guitar, mandolin; Bob Stroger, bass; Willie Smith, drums

Toronto, November 1 and 2, 2007

- $1,000 Dollar Bill — Electro-Fi 3405
- Love Me Baby — —
- Mellow Chick Swing — —
- New Jail House Blues — —
- Around This Old Juke Tonight — —
- Half-a-Pint — —
- Polly Put the Kettle On — —
- Decoration Day — —
- Squeeze Me Tight — —
- Black Gal Blues — —
- Collector Man Blues — —
- Rub-a-Dub — —
- Good Morning Little Schoolgirl — —
- Cut That Out — —
- Sugar Mama — —
- Tell Me Baby — —
- Springtime Blues — —

    Billy Boy Arnold Sings Sonny Boy (Electro-Fi)

Billy Boy Arnold, vocals, harmonica; Adrian Costa, Jimmy Reiter, guitar; Christian Rannenberg, piano; Alex Lex, drums

Bad Iburg, Germany, November 13 and 14, 2007

- Oh! Me! Oh! My! Blues — Electro-Fi 3435
- Angel Child — —
- Goodbye — —
- Move Back to the Woods — —
- Holiday Blues — —
- Please Remember Me — —

Add Keith Dunn, harmonica:

- Just One More Time — Electro-Fi 3435
- My Friends Don't Know Me — —

    The Walter Davis Project (Electro-Fi)

Billy Boy Arnold, vocals, harmonica; Billy Flynn, guitar; Johnny Iguana, keyboards; Felton Crews, bass; Kenny Smith, drums

Chicago, 2009

- My Little Machine — Raisin' Music RM1001
- She's Love Crazy — —
- Night Watchman Blues — —
- Memphis Slim USA — —
- I Wish You Would — —

    Chicago Blues: A Living History (Raisin' Music)

Billy Boy Arnold, vocals, harmonica; Billy Flynn, guitar; Johnny Iguana, piano; Felton Crews, bass; Kenny Smith, drums

Chicago, 2011

- He's a Jelly Roll Baker   Raisin' Music RM1004
    Chicago Blues: A Living History—The (R)evolution Continues (Raisin' Music)

Billy Boy Arnold, vocals; Billy Flynn, guitar; Johnny Iguana, piano; Felton Crews, bass; Kenny Smith, drums

Chicago, 2011

- I'll Be Up Again Someday   Raisin' Music RM1004
- My Daily Wish   —
    Chicago Blues: A Living History—The (R)evolution Continues (Raisin' Music)

Billy Boy Arnold, vocals, harmonica; Johnny Iguana, piano; Felton Crews, bass; Kenny Smith, drums

Chicago, 2011

- She Don't Love Me That Way   Raisin' Music RM1004
    Chicago Blues: A Living History—The (R)evolution Continues (Raisin' Music)

Billy Boy Arnold, John Primer, Billy Branch, Lurrie Bell, vocals; John Primer, guitar; Billy Branch, Matthew Skoller, harmonica; Billy Flynn, guitar; Johnny Iguana, piano; Felton Crews, bass; Kenny Smith, drums

Chicago, 2011

- The Blues Had a Baby (and They Named It   Raisin' Music RM1004
    Rock and Roll)
    Chicago Blues: A Living History—The (R)evolution Continues (Raisin' Music)

Billy Boy Arnold, vocals, harmonica; Eric Noden, acoustic guitar; Billy Flynn, electric guitar, mandolin; Beau Sample, acoustic bass; Rick Sherry, washboard, percussion, clarinet

Chicago, February 21, 22, and 23 and June 6, 2011

- Sweet Honey Bee   Electro-Fi 3430
- Going Back to Arkansas   —
- Girl in the Valley aka Water Coast Blues   —
- Key to the Highway   —
- Looking Up at Down   —
- Rider Rider Blues   —
- Willie Mae Blues   —
- Cell No. 13 Blues   —
- I Want You by My Side   —
- San Antonio Blues   —
- Living on Easy Street   —
- When I Get to Thinkin'   —
- I Love My Whiskey   —
- It Was Just a Dream   —
- Just Got to Hold You Tight   —
    Billy Boy Arnold Sings Big Bill Broonzy (Electro-Fi)

Billy Boy Arnold, vocals, harmonica; Duke Robillard, guitar, background vocals; Rich Lataille, alto sax, tenor sax; Mark Earley, tenor sax, baritone sax; Doug Woolverton, trumpet; Bruce Bears, piano; Brad Hallen, acoustic bass, electric bass; Mark Teixeira, drums, background vocals; Jack Gauthier, Anita Suhanin, background vocals

West Greenwich, Rhode Island, ca. 2014
- Coal Man   Stony Plain CD321378
- I'd Rather Drink Muddy Water   —
- You Give Me Nothing to Go On   —
- 99 Lbs.   —
- A Mother's Prayer   —
- St. James Infirmary   —
- Don't Set Me Free   —
- What's on the Menu Mama   —
- Worried Dream   —
- Nadine (Is It You?)   —
- Work Song   —
- Dance for Me Baby   —
- Ain't That Just Like a Woman   —
- Keep On Rubbing   —
    Billy Boy Arnold, *The Blues Soul of Billy Boy Arnold* (Stony Plain)

Billy Boy Arnold, vocals; Bob Margolin, guitar; Johnny Iguana, piano; Vincent Bucher, harmonica; Felton Crews, bass; Kenny Smith, drums

Chicago, 2017
- Play with Fire   Raisin' Music CBE1701
    Chicago Plays the Stones (Raisin' Music)

JOHNNY IGUANA

Billy Boy Arnold, vocals, harmonica; Billy Flynn, guitar; Johnny Iguana, piano; Kenny Smith, drums

Chicago, January 6–11, 2019
- You're an Old Lady   Delmark DE-864
    Johnny Iguana's Chicago Spectacular (Delmark)

Billy Boy Arnold, vocals; Billy Flynn, guitar; Johnny Iguana, piano; Kenny Smith, drums

Chicago, January 6–11, 2019
- Hot Dog Mama   Delmark DE-864
    Johnny Iguana's Chicago Spectacular (Delmark)

Index

Performers who used a nickname with their surname are listed under that surname; those whose stage names did not include their surname are listed under the first letter of the stage name. For example, Sonny Boy Williamson is listed under *W*, whereas Memphis Slim is listed under *M*.

Page numbers in italics refer to figures.

Vaughan, Jimmie, 257
Vaughan, Sarah, 25
Vee-Jay Records, 118–23, *119*, 131–
    39, *138*, 141–42, 145, 203, 231;
    overseas distribution, 139, 232.
    See also under Arnold, Billy Boy,
    sessions
Vernon, Mike, 6
Vinson, Eddie "Cleanhead," 21
voice, for singing the blues, 19, 22,
    29, 74, 84, 101, 117, 132, 142,
    147, 176, 249–50, 253; Detroit
    Junior, 196; Elbert, Donnie, 169;
    Hooker, Earline, 159–62; Howlin'
    Wolf, 179–80; James, Elmore, 182;
    Rogers, Jimmy, 98–99, 172

Wagon Wheel, 17, 195
Waldman, Dave, 255
Walker, Jimmy, 142
Walker, Joe Louis, 239
Walker, Johnny "Big Moose," 158, 163,
    225
Walker, Aaron Thibeaux "T-Bone," 68,
    194, 196, 254
Ware, Eddie, 99–100
Washington, Sylvester (Two-Gun Pete)
    15–17, *16*
Waterman, Dick, 65n6, 224
Watermelon trucks, 24–25, *25*, 171
Watson, Johnny "Guitar," 167–168,
    171, 234
Welding, Pete, 208–9, 219–21
West Side of Chicago, 13, 18, 186–87,
    198
WGES-AM, 203
Wheeler, Golden, 207
Wheeler, James, 207–8, 242, 255
white audiences, for black music and the
    blues, 206, 212–13, 222–24, 232

white college circuit, 224–25
White, Ed "Big," 22, *34*, 35–37
White, Zadie Belle, *34*
Williams, Fred, 50
Williams, Hank, 206
Williams, Jody, 71–75, 127, 131–32,
    151–56, *164*, 175, 179, 197, 207,
    220, 248
Williams, Joseph Lee "Big Joe," 56,
    56n1, 252
Williams, Ulysses, 226–27
Williamson, John Lee "Sonny Boy,"
    2–6, 9, 14, *22*, 33, *34*, 35–53, *36*,
    46, 79, 162, 176, 197, 204–5,
    253–56; death, 46–49, *49*, 56–57,
    218; influence on Billy Boy Arnold,
    20–23, 28–30; influence on Little
    Walter, 106–7, 109; meets Billy
    Boy Arnold, 40–45; recording
    sessions, 50–51; songs, 233, 241,
    244–45; traditional blues, 258;
    unique style, 249
Williamson, Lacey Belle, *34*, 40, 42,
    46–49
Wilson, Kim, 240, 244–45, 256–57
Wilson, Quinn, 152
Wise Fools Pub, 223
Witherspoon, Jimmy, 151
WLAC, 161n5
Wood, Randy, 161n5
Woodfork, Robert "Poor Bob," 83, 172

Yardbirds, 3, 139, 153, *228*, 231–32
Yescalis, Rich, 4
Young, Johnny, 81–83, *82*, 214
Young, Joseph "Mighty Joe," 207, 210,
    220, 223, 248

Zanzibar, 74, 78, *99*, 145, 149, 198
Zinn, Rusty, 237

CHICAGO VISIONS AND REVISIONS

Edited by Carlo Rotella, Bill Savage, Carl Smith, and Robert B. Stepto

Also in the series: